THE PRAXIS
OF SUFFERING

THE PRAXIS OF SUFFERING

An Interpretation of Liberation and Political Theologies

Rebecca S. Chopp

ORBIS BOOKS

Maryknoll, New York 10545

Second Printing, March 1989

The Catholic Foreign Mission Society of America (Maryknoll) recruits and trains people for overseas missionary service. Through Orbis Books Maryknoll aims to foster the international dialogue that is essential to mission. The books published, however, reflect the opinions of their authors and are not meant to represent the official position of the society.

Manuscript editor: Lisa McGaw

Library of Congress Cataloging in Publication Data

Chopp, Rebecca S, 1952–
  The praxis of suffering.

  Bibliography: p.
  Includes index.
  1. Liberation theology.   2. Christianity and
politics.   3. Suffering—Religious aspects—Christianity.
4. Theology, Doctrinal—History—20th century.
I. Title.
BT83.57.C466   1986   230   86–824
ISBN 0–88344–256–6 (pbk.)

To Mark and Nate Biddle

For the wound of the daughter of my peo-
ple is my heart wounded,
I mourn, and dismay has taken hold on me.
Is there no balm in Gilead? Is there no
physician there?
Why then has the health of the daughter of
my people not been restored?
O that my head were waters, and my eyes a
fountain of tears, that
I might weep day and night for the slain of
the daughter of my people!

                                          Jeremiah 8:22–9:1

Contents

Preface   **xi**

Introduction   **1**

The Witness of Theology   2

Different Voices in the Paradigm   4

1. Latin American Liberation Theology   **7**

The Historical Context   8

The Church and Aggiornamento   14

The Conversation with Marxism   16

The Influence of Modern Theology   19

The Sacrament of God and Basic Christian Communities   20

Basic Themes in Latin American Liberation Theology   22

     The Preferential Option for the Poor   22

     God as Liberator   24

     The Liberation of Theology   25

2. Political Theology   **28**

The Project of Modern, Western Theology   29

The Cultural Situation of Political Theology   33

     Ideology Critique   33

     Pluralism   35

     Relativism   36

     Praxis   36

Political Theology: Stage One   38

Political Theology: Stage Two   41

3. Gustavo Gutiérrez: A Theology for Historical Amnesia   **46**

The Power of the Poor   47

Faith: Poverty, Solidarity, and Protest   51

     Liberation and Salvation   52

     Eschatology and Politics   54

     The Church as the Sacrament of God in History   55

Theology as the Voice of the Voiceless   57

Conclusion   62

4. Johann Baptist Metz: The Subject of Suffering   **64**

Freedom as Autonomy and Future   65

Secularization   65
Eschatology   67
Deconstructing the Subject   71
The Subject of Suffering   74
A Practical, Fundamental Theology   78
Conclusion   80

5. José Míguez Bonino: The Conversion to the World   **82**
A Hermeneutics of the World   83
A Hermeneutics of the Word   87
Discerning the Logic of Death   92
Conclusion   98

6. Jürgen Moltmann: The Language of God as the Language of Suffering 100
The Origin of Moltmann's Political Theology   101
The Advent of Hope   102
The Cross and the Resurrection   106
The Spirit and the Church   112
Method, Suffering, and Praxis   115

7. Christ Liberating Culture   **118**
Human Existence: An Anthropology of Praxis   120
Christ and Solidarity   126
Christ and Culture   130

8. Toward Praxis: A Method for Liberation Theology   **134**
Thesis 1: The two sources for liberation theology are human existence and
Christian tradition   135
Thesis 2: Liberation theology interprets the source of human existence
politically, using, among other disciplines, the social sciences to
reflect on the full concreteness of historical existence   136
Thesis 3: Theology employs a hermeneutics of liberation, including a proj-
ect of deideologization in relation to the source of Christian
tradition   137
Thesis 4: The method of liberation theology can be characterized as a critical
praxis correlation, wherein praxis is both the foundation and the
aim of theological hermeneutics   139
Thesis 5: Liberation theology's method of critical praxis correlation is, by its
nature, a form of ideology critique   142
Thesis 6: Liberation theology must develop an adequate social theory to
attend to the full meaning of praxis   144

9. Conclusion   **149**
Notes   **155**
Index   **175**

Preface

This book draws upon the contexts and resources of Latin American liberation theology and German political theology to introduce the new paradigm of liberation theology. Interpretive studies of Gustavo Gutiérrez, Johann Baptist Metz, José Míguez Bonino, and Jürgen Moltmann express the rupture and the continuity of the new theology with its predecessors. These studies and the two introductory chapters illustrate the basic themes and fundamental characteristics of liberation theology. Two constructive chapters conclude the book: one identifies the systematic claims of liberation theology; one analyzes the theological method of liberation theology. This book interprets liberation theology through a decidedly theological lens, attending to the question of suffering, examining the turn to praxis, and investigating a "new way of doing" theology.

Many have helped me with this project and I can but thank only a few in this public space. Special thanks go to David Tracy, Langdon Gilkey, Martin Marty, Matthew Lamb, and Susan Shapiro. Mary Sturm and Elizabeth Lynn read different portions of this manuscript with great care and Ken Langston prepared the index with inestimable fortitude and attention—my deep appreciation for their efforts. I also want to thank Peter Browning and the ministry students at the Divinity School of the University of Chicago for their blend of theory and praxis and for their community, questions, and energy. Most of all I must thank my family—Mark for his support and his helpful suggestions on the manuscript, and my son, Nate, for his patience, his playfulness, and his prayers for the poor and those who suffer.

Introduction

History shudders, pierced by events of massive public suffering. Memory is haunted, stalked by the ghosts of history's victims, capriciously severed from life in genocide, holocausts, and extermination camps. The cries of the hungry, the shrieks of political prisoners, and the silent voices of the oppressed echo slowly, painfully through daily existence. Through the wounds, sores, and cracks of history, the possibility of nuclear war lurks, threatening to annihilate life itself and thus to prevent even the possibility of suffering.

For most of the world's population in the present and the not-too-distant past, to live is to suffer: to be born is to become a victim. Once, long ago, humanity struggled to survive the calamities of nature: floods, scarcity, plagues, and famines. Now humanity survives to endure its own disasters, to suffer from its own incessant desire to destroy. Matthew Lamb describes the world in which we live:

> The last eight decades have profoundly changed the understanding of "an anguished world." Increasingly, the anguish in the world has been shifted from the weary shoulders of mother nature to the proud shoulders of a male-dominated history so aptly described by Atlas. Anguish has taken an anthropocentric (indeed, androcentric) turn to the subject. The countless wars and the nuclear arms race are only more evident symptoms of this turn. Never before in human history have so many humans slaughtered their fellow human beings on such a massive scale. The Lisbon earthquake pales in comparison with Hiroshima and Nagasaki. Famines and plagues can hardly measure up to the demonic intensity of the holocaust. The terrors of nature have tended to take a back seat to the horrors of history.[1]

Until recently it was assumed that advances in technology, increases in knowledge, and growth in material production were proof that the human race was speeding along on a trajectory toward moral, social, cultural, and physical perfection. But as the calamities of nature once rattled the tower of divine omnipotence, so the disasters of history now explode the freeways of progress. Science and technology pollute and destroy the air, the land, the water, while our capacities to produce and consume divide the world into those who have and those who have not. The labors of freedom have produced the chains of oppression: the resources of emancipation for the few are the sources of the dehumanization of the many. Progress is exposed as modernity's plastic mask, an illusion of our origin and destiny. This progress is history's suffering; we are its origin, its destiny, its cause.

Concern for suffering is not new, either in social history or in the tradition of Christianity. Society has worried over its catastrophes, the acts of God as well as its isolated tyrants and mad persons. Bearing suffering in its central symbol of the cross, Christianity has always honored the prophet who alleviates suffering and elevated martyrs who suffer for their faith. But the events of massive public suffering in modernity do not settle in among previous concerns, concepts, and responses. Due to the sheer numbers of victims, the increased awareness of their plight, and the widespread belief that this suffering could be otherwise, these events erupt within history with shattering intensity. This suffering has what we shall call in this book a "nonidentity character," an inability to be fully expressed in theory or fully represented in symbols. Events of massive public suffering have no identity or completed meaning in history; they cannot be fully explained, understood, or represented. The nonidentity character of suffering means that suffering cannot be forgotten or ignored in history's interpretation or construction; once progress has shoved the masses of humanity onto life's margins, history is broken, its end forever 'n question, and its purpose lost in suspension.

Events of massive, public suffering defy quantitative analysis. How can one really understand statistics citing the death of six million Jews or graphs of third-world starvation? Do numbers really reveal the agony, the interruption, the questions that these victims put to the meaning and nature of our individual lives and life as a whole? Knowledge of suffering cannot be conveyed in pure facts and figures, reportings that objectify the suffering of countless persons. The horror of suffering is not only its immensity but the faces of the anonymous victims who have little voice, let alone rights, in history. Oppressed, impoverished, and marginalized, the victims of history speak through narratives, stories, and poems evoking their human passions, hopes, failures, sufferings. In their stories, the victims of modern history are revealed as survivors, for, in the words of Terrence Des Pres, modern history "has created the survivor as a moral type."[2] The survivor offers the testimony of suffering and yet of surviving, not only for oneself but for others, the others who suffered and did not survive.

THE WITNESS OF THEOLOGY

In contemporary theology the responses to such suffering—to its past, its present, and its future—appear in liberation theologies. Liberation theologies interpret the logos of the Theos, that is, speech and knowledge of God, within the interruption of those who suffer. In a variety of forms, liberation theology speaks with those who, through their suffering, call into question the meaning and truth of human history. Latin American Christians break out of the history of colonialization and development to rewrite and remake history. Feminist Christians criticize the male dominance of ecclesiastical structures and theological systems. Black Christians challenge the white pictures of Jesus and the segregation of Christian fellowship. German political theologians negate the bourgeois gospel of apathy and consumerism. These critiques introduce a religious quest for freedom and justice in history that recalls the exodus—the journey for freedom of an oppressed people. These interruptions open a new voice in history "to preach good news to the poor/ . . . to proclaim release to the captives/and recovering of sight to the blind,/to set at liberty those who are oppressed,/to proclaim the acceptable year of the Lord" (Lk. 4:18).

In the Christian church the theoretical implications of justice and righteousness have long been the special domain of social ethics. The academy contemplates social ethics by combining theological interpretations with philosophical principles such as equality, duty, and fairness. Beyond the academy the church enacts its social principles through individual actions and institutional structures. The victims of history are served by various church groups, ranging from small outreach committees to large charitable agencies. But liberation theology is not the simple identification of Christian theology with the region of social ethics, prophetic declarations, or charitable service. Bringing suffering into the midst of reflection, liberation theology rethinks human existence, Christian tradition, and present Christian experience. What can theology say to the problems of human suffering? Who is the human subject created by God and destroyed by humanity? Who is God and where is God when history is marked more by suffering than by caretaking? Is the Bible an occasion for existential encounter or a witness of memory and hope?

Such questions acknowledge the nature of liberation theology, that the knowledge of God is today discerned in the midst of suffering. To understand liberation theology, we must grasp one basic claim: suffering and its quest for freedom is the fundamental reality of human experience as well as the location of God, Christ, and the church in history. Liberation theology urges action, strategy, and change in human existence; it demands justice, equality, and freedom in Christian witness. Consequently liberation theology is a new language of God, seeking, in the present historical situation, to be the voice of those who suffer.[3]

As a new language of God, liberation theology is formulated in opposition to modern, progressive theology. Modern theology, in attempting to be a language of God in its historical situation, found its focal center in a quest for the authenticity of the subject. A similar quest arose in philosophy with the "turn to the subject," in politics with the emergence of individual rights, and in economics with the development of private property. But each age gives way to the next, and theology in its continual incarnation becomes reformed and transformed into a new encounter of tradition, reflection, and experience. In liberation theology the bourgeois individual is no longer the primary subject, and authenticity and meaning no longer the central crisis for theology. Now the focus of theology is the nonsubjects of history, those who have been denied any voice or identity in history by their fellow humans. Through this focus Christianity converts, becoming a praxis of solidarity with those who suffer and working for the transformation of human agency and social structures. Through this focal center the sacrament of God's grace makes visible the identification of suffering and hope, while the service of God's love opens faith toward a future.

This book argues that liberation theology is a new model of theology both in its systematic content and in its practical method. The systematic content of liberation theology relates Christian symbols and narratives to the focal center of the liberating activity of God. With God's liberating activity at its center, liberation theology offers a new understanding of human existence through the centrality of praxis and a new interpretation of Christianity through Christ's solidarity with those who suffer. The method of liberation theology demands that theology be a reflection on Christian praxis—a reflection aimed at interpretation, critique, and transformation. As a reflection on Christian praxis, liberation theology is a practical method, oriented to a specific praxis and situated within a particular context.

In formal categories this book argues that liberation theology represents a paradigm shift in theology.[4] A theological paradigm is the broad framework for interpretation; a paradigm shift involves a radical reorganization of theology, introducing new categories, new issues, and new metaphors. As a paradigm shift, liberation theology orders issues of justice and freedom as central to the Christian faith; it introduces social and political categories for theological interpretation. This new paradigm centers on the metaphor of liberation, a metaphor referring both to God's acts in history and humanity's nature and purpose in history. Within this broad paradigm, liberation theologians ask such questions as the following: What is the witness of the liberating gospel? How do Christians encounter God in those who suffer? What is the vision of freedom disclosed in the Christian Scriptures? How are suffering and hope identified in Christ?

DIFFERENT VOICES IN THE PARADIGM

This book concentrates on Latin American liberation theology and German political theology as two distinct voices within the paradigm of liberation theology.[5] The voice of Latin American liberation theology is the voice of the "other," the voice of those systematically oppressed within history. The voice of political theology is the voice of the bourgeoisie, questioning their own basic assumptions and seeking grace and hope in conversion. In the context of the history of suffering, German political theologians and Latin American liberation theologians follow different routes to talk of God.[6] Latin American liberation theology works with the church in actual situations of oppression responding to the specific needs and issues of the people. German political theology formulates a theoretical critique of modernity's understanding of freedom, the human subject, history, and God. Economic, cultural, and political dependency expressed through theories of development are criticized in Latin American liberation theology from the perspective of the poor, who have a privileged option to hear and speak of God. In solidarity with all who suffer, both the living and the dead, German political theology criticizes existentialism and existentialist theology for blindly accepting the fatalism of modernity's progress toward destruction. Latin American liberation theology draws upon the resources of Paulo Freire, Marxism, and modern theology to demand that theology be grounded in a concrete praxis of commitment to social justice. German political theology converses with modern theology, the Frankfurt School of critical theory, and its own cultural situation to mediate theology through practical reason in the categories of memory, narrative, and solidarity.

But in light of these major differences of context and sources, Latin American liberation and German political theologians agree not only on the major fact of contemporary life—events of massive, public suffering—but also on the need for new ways of understanding human existence, Christianity, and theology.[7] Indeed, it is precisely through their differences that Latin American liberation theology and German political theology provide a new theological paradigm. In order to understand the paradigm, each form of theology must be studied in its own context, with explicit attention paid to the particular voice of each theology. The testimony of each theological voice must be carefully recorded, for together they create, as Alfredo Fierro has said, "a new theological space," or as we shall argue in this text, a new paradigm of theology.[8]

This volume provides a framework for understanding the context, the substance, and the method of liberation theology. The framework begins, in chapters 1 and 2, by locating Latin American liberation theology and German political theology in their respective historical, theological, and ecclesiastical situations. Though German political theology inherits modern theology's distinct agenda of representing the freedom of the human subject, it radically challenges the form of this agenda through its solidarity with those who suffer. Emerging out of a history of colonization marked by oppression and domination, Latin American liberation theology engages the church in solidarity with the poor.

A study of four representative theologians constitutes the next part of the framework in chapters 3 through 6: this part provides an analysis of major figures in this theological paradigm and a consideration of central themes within liberation theology. Four theologians are analyzed: Gustavo Gutiérrez, a Roman Catholic theologian from Peru; Johann Baptist Metz, a Roman Catholic theologian from the Federal Republic of Germany (West Germany); José Míguez Bonino, a United Methodist theologian from Argentina; and Jürgen Moltmann, a Reformed theologian from West Germany. Gustavo Gutiérrez interprets theology and Christianity through his reflection on the irruption of the poor in history and their new way of Christianity. Johann Baptist Metz intensifies the basic themes of Christian faith—the human subject, freedom, the meaningfulness of history—to the point of a complete reformulation of anthropology and Christianity. Gutiérrez and Metz present the basic case for a paradigm shift of theology: they show the need for a new way of action and reflection; they provide a new subject and a new form of

Christianity; they argue for a new method of and purpose for theological reflection. Míguez Bonino and Moltmann, on the other hand, function more specifically to call our attention to methodological and substantive issues within liberation theology. José Míguez Bonino concentrates on the important issue of the socio-historical mediation of all theology in developing a liberating hermeneutics of the Word and the world. Jürgen Moltmann forces us to recall the narratives of God in hope and suffering, narratives that demand the rupture of Moltmann's own theological method.

Finally, the framework for liberation theology is finished by the construction of two models: "Christ Liberating Culture" and "Toward Praxis: A Method for Liberation Theology." The first model of Christ liberating culture, the subject matter of chapter 7, considers the fundamental claims of liberation theology to relocate human existence in praxis and to reinterpret Christianity as a praxis of solidarity with those who suffer. In this substantive interpretation of liberation theology, Christianity follows a model of Christ liberating culture. In chapter 8, the second model, a model of critical praxis correlation, investigates the methodological claims of liberation theology. Through the identification of six theses, this formal model sketches the new nature and process of theological reflection through the use of practical hermeneutics, ideology critique, and social theory.

By building this framework of context, representatives, and interpretive models, this book contributes to the paradigm of liberation theology. It introduces the themes, issues, and categories of this new paradigm and it critically interprets the claims, arguments, and symbols within liberation theology. This book is written with an openness toward the turn to practical reflection in disciplines other than liberation theology: the turn to praxis and the concern for suffering mark much of the theoretical and practical activity of our present world. This suggests that liberation is itself a situated theology: a response to the needs of the day and an expression of the general ethos of the contemporary situation. But through this interpretation of liberation theology and in this broadening of its location, it is hoped that those who suffer will speak: for any interpretation of liberation theology must be radically ruptured by the claims and the cries of those who suffer. Any reflection on God—the God who creates, redeems, and liberates history—must today be interrupted by God who freely chooses to be with the victims of history.

1

Latin American Liberation Theology

There is no central founding event for Latin American liberation theology. The faces of the poor, the midnight roundups of political prisoners, the gradual genocide of Indian races, and the constant fear of the masses are all points of origin for this theology that speaks of God and the poor as always together. If we are to understand this theology, then we must understand where it begins— with the poor, in a history of domination, oppression, and colonialism. But it is not enough to understand the history of the poor; rather, we must, with this theology, wager that it is with the poor that God is found in Latin America. "The theology of liberation," writes theologian Ignacio Castuera, "reveals to us that theology is done by the *pueblo oprimido,* the oppressed people, those who are at the same time the *señor de la historia,* the Lord of history."[1] It is a wager that we must travel along history in the journey of the poor—a journey of faith, which will lead to greater understanding that is at the same time a transformation.

Having taken this wager that God is with the poor, we can begin to travel along with the Latin American liberation theologians. Segundo Galilea identifies the three assumptions of Latin American liberation theology: "(1) the present situation is one in which the vast majority of Latin Americans live in a state of underdevelopment and unjust dependence; (2) viewed in Christian terms, this is a 'sinful situation'; (3) hence it is the duty of Christians in conscience, and of the church in its pastoral activity, to commit themselves to efforts to overcome this situation."[2] These assumptions force our theology to be concrete and social, and require us to investigate the conditions of poverty, dependence, and injustice. We must, in this sinful situation where we are committed to transformation, take the tradition of past theology and find new ways of understanding Christian symbols such as sin, redemption, and grace. With these assumptions, we must enlarge our conversation partners and consider issues that may seem oddly nontheological to those who are new to the journey of the poor. Yet in dialogue with Marxists or in working with the liberating educational methods of Paulo Freire we find a new experience of Christian witness and new ways of speaking of God.

7

Located within the church, which is one of the few sources of resistance and creative transformation in society, Latin American liberation theology is best understood as faith seeking understanding among the poor of Latin America. It is a church theology in its intentional focus on issues such as ecclesiology, pastoral practice, and the relation of church and world as well as in its clear intent to be located within basic Christian communities. This logos of the Theos is a new way of doing theology both because it interprets anew human existence and Christian tradition and because it understands the purpose of theology to be that of reflecting on and guiding Christian praxis. But most important of all, Latin American liberation theology is, in its own wager, a response to a God who is with the poor and whose presence is made visible by the witness and service of the church.

THE HISTORICAL CONTEXT

The people of Latin America are hungry. Two-thirds of the population is "undernourished" to the point of starvation; in some areas of the continent, people chew cocoa leaves and eat mud to dull the hunger pains. Children in the rural areas survive on clay when the scanty supplies of rice and beans are depleted; children in the cities scavenge through garbage on the streets. Five percent of the population holds 80 percent of the wealth. The masses of Latin America are landless. Two-thirds of the usable land is in the hands of a few Latin Americans and foreign multinational corporations. The corporations that own the land reap the profits from the land.[3]

The people of Latin America are poor. High rates of unemployment are due to the ownership of the land by multinational corporations and to the unstable political situations. Those who are fortunate enough to work do so for almost nothing. According to Arthur McGovern, "Brazilian sugar cane workers make about two dollars a day. Near Recife in Brazil a father picks corn and cotton for rich landowners to support his family on 65 cents a day. In Caracas, Venezuela, slum dwellers spend six hours a day commuting to work."[4] The people from Latin America are deprived of education and medical attention. One-half of the people suffer from disease; in some countries, as many as three-fourths of the people are illiterate. Latin America lives in a constant state of war and siege. Governments use torture, mass media, and the suspension of basic rights to stifle movements of dissent or reform.

This is the concrete situation with which Latin American liberation theology begins its theological reflection. But this concrete situation exists in a history of continued dominance and repression; the history of the people of Latin America is a history of the "other," a history of the "underside." Latin American liberation theology attempts to speak for a people whose lives have been determined by a centuries-old system of structural oppression, a system that has used Christianity time and time again to secure the dominance of the few over the masses. In recalling this history, Latin American liberation theology finds the resources to criticize the origin, the function, and the nature of the oppression of the poor. It finds, as well, symbols, stories, and memories that reveal a new identity and vision of the human subject in history.

Christianity came to Latin America as part of the Spanish mission to conquer the New World for the honor of Spain and the glory of God. The first period of Latin American history is marked by the Spanish colonization of the sixteenth century. Spain's "temporal messianism" combined the conquest of foreign lands with the religious project of converting heathens and pagans. Indeed, before the first explorer ever set foot on American soil the early destiny of Latin America was settled through the promulgation of the patronage system by the Holy See, which established the fundamental principle of conquest and Christianization.[5] Through the patronage system, the church was responsible to the Spanish crown, and the crown had the power to appoint bishops, replace clerics, and seize part of the tithes collected by the church as reimbursement for the heavy costs of the "Christian" conquest. When the conquistadors arrived in Latin America, they brought with them the semi-feudal social structures of Spain—a country where, as Míguez Bonino observes, "obedience to the great king of Spain and submission to the King of Heaven were demanded as one single act."[6]

The Spanish system of "conquering" territories consisted of subduing local residents, establishing towns on the model of Spain's cities, and allocating Indians (nonpersons) as serfs to the conquerors. Spain established its fiefdom by virtually destroying Indian civilization, including the impressive Inca, Aztec, and Mayan cultures.[7] The Cortez conquest exemplifies the destructiveness of Spanish conquistador practices. In 1519 Cortez set out to conquer Mexico—a land rumored to be overflowing with jewels and gold.[8] Natives were bewildered and terrified when the conquistador landed with armor, guns, and horses. Montezuma II, the Aztec emperor, sent Cortez gifts but also demanded the invader and his men return to their boats and leave immediately. Cortez responded by burning his boats, establishing the city of Veracruz, and marching his men to Tenochtitlán, the center of the Aztec empire. Cortez seized Montezuma and demanded gold, silver, and jewels. After several battles in which the Aztecs were nearly victorious, the Spanish warrior succeeded in leveling Tenochtitlán to the ground and forcing the new Indian slaves to build a city in the Spanish rectangular form. Cortez rewarded his men with gifts of *repartimientos*—groups of Indians as pay for the officer's services. As with Cortez in Mexico, so with Pizarro in Peru, and with Valdivia in Chile: thus Spain subdued the New World.

The Spanish conquistadors, seeking honor for their king, were accompanied by missionaries, seeking to glorify their God. Under the patronage system, missionaries worked for the mass conversion of the Indians to Christianity and their acculturation to the Spanish worldview. Through this ostensibly Christian act of service, the church functioned to establish and secure class stratification and land ownership. Spanish Christendom's "natural order" established a hierarchy with God at the top, the king next, then the landowner, and finally the serf. But while attending to the formal establishment of God's intended order, on the level of daily religious practices Christianity settled in and around the indigenous religions.[9] The new Latin American Christianity, though formally following the pattern of Spanish Christianity, often included Indian beliefs in its liturgies and transformed Christian rituals to fit local religious practices.

Yet the relationship of church and state was not confined solely to the church's function as a dominant acculturating and controlling branch of the state. Gutiérrez contends that throughout the history of Latin America "the religious motivation not only justified but also judged, the colonial enterprise."[10] Notable individuals criticized the domination and the abuse of the Indians. Bartolomé de las Casas was a wealthy holder of *encomiendas*, plantations given by the king to Spanish lords as land grants, plantations on which the Indian serfs were worked and converted. Las Casas gave up the extravagant way of life on his *encomiendas* at the age of forty to work for the Indians, and he traveled to Spain to present the case of the Indians to the king.[11] Las Casas, understanding the crucial link between liberation and salvation, argued that the Indians were free human beings and that conquest was not a means of conversion. Others attempted to provide alternatives to the destructive *encomienda* system. The Jesuits, for instance, were especially active in Paraguay working with the Gurani Indians in mission houses known as *reducciones*, where the Indians received instruction in the manual arts and instruction in Christianity.

But these attempts did not stem the prevailing tide of conquest and Christianization. For many of the peoples of Latin America, Spanish colonization resulted in the domination, the oppression, and even the destruction of their own cultures. Indigenous societies, now termed "pagan" and "uncivilized," were governed by a "Higher Authority" and the people themselves, in their own land, became the dominated, the dispossessed, the despised, the "other." By and large, the first period of Latin American history consisted of the establishment of a patronage system granting to the Spanish conquerors the blessing, the right, and the responsibility to Christianize and colonize the existing cultures of Latin America.

The second major period of Latin American history began in the nineteenth century and contains both the independence movements and the beginnings of British neocolonialism and capitalistic imperialism. Until about 1808 the Spanish crown was able to contain dissent among the *criollo* minority (American-born Spanish) against the ruling *peninsulares* (Spanish natives). After 1808 revolutionary movements sprang up in many different areas of the colonized continent. *Criollos* agitated for more liberty, demanding greater freedom of thought, more political emancipation, and increased economic opportunities under the *peninsulares*. These revolutionary movements were heavily influenced by the North American revolution of the United States, by Napoleon's capture of Spain, and by eighteenth-century Enlightenment thought. Many of the revolutionary leaders were educated in Europe or the United States, where they studied the works of Rousseau, Hobbes, Locke, and Spinoza. By 1810 *criollo* juntas had taken over many of the cities in the course of resisting the French usurpation of the Spanish throne. This temporary exercise in self-government both increased the drive and aided the public training for independence; as the historian Pendle observes, "what had begun as resistance to France developed into war against Spain."¹² Independence also found sanction as a movement for the rights of the Indians and for the mestizos (persons of mixed heritage).

By 1830 the established nation-states of Latin America began to develop trade and communication with other non-Latin American nation-states. As the supplier of aid and personnel to the revolutionary movements, Great Britain was a natural ally. This relationship between the nation-states of Latin America and Great Britain resulted in a "neocolonial" pact: the New World supplied the raw resources and the industrial country supplied the manufactured goods. The rapid industrialization of Great Britain at that time meant new goods, gold, and technology to develop the resources of Latin America. The building of railroads allowed resources to be brought from the rich inlands of Latin America to the coasts, from there to be exported by ships. Railroads also made possible the settling of the inland with cattle ranches and farms. Capitalist imperialism demanded that the resources and profits from Latin America become an integral part of Britain's economy; thus Latin America became more dependent as economic expansion moved from the sporadic state of colonialism to the regular, systematic control of neocolonialism.¹³

The church, identified institutionally and ideologically with the Spanish crown, suffered a great deal of disorganization and disruption during this period. Much of the European philosophy popular in this period was anticlerical and critical of the church for its wealth and power.¹⁴ As a result of the independence movements, the patronage system was overthrown in many countries. The initial reaction from the Vatican was the swift condemnation of revolutionary movements, as expressed in the encyclicals *Etsi Longissimo* (1816) and *Etsi Iam Diu* (1824). In some countries the church simply transferred its loyalty to the new ruling power; in other countries the church attempted to forge its primary ties to Rome. In general the church lost many of its previous economic and political advantages.

Yet even in the midst of its own turmoil, the church often criticized ruling juntas. Occasionally the church aligned itself with revolutionary movements, even though it realized that independence would result in the diminishment of its own power. Many priests not only supported the revolutions but also called for ecclesiastical reforms such as a revival of Scripture reading, Mass in the vernacular, the establishment of a "poor" church, greater freedom of conscience, and a reform or abolition of the Roman Curia. ¹⁵ After a time of being pressured both by his own loyalty to Spain and by the new Latin American countries, Pope Gregory XVI issued *Sollicitudo Ecclesiarum* recognizing the new American republics.

This second period also marks the entrance of Protestantism into Latin America—a tradition often described as the religion of the investors and developers and as the religion of democracy, progressivism, science, and culture. With its emphasis on individualism and freedom, the Protestant conversion process complemented the reigning ethos of individualism and freedom in the enlightened world. Just as Catholicism had functioned as an ideological justification for colonization in the first period, so Protestantism performed the same service for the neocolonialism of the second period. Protestant missionaries, after their arrival in the early years of the twentieth century, often supported democratic ideology as the truly "Christian way" or, alternatively, argued that religion had nothing to do with business and politics. Yet Protestantism, like Roman Catholicism, was not to be identified only with the reigning powers. As early as the Panama Conference on Christian Work in Latin America (1916), missionaries talked about the relevance of the social gospel in Latin America. Protestantism exhibited the tension of both supporting and criticizing the ruling powers and ideologies—a tension it shared with the history of Roman Catholicism in Latin America.

The third period is marked by a shift in Latin American neocolonialism, from a dependence on Great Britain to a dependence on the United States. From the beginning of the independence movements, the United States indicated special interest in Latin America, expressed in the Monroe Doctrine of 1823 stating that European involvement in the independent countries of the Western hemisphere would be considered a "manifestation of an unfriendly disposition toward the United States."[16] After 1890 the United States began to take an increasingly important role in the political and economic affairs of Latin American countries. In 1895 it invoked the Monroe Doctrine against Great Britain in Britain's attempt to expand Guinea into Venezuela. Three years later the United States went to war with Spain over Cuba. Along with these military interventions, the United States secured its involvement in Latin America through economic investments in sugar plantations, the construction of railroads, and the importation of United States manufactured goods. The 1903 revolution in Panama provided the United States with an opportunity to construct successfully a canal and thus to realize a plan for increased military efficiency and economic opportunity. In 1904 the Roosevelt corollary to the Monroe Doctrine gave the United States the right to intervene in cases of wrongdoing or civil disorder in the nation-states of the Western hemisphere. The corollary provided the rationale for later United States intervention in the Dominican Republic (1916–24), Haiti (1915–34), and Nicaragua (1912–33).

During this period the church attempted to develop some significant new political positions. The New Christendom movement, one such development, represented a progressive, if moderate, attempt to acknowledge the autonomy of the temporal sphere and to advocate justice in the world while maintaining the importance of the spiritual sphere for evangelization and inspiration.[17] Alfredo Fierro cites three assumptions central to the New Christendom movement: "(1) the lay character of political institutions; (2) the underlying Christian inspiration of the state; and (3) the full incorporation of non-Christians into the state by virtue of its temporal aims as a civil society."[18] This new "social" Christianity envisioned a third political option between capitalism and socialism that would permit Christian involvement in the world but still keep the sphere of faith distinct from the world. The writings of Jacques Maritain greatly influenced "social" Christianity and its expression in movements such as Catholic Action and Catholic Trade Unions.[19] In continuity with earlier Catholic positions, the New Christendom model continued to distinguish the salvific work of the church from the profane work of the world. The model did, however, recognize that Christian principles could and should inspire and direct laypersons in this worldly activity. The church still believed in two planes, one temporal and one spiritual—but the planes were now to be differentiated rather than totally separated. Thus the third period is marked by significant new activity for the Roman Catholic Church, by the increasing call for reform and independence among the Latin American people, and by the emergence of a neocolonial relationship between Latin America and the United States.

The fourth period of history covers the years from 1950 to the present writing (1980s). This period continues to be marked by Latin American dependence and capitalist imperialism; that imperialism is now the work of multinational corporations. The first stage of this period, in the 1950s and early 1960s, covers the model of development represented by the United Nations Decade of Development. Based on the distinction between developed and underdeveloped countries, this model assumed that, with the proper financial aid and technological knowledge, underdeveloped countries could become like their first-world counterparts. The project of development also required certain cultural "improvements": democracy, a large middle class, mass advertising, high literacy rates. The plan was given popular expression in Walt W. Rostow's *The Stages of Economic Growth: A Non-Communist Manifesto.*[20]

The second stage of this fourth period in Latin American history begins with the failure of the developmentalism model. Ten years of development had resulted in an even worse situation for the poor and oppressed in Latin America: the befriended countries faced growing political instability, increased repression of political dissent, and a larger economic gap between rich and poor.[21] Neither a middle class nor a democracy had developed; instead, military dictatorships were seizing political control and suspending the basic rights of the masses. International investors were taking out more profits than they were putting in aid, and loans from governmental agencies were mere financial tokens beside the so-called investments of multinational corporations. The model was further discredited by political events such as the Brazilian coup of 1964 and Chile's failed Christian Democracy, not to mention the revelation of the involvement by the United States in the Dominican Republic.[22]

The solution to the failure of the development model came in the form of the concept of a "national security system." José Comblin, in *The Church and the National Security State*, describes its principles as "integration of the whole nation into the national security system and the polity of the United States; total war against communism; collaboration with American or American-controlled business corporations; establishment of dictatorships; and placing of absolute power in the hands of the military."[23] The concept of a national security system was incompatible with the notion of development and its necessary correlates of freedom and democracy. Instead, cooperation between oligarchies and multinational corporations, a cooperation secured by dictatorships and protected by the military, became the dominant reality. The national security system thus defends the interests of corporations, foreign governments, and the elites of Latin America. It uses the issues of geopolitics, military strategy, and security from war to create a comprehensive system that, in the words of Robert Calvo, "reflects a predominately military vision of society, the economy, and culture. The basic elements of society are seen through the world-view of the professional soldier."[24]

The situation of the church in this fourth period is the immediate context for Latin American liberation theology. The system of domination and repression in which the church and liberation theology find themselves is but a continuation of a history of imperialism. The history of Latin America is characterized by the ideological use of Christianity to further the interest of the ruling party, on the one hand, and, on the other hand, the painful suffering of the poor whom the church serves. In recent years, however, the church has taken a much stronger stand *with* the poor *against* both the ideological distortion of Christianity and the history of domination and repression in Latin America.

THE CHURCH AND AGGIORNAMENTO

The foregoing brief and fragmentary summary of Latin American history illustrates that, though particular individuals and even groups have sided with the poor, by and large the church functioned for centuries to justify the systematic oppression of the "other," the poor. In part this was due to the theological separation of the spiritual and temporal spheres, a separation that resulted in little importance being placed on justice and righteousness in social structures. Along with this theological tendency to confine faith to a separate sphere, the Roman Catholic Church sheltered itself from conversation with modernity, preferring to remain in the Christendom mentality of an earlier era. In 1864 Pope Pius IX's "Syllabus of Errors," an appendix to the encyclical *Quanta Cura*, concluded by stating, "if anyone thinks that the Roman Pontiff can and should reconcile himself and come to terms with progress, with liberalism, and with modern civilization, let him be anathema."[25] It was, then, a startling change when, in 1960, Pope John XXIII announced a second Vatican Council in order "to open the windows of the church to let in fresh air from the outside world."[26] This new movement of "aggiornamento," or renewal, is a major shift in the church's theological formulations, liturgical practices, and relationships with the modern world. In Pope John's encyclicals and the Vatican II documents the church begins to appear as a social actor, ready to serve and transform human life in history. Pope John's *Mater et Magistra*, published in 1961, advocated advances in social relations for the sake of human rights.[27] Vatican II documents such as *Populorum Progressio* and *Gaudium et Spes* emphasized worldly transformation as integral to the salvation of humanity. *Gaudium et Spes,* published in 1965, argued the need for structural change and indicated the special role of Christianity in working for human dignity. Two years later, in 1967, *Populorum Progressio* attacked oppressive social structures and called for the church to work with others in human solidarity. In the papal encyclicals and in the Vatican II documents, two basic themes received special emphasis: the dignity of all people and the interrelatedness of the peoples of the world. Vatican II marked a new form of critical dialogue with modern thought and historical involvement in the world. The temporal and spiritual spheres were no longer separated; the careful distinctions of the New Christendom model were blurred both theologically and pastorally. Faith, according to the spirit of Vatican II, has a new location of historical engagement—a radical involvement with the world.

In 1968 the Second General Conference of Latin American Bishops (CELAM II) met at Medellín, Colombia. The purpose of the Medellín Conference was to address, in light of Latin America, Vatican II's concern for human rights and historical transformation. The ensuing documents of Medellín serve as the founding documents of Latin American liberation theology; they determine, as well, a direction of solidarity and liberation through the creation of grassroots communities. At Medellín the bishops and theologians dealt with three general topics: (1) the pursuit of justice and peace, (2) evangelization and spiritual growth, and (3) ecclesiological structures.[28] Key words in almost all the Medellín documents are "conscientization" and "participation"—both of which stress the need to facilitate the active involvement of the masses in decision-making at all levels. Offering an analysis of the unjust situation in Latin America as a result of internal colonialism as well as external colonialism, the Medellín documents criticize both socialism and capitalism. These documents recognize the reality of class conflict in Latin America, speak of international tensions, call for the involvement of the poor, and acknowledge the need for agrarian reform. Any struggle for change, according to the bishops and theologians who authored the documents, must be a struggle against "institutionalized violence"—the violence of the rich against the poor institutionalized in structures, systems, values, and worldviews. The documents of Medellín thus portray a new location and foundation for Christian faith in the Latin American situation, proclaiming: "We wish to affirm that it is indispensable to form a social conscience and a realistic perception of the problems of the community and of social structures. We must awaken the social conscience and communal customs in all strata of society and professional groups regarding such values as dialogue and community living within the same group and relations with wider social groups (workers, peasants, professionals, clergy, religious, administrators, etc.)."[29]

Many individuals and groups in the Latin American church opposed the "liberal" stance taken at Medellín and, by the time of the Third General Conference of Latin American Bishops (CELAM III), held at Puebla, Mexico, in 1979, a strong reactionary movement had developed. With Bishop López Trujillo, one of the leaders of the opposition to the Medellín stance, as the new president of CELAM, it appeared that the Medellín documents might become mere historical citations. The meeting was prefaced by intense debates and contradictory preparatory documents. Yet the documents of Puebla maintain the basic theme of liberation in the midst of a rather conservative text that stresses the independence of the church from the powers of the world. Continuing Medellín's option for the poor and the critique of the dependency of Latin America, the final documents of Puebla praise the basic Christian communities but call for serious caution toward the authority and ideology of popular religion.[30]

Protestant churches also offered resistance to the political and economic situation in Latin America. In 1968 the Third Latin American Evangelical Conference (CELA) focused attention on the present problems in Latin America. As at the Puebla Conference, positions taken ranged from identifying the church with the revolutionary struggle to wanting the church to maintain a hands-off attitude toward all political positions. In 1978 the Latin American Council of Evangelization, held in Oaxtapec, Mexico, considered papers on topics such as power structures in Latin America, indigenous communities, and human rights.[31] Christianity, in both its Protestant and Catholic expressions, was becoming institutionally and theologically identified with the oppressed and the struggle for justice in the third world.

THE CONVERSATION WITH MARXISM

As the church became identified with the oppressed, many Latin American liberation theologians found themselves in conversation with Marxism—a conversation called for by the need for specific tools of social analysis, the search for a new understanding of history and anthropology, and the demand for new political options. Marxism is, by now, as much a general attitude emphasizing the historical and transformative nature of all action and reflection as it is a specific political structure or set of philosophical assumptions.[32] The importance of praxis, practical reason, and solidarity may be held by those who have never read Karl Marx as well as by those who have mastered the works of Marx and have studied all the varieties of revisionary Marxism.[33] As Latin American liberation theology developed, it became clear that no one particular system of Marxism was essential to its interpretation of the Christian faith or necessary for its political strategy.[34] Latin American liberation theology carries on a *critical* dialogue with Marxism in at least three areas: (1) the general economic-social-political climate of Latin America, (2) the philosophical categories of history and anthropology, and (3) political options in specific situations.

In some ways the greatest effect of Marxism on Latin American liberation theology may be the latter's analysis of the general climate of Latin America, an analysis emphasizing class conflict, oppression, and revolutionary ferment.

A Marxist analysis of the ownership of the mode of production and the Marxist insistence on the necessity for revolutionary change readily apply to Latin America's massive gap between the rich and the poor, the "haves" and the "have-nots."[35] Indeed, the initial criticism made by Latin American liberation theology relied upon a Marxist-influenced analysis of the model of development.[36] The theologians elaborated their critique of developmentalism through the notion of dependency, a notion taken from the work of Fernando Henrique Cardoso and Enzo Falleto, *Dependencia y Desarrollo en América Latina*, which says of the notion of dependency, in sum: "the relationship of dependency presupposes the insertion of specifically unequal structures. The growth of the world market created relationships of dependence (and domination) among nations."[37] This analysis demonstrated that the developmentalism of the 1950s and 1960s presumed a progressive view of exponential growth similar to the growth found in Western democracies, especially the United States. Utilizing the dependency theories of the social scientists, Latin American liberation theologians argued that, ten years after the beginning of development, the countries targeted for the efforts suffered even wider gaps between the rich and the poor, greater political instability, and fewer human rights than ever before.[38]

Through this analysis of dependency, Latin American theologians understand their context and their history as being structurally, culturally, and ideologically dominated by imperialistic systems. In their effort to analyze this context of oppression and domination, Latin American liberation theologians stress the importance of critical dialogue with social scientists, especially those scientists influenced by Marxism.[39] Marxist social sciences offer to liberation theologians an analysis of the systems of oppression between their countries and the first-world "empires." Minimally, it can be said that Latin American liberation theology grows out of a situation in which Marxist analysis provides some of the interpretations of the social situation.

Latin American liberation theologians are influenced also by certain "philosophical" categories set forth by Marx. In "The German Ideology" Marx argued that humanity committed the first historical act in its production of the means of subsistence, so that the mode of production is a definite form of the expression of human life. Humanity produces the means to satisfy needs that in turn creates new needs and humanity reproduces the species. The production of life, both of one's own labor and of new life, appears as a double relationship, as Marx himself indicates: ". . . on the one hand as a natural, on the other, as a social relationship. By social we understand that cooperation of several individuals, no matter what conditions, in what manner and to what end. It follows from this that a certain mode of production, or industrial stage, is always combined with a certain mode of cooperation, or social stage, and this mode of cooperation is itself a 'productive force.' "[40] For Marx a certain mode of production is always combined with a certain stage of cooperation so that consciousness is itself a social product. The division of labor in society, arising from needs and natural dispositions, means that the forces of production, the state of society, and consciousness must come into contradiction with one another.

Somewhat like Hegel's self-realization of the Absolute Spirit, Marx understood history as evolving through different stages.[41] Inherent in each stage are the seeds of conflict and destruction of that stage as well as the birth of the next stage. Alienation arises out of the pattern of ownership in society and occurs when the human subject becomes estranged from his or her productions. Alienation, in Marx's work, has four basic characteristics: (1) human subjects are estranged from their products, (2) there is no intrinsic satisfaction from work, (3) humans become estranged in their social relationships, and (4) humans do not fulfill their nature as social beings, what Marx calls "the species-being."

One of Latin American liberation theology's central theological base points is the demand that the primary arena for God and human action is history—the social, political, and economic realities of daily existence. Latin American liberation theology is openly indebted to Marx for pointing out the importance of history: "It is," Gutiérrez has written, "to a large extent due to Marxism's influence that theological thought, searching for its own sources, has begun to reflect on the meaning of the transformation of this world and the action of man in history."[42] Latin American liberation theology revises the Marxist understanding of history to include liberation in a mediate relationship to redemption and to argue that all method is bound by historical conditions and must be conscious of its own interests, priorities, and goals.

Latin American liberation theology is influenced, as well, by Marx's social anthropology, especially his understanding that humans both produce and are produced by history. For Latin American liberation theology this social anthropology necessitates an analysis of human existence in relation to its social context.[43] Latin American liberation theologians also revise Marx's category of alienation so that alienation contributes to and expresses human sinfulness. Though Latin American liberation theology uses Marx's philosophical categories to mediate and transform theological categories, that theology is nonetheless critical of Marxist theory.[44] Marx's theory, Latin American liberation theologians accuse, promises to solve fully the problems of history—a promise no theory can keep because of the nature of sin. Alienation, as Marx taught, may well be constituted by and expressive of systemic structures of oppression, but as such alienation is also an expression of the tragic relationship between history and salvation. Likewise, even Marx's categories of history and anthropology are, for Latin American liberation theologians, adequately understood only in light of the Christian notions of creation, sin, and redemption.

The third area of conversation between Marxism and Latin American liberation theology exists in the consideration of specific political options for the Latin American countries. This conversation takes place in a context in which Marxist-influenced groups and Christians sometimes work together to develop new political systems. The 1970 election of Salvador Allende in Chile marked both the election of a Marxist head of government and the cooperation of Christians toward this end. In 1972 Christians for Socialism, meeting at Santiago, identified socialism as the only acceptable political option but also called for criticism of Marxist dogmatism. Frequently Latin American liberation theologians argue for a form of socialism as the most adequate political structure for the present situation of their countries. Socialism is "Marxist" in the sense that it advocates that the ownership of the means of production belongs to the people as a whole or, in Juan Luis Segundo's definition, "a political regime in which the ownership of the means of production is taken away from individuals and handed over to higher institutions whose main concern is the common good."[45] Latin American liberation theologians contribute to the quest for a particular form of Latin American socialism, one that would avoid the problems of communism and capitalism. In sum, within the general climate of Latin America, Marxism is a resource and conversation partner for liberation theology. Latin American liberation theology is critical of its own use of Marxism, yet it remains in dialogue with Marxist social science, Marx's philosophy, and with various forms of socialism.

THE INFLUENCE OF MODERN THEOLOGY

Though Latin American liberation theologians may dialogue with social sciences, political theory, and various forms of philosophy, they nonetheless are centrally engaged in an ongoing conversation with modern theology. Latin American liberation theologians, trained in twentieth-century theology, retrieve the notions of freedom, grace, sin, obedience, and redemption as a way to interpret Christian praxis. In this hermeneutics of retrieval within modern theology, theological concepts are often radically transformed. For instance, Karl Barth's stress on obedience to the revelation of God comes to the surface in José Míguez Bonino's vision of theology as the discernment of God's actions in concrete situations. Likewise, Karl Rahner's interpretation of the experience of salvation mediated through the affirmation of the self contributes to Gustavo Gutiérrez's notion of salvation mediated through historical self-realization. Many Latin American liberation theologians are influenced, as well, by Pierre Teilhard de Chardin's emphasis on the process of history as the conquest for new ways of being human, an emphasis that, in the works of these theologians, becomes constructed through social and political structures.[46] Latin American liberation theology continues modern theology's concern for the subject, the representation of freedom by Christianity, and the experience of faith in history but, in a radical reformulation, defines the subject as the poor, reinterprets freedom to include political self-determination, and envisions history as the arena for both liberation and redemption.

In its early years Latin American liberation theology understood itself as having real affinities to German political theology. Latin American liberation theologians agreed with German political theology that faith and world could no longer be two separate realms; and they agreed that earlier forms of modern theology had functioned ideologically to justify the ruling powers of bourgeois society. The critique made by Johann Baptist Metz and Jürgen Moltmann of the privatization of religion in the first world was understood by Latin American liberation theologians as an example of the need for self-critique in theology. To the Latin American liberation theologians, political theology suggested new categories of religious language, introducing distinctively political concepts such as liberation, privatization, ideology, and oppression through its political hermeneutics. The language of salvation and redemption now designated concrete historical conditions, thus providing new possibilities for understanding and speaking to the pressing problems of oppression, suffering, and poverty. And Latin American liberation theologians discovered an ally in their German counterparts in the demand and desire for a new interpretation of Christian witness—a witness opposing false consciousness and injustice while working for human fulfillment in history.

Perhaps the most significant area of both agreement and disagreement between German political theology and Latin American liberation theology was the vision of faith acting in a *critical* relationship to the world. Jürgen Moltmann, in *Theology of Hope*, argued for a Christian faith that disturbs and calls history into question, a position to which Latin American liberation theology gave its hearty assent. In light of this critical relationship of Christianity to the world, political theology identified the church as an agent of historical freedom. Metz's notion of the church as a critical institution provided a new vision of the nature as well as the role of the church in the world. But the understanding of how the church could fulfill its role as a critical institution was significantly different in Latin America from that in secularized West Germany.[47] In Latin America the church's size, power, and influence could provide it with many different opportunities for political influence, education, and service. Latin American liberation theology located its disagreement with political theology in the dual issues of *how* the church should be a critical institution and the *nature* of theology as a political activity. Locating the critical activity of the church through its political, educational, and social activity with the poor, Latin American liberation theology committed itself not only to interpreting critically the world, in the tradition of its German counterpart political theology, but also to transforming that world.

THE SACRAMENT OF GOD AND BASIC CHRISTIAN COMMUNITIES

At the heart of Latin American liberation theology is the reinterpretation of Christian faith as a radical engagement of the church in the world. In the journey of the poor with God, the purpose of the church becomes one of acting in history as a witness to the God that creates, liberates, and redeems history. As this witness, the church—and through it Christianity—is a making visible of the invisible, a sacrament of God's action in history. Gutiérrez captures this new interpretation of the transforming activity of the church in the world: "as a sign of the liberation of man and history, the Church itself in its concrete existence ought to be a place of liberation. A sign should be clear and understandable. If we conceive of the Church as a sacrament of the salvation of the world, then it has all the more obligation to manifest in its visible structures the message that it bears."[48]

Much of the transforming activity of the church takes place in basic Christian communities, or *comunidades eclesiales de base*. Basic Christian communities include a wide variety of small, loosely structured religious groups involved in projects ranging from Bible study to political action.[49] Through working on concrete problems or specific tasks, basic Christian communities function as a locus for conscientization, educational activity that enables persons to participate more effectively in a variety of political, religious, and social projects. This education is based on Christian commitment and has a Christian goal; the commitment is to the privileged option for the poor as the place of the church and the goal is one of witness and mission to Latin American society. The commitment and goal often express themselves through an attempt to work on some local project such as improving the water system in a neighborhood. Before persons can improve a water system, they must study the political systems in their society and understand their rights and duties as citizens; they must educate themselves to do the necessary tasks and they must accept, through the process of conscientization in basic Christian communities, the basic religious responsibility for changing this historical situation.

The major strategy of conscientization developed out of Paulo Freire's project of liberating education, articulated in his major work, *Pedagogy of the Oppressed*.[50] This work has been used widely in literacy campaigns in Brazil, Chile, and other Latin American countries. Freire proposes that education should be "liberating" and that it be structured as a mutual ongoing process between co-learners. Education, in the understanding of Freire, is the practice of freedom and depends on a political decision to make persons fully active in their concrete situation. Liberating education stimulates consciousness to emerge through constant problem-posing in which persons think about the problem and its social context in a critical fashion. The purpose of liberating education is for persons to be able to "name the world," to be subjects in their own history.

Latin American liberation theologians adapt from Freire's work the process of conscientization, a type of critical theory that helps persons to become emancipated agents in their social contexts. Conscientization, in this understanding, is not only a matter of undertaking new projects and learning new skills; more fully considered, conscientization enacts freedom, creating a new human subject. Latin American liberation theologians revise conscientization to name the activity of faith: becoming human in solidarity with God and with the poor. The enactment of freedom is not only a process of education but also a process of grace, dependent upon God's activity with the oppressed. Thus adapted, conscientization becomes a process of conversion to the neighbor based on a spirituality of gratuitousness. This conversion to the "other" and the spirituality of gratuitousness is, in Latin American liberation theology, a way of procuring the dignity of human persons and a way of realizing freedom in history. Conscientization is, in liberation theology, a project of freedom that takes place in small, basic Christian communities where persons engage their faith, experience God, and work together for justice.

Basic Christian communities model an ecclesiology that is very much "of the people" and "in the world." Because basic Christian communities are located in the concrete praxis of the poor and because they envision a new way of life for both the church and the society, they serve as the ecclesiastical context for many Latin American liberation theologians. Those theologians find in the basic Christian communities a new way of experiencing and reflecting on Christianity through the poor, as Gutiérrez remarks:

> Only these base-level Christian communities, rising up out of the oppressed but believing people, will be in a position to proclaim and live the values of the Kingdom in the very midst of the common masses who are fighting for their liberation. The practice of these communities continually leads them beyond themselves. The CCBs are a means, a tool if you will, for the evangelization of all nations from the standpoint of the poor and exploited. That is why they are transforming our way of understanding Christian discipleship. . . . They arise in the very process of living out what Christ means for the common masses, of showing how the gratuitous gift of the Kingdom is accepted in their efforts to free themselves from exploitation, defend their rights as poor people, and fashion a human society that is free and just.[51]

BASIC THEMES IN LATIN AMERICAN LIBERATION THEOLOGY

Though Latin American liberation theology began with an economic critique of developmentalism, it soon expanded its critique to the cultural realm and the humanistic sciences of cultural interpretation. As theologians worked in basic Christian communities, attempting to make sense of the situation in light of their own theological training, they began to question the nature and method of modern theology. In the midst of criticizing modernity and serving the poor, Latin American liberation theology forged a new theological paradigm: representing a "new" subject outside the realm of modern history; testifying to an experience of God not found in modern theology; and calling for a new way of doing theology. Consequently the basic themes of Latin American liberation theology are three: (1) the "preferential option for the poor," (2) God as liberator, and (3) the liberation of theology.

The Preferential Option for the Poor

The church's turn to worldly transformation and to concrete issues of justice results not in a call for charitable sympathy, but for the recognition of the rights of the poor. The poor are not simply to be helped, assisted along as the chronically "underprivileged," but must be granted their rights to speak, to eat, to work, to think. The bishops at Puebla affirmed the church's preferential option for the poor that Medellín had established and Latin American liberation theologians had adopted as *a*, if not *the*, basic characteristic of their theology: "With renewed hope in the vivifying power of the Spirit, we are going to take up once again the position of the Second General Conference of the Latin American episcopate in Medellín, which adopted a clear and prophetic option expressing preference for, and solidarity with, the poor."[52] The preferential option for the poor is the most fundamental theme of Latin American liberation theology: it illustrates the massive poverty and oppression of the third world as the major theological concern; it identifies the Christian faith as a spirituality of evangelical poverty; and it expresses the experience of God in the journey of the poor. In sum: the preferential option for the poor locates a paradigm shift in Christian experience and reflection. The preferential option for the poor is the solidarity, in memory and hope through Jesus Christ, of Christianity with the poor, with the despised and dispossessed of the earth.

The option for the poor reminds us of the situation of Latin America, a situation that must be seen not through the eyes of those who "make" history, but through the eyes of those who suffer history. Any critical understanding of the situation begins in the faces of starving young children, of adolescents who cannot find productive work, of the indigenous people (often the poorest of poor), of peasants exiled from the land that belongs to them, of laborers refused their rights, and of the aged who have lost their "value" along with their ability to produce. "In these faces," the bishops at Puebla said, "we ought to recognize the suffering features of Christ our Lord, who questions and challenges us."[53] The poor are not abstract economic statistics, but represent an actual way of being in the world—a way of being conditioned by cultural, economic, social, political, and international factors. The poor, the victims of history, are the majority of the Latin American populace.

The preferential option for the poor also recognizes the existence of popular movements for liberation in Latin America. Indeed, for Latin American liberation theology, the *most* important fact in recent history is what Gustavo Gutiérrez calls the "irruption of the poor," the quest of the poor or the nonperson for self-realization in history.[54] This irruption of the poor, with its various popular movements, is a struggle not only for economic justice but also for a new way of becoming human. The struggle seeks to find a new way beyond the oppressive consumerism of capitalism and the totalitarian control of communism. This quest is called "liberation" and works for improved economic, cultural, political, educational, and psychological conditions.

In Latin American liberation theology the preferential option for the poor identifies Christianity with this quest for liberation. Christianity takes a preferential though not exclusive option for the poor; it extends its solidarity with all persons through its solidarity with the poor. The poor, in Latin American liberation theology, represent the quest of all persons in the historical project of humanity. Consequently, the preferential option for the poor is the identification of Christianity with the human subject. As Gutiérrez indicates, "solidarity with the poor, with their struggles and their hopes, is the condition of an authentic solidarity with everyone—the condition of a universal love that makes no attempt to gloss over the social oppositions that obtain in the concrete history of peoples, but strides straight through the middle of them to a kingdom of justice and love."[55] The Scriptures reveal that God in God's gratuitousness chooses to be on the side of the poor; therefore, the privileged option for the poor is always a religious option and a religious experience for the Christian.

The option for the poor necessitates a spirituality of evangelical poverty, since Christianity is itself now a form of poverty, of becoming poor in imitation of Christ. This praxis of following Christ involves the identification of the love of God with the love of neighbor.[56] Indeed, the option for the poor suggests a new reality for Christianity—a reality now characterized by a praxis of solidarity, a discipleship of service, a representation of the poor of the world. Christians renounce their attachment to material goods both as an identification with Christ and neighbor and as a protest against sin. In this spirituality of poverty, Christianity does not idealize poverty but takes it on in order to abolish it. The option for the poor identifies a new form of Christian life, a mystical/political spirituality of poverty, which, in representation and service, satisfies the world's hunger, interrupts humanity's sinfulness, heals history's diseases, and liberates the oppressed.

God as Liberator

At its center Latin American liberation theology embraces the metaphor of God as liberator. As in other theologies, the metaphors, symbols, and concepts of this theology are influenced by culture but are formed as uniquely Christian in light of Scripture, Christian tradition, and church teachings. The metaphor of God as liberator provokes the movement of liberating praxis, judges historical situations, recalls the dangerous memories of Christian tradition, and gives hope for the journey into freedom. As the central metaphor, God as liberator relates to other symbols popular in Latin American liberation theology—to the suffering Christ, to the church as sacrament of history, to Christ liberating culture, and to the symbols of popular religion.

For this founding metaphor of God as liberator, the exodus serves as the paradigmatic event: it unites creation and redemption in the promise of historical fulfillment. The unity of creation and redemption in liberation is a basic foundation for the systematic content of Latin American liberation theology, as Andrew Kirk, author of a text on biblical themes in liberation theology, observes: "the close line between creation and historical acts of liberation in a unitary, overall design of God for the world, gives to liberation theology its chief biblical/theological basis for considering man's history as an open-ended process for which he is fundamentally responsible."[57] God as liberator indicates that history is open-ended, with no predetermined finish or final event, and that salvation is always mediated through history. Latin American liberation theologians thus claim that "history is one," meaning by this that there is no special salvific realm above or beyond history. The metaphor of God as liberator signals the providential relation of God to the world, God acting in history through human activity for the coming kingdom. Sin both constitutes and is expressed through historical structures of oppression; it is the whole of creation, both natural and social, groaning in travail. This is not to exclude the notion of sin as the willful act of an individual turning away from God; it is, rather, to make sense of human pride, hubris, and concupiscence in relation to all of God's creation. Sin is inclusive of alienation, and alienation must be understood through social categories.

Christ's person and work must, Latin American liberation theology tells us, also be considered through the metaphor of liberation.[58] Christ is the suffering Christ, the identification of God with those who suffer under oppression. In his identification with the poor and in his prophetic teaching that blesses the poor, Christ models liberation in his revolt against worldly authorities. Christ gives liberation, for his resurrection victory sets free the power of faith. Christ discloses the praxis of solidarity and transformation that Christianity represents: the work of Christ is both a fulfillment and a transformation of history itself.

As the representation of Christ in history, the church is a sacrament of history, the visible presentation of God's invisible liberating grace. As such, the church is the sign of God's liberating activity, witnessing to that which it signifies through its own praxis of solidarity with the poor. The role of the church is evangelization, the bringing of good news to the dispossessed of the earth. The activity of the church proclaims the gift of God's liberation and operates prophetically in each historical situation.[59] The church is a "sign and instrument of the transformation of society" in relation to God as liberator.[60] All these symbols and others are interpreted through the central metaphor of God as liberator, and thus this metaphor becomes the systematic center of Latin American liberation theology.

The Liberation of Theology

Through the privileged option for the poor and through the root metaphor of God as liberator, Latin American liberation theology elaborates a new understanding of human existence and a new interpretation of Christianity. Its interests are the quest for freedom, equality, and justice on the part of the poor, those who have been continually victimized in history; its concerns are false ideology, structural oppression, human dignity, and a liberating faith. The language of Latin American liberation theology is that of freedom, oppression, liberation, spirituality, and politics. It understands the Christian faith as a force in history that holds the possibility of helping all persons to become, within history, new people. With these new interests, concerns, and language, Latin American liberation theology provides a new way of doing theology, a new form of theological method.

Consistent with its history and location, Latin American liberation theology is a church theology—speaking to the church and guiding, more often than not, basic Christian communities. Within basic Christian communities, faith is experienced and understood as a praxis; theology is, quite simply stated, reflection on this praxis. Theology is the work of the corporate community of Christians reflecting on their faith; it is a task of faith seeking understanding. As a reflection on praxis, Latin American liberation theology draws upon the social sciences as well as upon philosophy. As a reflection on faith, it uses the symbols and rituals of popular religion. Within faith, then, theology is always a second act; it follows faith as a reflection upon the praxis of the community. In Latin American liberation theology, theology *is* a form of practical reflection: the activity of interpreting, guiding, and criticizing Christian praxis.

Latin American liberation theology faults modern theology for becoming a theory that functions as an ideology for the bourgeois, securing freedom as individual and ahistorical. Arguing that there is no "objective" theory unaffected by the thinker's historical particularity, Latin American liberation theology claims that theology must be self-consciously grounded in praxis. The norms and criteria for understanding and guiding human life exist in the praxis of particular communities; as Míguez Bonino notes, "there is no possibility of invoking or availing oneself of a norm outside of praxis itself."[61] Theology must be constantly self-critical, acknowledging its own participation in history and attempting to position itself in its own social location.

As the foundation of theology, praxis also suggests that human action and reflection are inherently oriented toward transformation. Latin American liberation theologians argue that the truth of theology involves reason as yet to be realized in history and is therefore temporal and transformative. Jon Sobrino, in a speech delivered to the Encuentro Latinoamericano de Teología in 1975 in Mexico City, noted two phases in the Enlightenment, phases that correspond to the differences between European theology and Latin American liberation theology. European theology, responding to the first phase of the Enlightenment, believes liberation to consist of the independence of reason and locates truth in theoretical rationality. Within the boundaries of reason, European theology demonstrates the truthfulness and meaningfulness of religious claims, thus, as Sobrino states, "liberating the faith from any elements of myth or historical error."[62] Latin American liberation theology, within the second phase of the Enlightenment, responds to the need to confront and change a given historical situation, "a liberation from the misery of the world."[63] In this second phase of the Enlightenment, the task of theology is not simply to describe the "is" of each historical situation but also to suggest the "ought," a new way of being in light of Christian faith and worldly existence. Sobrino describes theology in the second phase of the Enlightenment: "Latin American theology is interested in liberating the real world from its wretched state, since it is this objective situation that has obscured the real meaning of faith. The task, therefore, is not to understand the faith differently, but to allow a new faith to spring from a new practice."[64]

In sum: Latin American liberation theology is a new interpretation of the Christian faith, combining spirituality and politics as part of the ongoing process of Christian conversion to God and neighbor. It understands human existence in terms of social agency, and history in terms of liberation. It reflects on a new subject, the poor, and reads the Scripture in light of a liberating God. This theology is a practical reflection, a process of discerning, judging, deciding, and becoming within a specific community.

As Christian theology always has, Latin American liberation theology represents faith seeking understanding, a faith of the poor and an understanding that transforms history. To the first world, Latin American liberation theology is the voice of the "other" coming from the underside of history. It is a strongly Christian voice, speaking out of its journey with God and reinterpreting the Christian tradition in light of its own context of suffering. To understand this voice we are asked to view history with other eyes, to displace our own knowledge of God into the irruption of the poor. Having taken this wager with the victims of history, we may, in turning to political theology, now hear another voice and another testimony: the rupture of modern culture, bourgeois religion, and progressive theology by those who in any account are themselves the victors of history, but victors deeply aware of the failings, the fragility, and the faults of their victory.

2

Political Theology

German political theology arose in the 1960s during a period of intense secularization for the culture and churches of Western developed nations. Western churches sought to take a new global role in Vatican II and the 1966 Geneva Assembly of the World Council of Churches. In the academy, theologies of secularization became popular, embracing the secular world as the natural outcome of the Christian tradition. These theologies spoke of play, the city, the Dionysian person, and student protests as a part of the Christian blessing on the world. Yet the euphoria of the 1960s gave way to a mood of sobriety with the horrors of Vietnam, the failures of student protests, and the recognition of massive corruption in governments. Disenchantment with the secularized world was accompanied by increasing dismay at the positivist approaches in science, philosophy, government, and technology—approaches that sought to plan and control both developed and underdeveloped societies.[1]

In the midst of this ambiguous cultural situation, political theologians declare that only a radical transformation can save the human subject and the Christian tradition. Western society and modern Christianity, the political theologians argue, have elevated themselves at the expense of those who suffer; the West has become a tower of success for a few victors on a human platform of many victims. Events such as Auschwitz, political theology maintains, reveal not only the dreadful plight of our times but also locate the "new" subject of modernity's collapse, the subject of suffering. The true purpose of Christianity, maintains political theology, is to represent this human subject, the subject who suffers, through the retrieval of the dangerous memory of Jesus Christ. To oppose the suffering that Western culture and religion have both caused and forgotten, political theology urges conversion to a new way of being human and a new way of following Christ.

Political theology relocates the subject in suffering and reinterprets human existence through the praxis of freedom; political theology continues the Christian tradition only through its insistence that Christianity is the continual transformation of suffering and hope in the dangerous memory of Christ. But in the radical reinterpretations of the subject and Christian tradition, political theology carries forward the project of modern theology—the project of understanding the human subject by the mediation of Christian tradition and contemporary existence. Consequently, to understand political theology, we must begin by following the project of modern theology, paying special attention to its own change and development through its engagement with culture. By following the project of modern theology we shall come to dwell, for a time, in the contemporary context, the cultural home, of political theology, arriving at an understanding of political theology as a "situated theology." In its own cultural home, political theology attempts to respond to the issues of ideology critique, pluralism, relativism, and praxis. Finally, we shall explore the rupture and transformation of modern theology that characterizes political theology: very much a part of its own culture and an inheritor of modern theology's project, political theology seeks not only to understand the subject, mediating tradition and existence, but to form the subject, transforming both tradition and existence in a practical, fundamental fashion.

THE PROJECT OF MODERN, WESTERN THEOLOGY

Before modernity the worldview of Christendom centered on God who, in turn, determined the very parameters of life. God started the world by shaping, molding, creating it out of nothing; undoubtedly God would end the world in judgment and glory. God caused miraculous events to occur in a natural order that, for its very rhythms, depended on God's desires. Jesus was a God-Man, both divine and human, supernatural and natural, bearing the special gift of grace that added to or completed nature. Life, lived in the realm of the natural infused with the supernatural, was but a temporary passage full of travails and sorrows, leading to a fulfillment that existed beyond this world. There were two planes—one eternal, never changing, the realm of God, and the other tragic, full of hardships, the sphere of human life. That sphere, the world, was imposed as fate; religion was bestowed upon the world to point above to eternal, unchanging salvation. Theologians reported on eternal truths given by God, enshrined in doctrine, and protected by the holy church.

In the modern world this worldview was shattered by the progressive autonomy of Western "man."[2] Humanity gained the powers to determine, if not the very parameters of birth and death, then certainly the quality, values, and substance of life. The genesis of the world was interpreted through the theory of evolution, and the telos of life was located in history, a history that was rapidly progressing toward perfection. Modernity viewed the world as material for construction and envisioned the goal of life to lie in present satisfaction. As the intellectual partner of modernity, the Enlightenment threw off traditional authorities—especially traditional religious authorities—for the sake of free, autonomous reflection: with almost total reverence for the autonomy of the human person, the Enlightenment fervently worshiped history as the representation of the human subject. Philosophy and theology reflected on human subjectivity and human consciousness. Disciplines like sociology and psychology were designed to study "humanity," who now contained a psyche that could be adapted, reformed, and revolutionized to meet changing needs. Science explored nature as an environment that could be influenced, manipulated, and controlled. Knowledge, culture, economics, science, the arts, politics, and history all found their center in the human subject.

Modernity achieved its freedom, in part, through the destruction of the intimate ties between religion and society; the medieval marriage between church and state was forever rent asunder by society itself. Major religious foundations were not merely questioned; they were destroyed. The particularistic myths of religion were surrendered to the realms of the private, retained as superstitions for the weak-minded or ignorant. On the other hand, the formal ritual of religion received special recognition for its social usefulness in maintaining the state. Modernity was, after all, a leap from a religious-mythical, natural world to a rational-functional, historical world. This leap from a divinized to a humanized world demanded more than the mere dismissal of individual beliefs about the location of heaven, the creation of the world, or the role of miracles in nature.[3] Modernity depended on the ability to experience and reflect on life in a historical fashion. Historical knowledge construes events in relation to causes and effects; it considers events in relation to other events, a consideration that excluded the possibility of human knowledge of supernatural events.

Theologians such as Friedrich Schleiermacher and Ernst Troeltsch recognized the challenge that historical knowledge presented to Christian theology. Ernst Troeltsch identified three principles of historical inquiry: (1) the principle of criticism—no absolute truth or falsity can be assured, but only degrees of probability; (2) the principle of analogy—judgments can be made on the basis of similarity between present and past experience; and (3) the principle of correlation—one occurrence has effects on an entire set of relations.[4] Troeltsch correctly understood that these principles necessitate, among other things, that miracles cannot be a subject for historical inquiry, since miracles exclude probability, deny any similarity in history, and preclude correlation with other historical events. Moreover, these principles of historical inquiry create a divided loyalty for the theologian; the theologian, as Van Harvey suggests, must now live by the canons of historical inquiry as a modern person, as well as by the canons of church teaching as a Christian.[5] On the one hand, as a citizen of modernity and a member of the modern academy, the theologian must abide by the guiding propositions and ruling methods of historical inquiry. On the other hand, as a believer in religious doctrine and loyal member of the church, the theologian must remain faithful to traditional teaching and dogma. Would the theologian part company with the church and not reflect on the logos of the Theos? Or would the theologian forgo his or her place in modernity and thus never be heard in the academy? Did the theologian (and the believer) have to choose between being rational and being religious?

Or could the rational itself be religious, grounded in a Christian acceptance of history? Believing that modernity was based on a Christian impulse, liberal

Protestant theologians sought to reinterpret archaic, misplaced, and even superstitious religious beliefs.[6] Unabashedly modern people, the liberals were committed to modern historical inquiry and to the belief that history was progressively improving. Well within the ethos of their times, they formulated an optimistic theology, based on the belief that the force progressively improving nature, morality, and knowledge was understood correctly as God. In this way liberal theologians demonstrated that theology need not be opposed to rational inquiry and that religion need not be opposed to modernity.

Liberal theology reconciled modernity and religion: modernity corrected the artificial trappings of religion, and religion in turn used its essence to ground and bless modernity. Religion did not depend on miracles, the liberals exclaimed, for history itself displayed the impulse of the religious.[7] Theologians used historical criticism to explain the person of Jesus as a great moral figure, as a religious archetype, as a privileged picture of love and charity.[8] Hand in hand with modernity, liberal theologians studied the human subject as the location and realization of religion; though the object of religion, God, could no longer be studied directly, human consciousness provided a subject that, when properly interpreted, reflected the "whence" of existence, God.

Liberal theology was, as Langdon Gilkey has noted, a courageous and important movement in theology.[9] Liberal theologians made Christianity relevant to human history and bestowed upon the faith a new identity—the identity of representing the ultimate essence of free human life. In so doing, liberal theology established an agenda of an ongoing conversation between modernity and Christianity, a conversation that continues even in contemporary political theology. But in the manner in which it formulated the agenda, liberal theology was largely a project of accommodation. Christianity's content was replaced by a picture of the historical Jesus; its form was dependent on the progressive evolution of history; its telos was tied to the Enlightenment ethos of optimism. Liberal theology became a member of modernity, but preserved little, if any, of Christianity's non-identity with the world. Christianity, in liberal theology's version, was reduced to being entirely "of this world."

Liberal theology met its demise with the turn of the twentieth century and the almost total breakdown of any belief in moral and evolutionary progress.[10] Optimism was replaced with pessimism; life was not characterized by progress, pleasure, and reason but by anxiety, fear, and despair. Alienation existed as a break in the meaning of history rather than a temporary delay in progress. In both East and West, freedom became threatened by the technical manipulation of society. Two world wars failed to solve the problems of aggression and violence, of right and wrong, of oppression and totalitarianism.

Modern theology responded to these times of despair with neo-orthodoxy, which included various forms of existentialist, transcendental, and personalist theologies.[11] For the neo-orthodox theologians, the meaning of life and the experience of God could not be identified with this empty, broken mess called history. If life had any meaning, any hope, any religious value, it had to come from that which is beyond or outside of history. Only a Wholly Other God, as

Karl Barth said, could both judge and save human life.[12] Reflecting its own cultural situation, neo-orthodoxy refused to put any faith in historical progress. Nor would it depend on historical knowledge to secure the essence of Christianity by recovering the religion of Jesus. Indeed, historical inquiry and scholarship, as important as they were, could and must be kept separate from religious faith. Faith could not depend on the vicissitudes of scholarship any more than it could depend upon the changes of history. To the liberal puzzle of the proper adjudication between historical knowledge and religious truth, neo-orthodox theologians offered the strategy of demythologization, using historical-critical methods to strip away the dated vessels of biblical myths in order to occasion a new encounter with the Christ of faith.[13] The Bible could be home, both for the historian who studies it through historical inquiry and for the religious believer who receives it in encounter and engagement.

It is significant that neo-orthodox theology secured faith outside the process of history. Neither faith nor God could be arrived at through limited, changing reason but only through the unlimited gift of revelation in Jesus Christ. As Karl Rahner suggested, God gives, through grace, an immediate relationship that fulfills and authenticates the human subject.[14] This was not to deny the autonomy of reason; indeed, it courageously distinguished the realms of revelation and reason. Revelation could not be reduced to scientific facts or sublated within the general ordering of human history; though revelation occurred through human history, it was never to be identified with history. But neo-orthodoxy, despite its name, did not return to a premodern view of revelation as supernatural "truths" buttressed by the belief in miracles.

Neo-orthodoxy committed itself to the modern world; it accepted science and historical inquiry but it also confronted the despair and meaninglessness of the twentieth century. Formally, the problem of neo-orthodoxy was the problem of liberalism—how to *understand* and give meaning to the human subject in the modern world. Though the world was, for the neo-orthodox theologians, pessimistic and tragic rather than optimistic and progressive, it nonetheless presented a cognitive challenge—a challenge neo-orthodoxy answered by locating faith in an encounter between the individual and God. Neo-orthodox theologians portrayed faith as personal, individual, and interior; thus, said its critics, neo-orthodoxy worked through history to get beyond history.

Like liberal theology before it, neo-orthodoxy paralleled the mood and ethos of its historical situation; like liberal theology, it maintained the relevance of Christianity by making it the true representation of human meaning, value, and worth. But neo-orthodoxy contradicted liberalism, emphasizing the non-identity of Christianity with the world and making the "not being of this world" the locus of faith. Neo-orthodoxy replaced the immanence of the liberal God, who threatened to become a deification of humanity, with the transcendence of its Wholly Other God as Lord and Judge of all.

Neo-orthodoxy and liberalism might be warring neighbors, but they did live in the same neighborhood—the dwelling of progressive Christianity within a modern world. Though the forms, understandings, and answers might be radically different, theology was, nonetheless, the interpretation of human existence and Christian tradition in the present situation. In so doing, through both liberalism and neo-orthodoxy, theology set for itself a distinct agenda: (a) understanding and giving meaning to the human subject, (b) the creative reinterpretation of tradition as the faithful representation of tradition, and (c) the interpretive role of theology in mediating the relationship of human existence and Christian tradition. With this agenda we move on to a cultural situation different from that of either neo-orthodoxy or liberalism, a situation that summons forth a new form of modern theology—a form that, in continuity with the agenda of modern theology, reinterprets both Christianity and human existence.

THE CULTURAL SITUATION OF POLITICAL THEOLOGY

The 1960s were, altogether, a period of radical questioning in the form of various critiques—the "opting-out" of flower children, the radicalism of antiwar protesters, the emphasis on environmental ethics, a philosophical utopianism, growing resistance to governmental controls and planning, and demands for the liberation of women, blacks, and other minorities. These critiques shared the common sentiment that something was wrong on a massive global scale and that the future must be radically different from the present. The critiques also indicated the emergence of a new cultural situation: modernity was becoming aware of its many different members. This recent period of modernity, with its critiques and questions, is the context for political theology. It can be explored through the examination of the following four features: (1) ideology critique, (2) pluralism, (3) relativism, and (4) praxis.

Ideology Critique

The first feature of the contemporary period, ideology critique, points to the social distortions of modernity, distortions calling into question the very rationality and freedom of the project of modernity. In recent years ideology critique has become a nightly media event, a ritual unveiling of modernity's illusions, contradictions, and distortions. Scientific "advances" tempt the destruction of this planet; manufacturing techniques result in acid rain that destroys plant life. The ability to control nature threatens in the end to destroy the human race, which seems to have forgotten its own dependence on nature. Bureaucratic organizations routinely command human actions—in a bureaucracy persons are parts that can easily be discarded and replaced. Equality is determined more in the marketplace than in the voting booth. Modern freedom and reason create the power of nuclear weapons, with which humanity is at the center of not only experience, history, and knowledge but even time and space. What could be more free and autonomous? What could be more irrational and oppressive?

The victims of history accuse modernity of building its progress upon their suffering. The Jews recall the memories of the Holocaust; the survivors testify to modernity's project of "extermination." Women accuse patriarchal modernity of ensuring misogyny by representing women as inferior through biology, sociology, psychology, religion, and history. Blacks realize that their emancipation from slavery was far too often liberation into hunger, homelessness, and joblessness. Latin Americans denounce their history as the industrial colony of the first world.

These various forms of ideology critique question the prevailing structures and systems of reality, especially as those systems are reflected in symbolic, structural, and epistemic "views of reality." Many of the critical theories of the nineteenth and twentieth centuries have been powerfully retrieved, elucidating the various distortions within modernity. These modern masters of suspicion include Karl Marx, who accused the bourgeoisie of hiding behind an ideology that masks their greedy interests, keeps the poor impoverished, and protects their privileged existence. Sigmund Freud disclosed to us the power of the unconscious in influencing our meanings, motivations, and behaviors. Friedrich Nietzsche warned that our conscious reflections on freedom disguise our unconscious drives for individual power. In recent years the critiques of modernity have increased and expanded even beyond those who place themselves in the tradition of Marx, Freud, or Nietzsche. Hans-Georg Gadamer denies the very notion of autonomous reason and argues that reason is always based on tradition.[15] Michel Foucault argued that the "human subject" is a construct of society;[16] Alasdair MacIntyre accuses the Enlightenment project of being incapable of morality because of its inherent emotivism.[17] Jacques Derrida criticizes modernity's "metaphysics of presence" for covering up the irreducibility of "differance" that constitutes all of life.[18] The critiques of modernity arise not only from its victims, but also from its citizens.

In sum, the cries and demands of its victims and the internal critique by its own "citizens" threaten to rupture the very project of modernity: together they accuse modernity of the distortion of reason and of the systematic oppression and repression of humanity. Modernity is built on a foundation, a foundation of its victims, whom it pushes into and past the very margins of its history.[19] The Enlightenment is grounded in a reason that denies its own location and seeks to cover its own irrationality. Modernity is guaranteed by its freedom, the freedom of a greedy culture that stuffs itself with goods and services and forgets its memories and its wounds. Ideology critique—be it on picket lines, in consciousness-raising groups, or academic texts—reveals that the freedom of modernity is defined through control and domination.

Religion is understood by many of the masters of suspicion as yet another false ideology, one more illusion. Marx, following Feuerbach, called religion the "opiate of the people" and regarded it as one more form of ideology. Jews and women question the ideological distortions alive in the Christian Scriptures. Indeed, simple observation indicates that religion is far too often used to placate those who suffer and to siphon off any critical energy through charitable goodwill. Christians, however, are also among the voices both on the margins and in the center, crying out against the distortions within modernity. A new form of Christian witness and reflection begins emerging in various grassroots movements and base communities. Seminaries and churches reassess their witness in light of Christian tradition and reconsider their mission in light of cultural needs. But is this too another illusion? Or do religion and theologians have something to contribute? On which side of the dialectic of Enlightenment does Christianity stand?

Pluralism

Contemporary existence may well be best characterized by the word "pluralism": the reality of a multiplicity of worldviews, ethics, religions, roles, and people. Once human existence was described in the language of "common," "shared," "we," and the stranger was encountered only in exotic travels or in extraordinary, chance encounters. But now our language refers to "difference," "variations," and "the other," and now the stranger lives next door: the pluralism of modernity is a basic fact of human existence. Most surprisingly of all, we realize that the modern Western world is not a monolithic culture: culture is not a melting pot but a smorgasbord of different beliefs, work habits, and ways of leisure. Pluralism is the reality of otherness and difference on both a common-sense and a philosophical level. Considered alternatively as different representations of the same mass culture or as differences in constituting values, worldviews, and belief structures, pluralism is both a fact and a value in the present situation. Pluralism can be understood as a fact—the fact of otherness and difference within the present period. Pluralism can also be understood as a value—the value placed upon living together, not despite but through the differences.

But pluralism also connotes that any one person lives in many different worlds; a person may work in one part of town, live in another, and belong to a club in still a third area. And each of these areas may be totally unrelated, with the only intersection being the person. In each area the person plays a different role: in one, the person might be an attorney, in another a mother or father, and in the third a friend, or ballplayer, or member of an interest group. Different value structures, symbolic worlds, and community ties may operate in the different worlds of any one individual. Pluralism is the variety and the intensity of different ways and dimensions of living.

In religion pluralism means that the social world of the believer is no longer composed of persons who attend the same church, hold the same beliefs, or even worship the same God. Consequently families may combine a mixture of religious beliefs—beliefs that ancestors fought wars to keep apart. Such religious pluralism poses a question: Do these differences in belief make any real difference? Moreover, pluralism does not simply refer to the different groups within Christianity; it also acknowledges the awareness of religions other than Christianity. What can Christianity learn and what can it contribute to world religions? Theologians ponder the radical monotheistic God in Christianity: Is

God one among the many? Theologians wonder where and how religion fits in all the pluralism of an individual life: Does religion bind together all the various pieces, ground the whole of life, or exist as one function among many? Finally, in this reality of pluralism the theologian must speak to the different publics of church, society, and academy. David Tracy has argued that in these different publics the theologian must struggle with all the implications and questions of pluralism: the diversity of interpretations, multiple claims for truth and meaning, a variety of conceptual schemes, and differences in beliefs and values.[20]

Relativism

In the contemporary period pluralism exists hand in hand with relativism. Relativism names the belief that there is no underlying unity, no becoming, no transcendence in or beyond history. There is, in the most extreme expressions of relativism, no possible method or process capable of making translations or comparing different conceptual schemes or value structures. Philosophically, relativism maintains that even the concepts we use to comprehend reality—concepts such as history, humanity, and natural rights—are themselves culturally conditioned. Reason is not only historical; it is also culture-bound. There are no universal, transcendental, or general rules even for conversation. Indeed, any attempts at translation or comparison are simply ideological cover-ups for some latent form of imperialism or universalism. In this sea of relativism, we may wonder if there is any way to settle the difference: you believe one way because, by an accident of birth, you were born in a particular culture; I believe another way because I, through my own birthright, inherited a different cultural code. Relativism confronts the contemporary age with a multiplicity of options without any criteria for choosing among these options.[21]

Is religion just another conceptual system, belief structure, or worldview? Furthermore, is the very concept of religion bound to Western culture itself? Are the differences between religions reducible to differences in cultures and systems? Is dialogue even possible? For the theologian, relativism questions the role of religion (Is it a conceptual system?) as well as its relativity (Is it just one more conceptual system, no better or worse than the others?). If the most extreme assertions of relativism are true, then Christianity's claims to universalism, by way of universal redemption or in speaking for the universal human subject, are but two forms of the same cultural illusion.

Praxis

Increasingly, discussions of ideology critique, relativism, and pluralism lead to a consideration of praxis. Praxis is, positively stated, the realization that humans make history and, negatively stated, the realization that humans cannot rely on any ahistorical, universal truths to guide life. In recent years we have come to understand praxis as foundational, recognizing ideology critique, relativism, and pluralism as appealing to human praxis for criteria and norms of both reflection and action.²² Hence, even though the relativist makes a theoretical case for the inability to compare different value systems, in practice humans with quite different systems live, work, and act together. Likewise, the pluralism that composes present human praxis provides possibilities for growth and enrichment in various political, cultural, and personal spheres. In attending to the ongoing norms and meanings in concrete human activity, praxis also entails the fact of power and interest in human interactions.²³ Though praxis is no less ambiguous than theory, concrete action contains suggestions and possibilities for critical evaluation and transformation.

Praxis suggests, then, a bringing together of action and reflection, transformation and understanding. This new marriage of action and reflection depends on accepting human life as fundamentally practical. It is through this foundation of praxis that there may be a transformative influence of critique, a powerful enrichment of pluralism, and a continual adjudication of relativism. Within the rich possibilities of praxis, there are, of course, different forms and versions of how praxis provides new possibilities for action and reflection. Some attend to language itself as the most basic form of human activity, seeking in language the norms for human action and reflection. Others study the traditions of literature, memories, stories, and symbols for visions that might criticize situations of oppression and provoke new cultural possibilities. Still others commit themselves to particular movements of emancipatory activity, hoping to influence human praxis through particular political activity. Whatever the form praxis takes, it involves the constructive attempt to take seriously the relativism, the pluralism, and the distortions of modernity.

In this factor of the present cultural situation, Christianity is understood as a particular religious praxis, and religion is understood as part of human praxis. Two issues popular with contemporary Christians are social action and spiritual development, both forms of concrete praxis. Christians struggle to "live out" their faith through prayer, meditation, and religious discipline or through action, witness, and prophetic testimony, or through both. Christian theologians follow different routes to place praxis at the center of theological reflection. Critical of the Enlightenment tendency to locate religion in common human experience, some theologians advocate a radical Christian praxis, a way of life that is set apart from the rest of the world.²⁴ Other theologians place the practical activities of appropriation and transformation at the center of theological hermeneutics.²⁵ Still other theologians find the turn to praxis a way of making theology less a false ideology, less an academic illusion, and less an incoherent abstraction.²⁶ Indeed, practical theology, theology as praxis, and theological reflection on praxis become new forms of theological method.

Taken together, these cultural factors portray a central paradox of modernity—the quest for both particularity and universality. We live in a global culture, constantly aware of ourselves as citizens of a world. But we inhabit history through particular ways, with particular traditions, symbols, dreams, and desires. Any quest for a global community will succeed only as it assures the radical otherness and difference within history itself. This paradox is not simply a theoretical or ecclesiastical concern; it is the living reality of most if not all men and women. The paradox is experienced as a crisis: a crisis that the theories and institutions and symbols of the past may be false and oppressive; a crisis that the particularity of Western modern culture has been universalized as the true, the good, and the beautiful. The paradox must also be experienced as a possibility—the possibility of learning, perhaps for the first time, to live together with our differences and to recognize others without having to identify the other as inferior.

It should be clear that neither the crisis nor the possibilities of the present situation can be fully addressed through neo-orthodoxy with its despairing individual before the radically transcendent God. Just as neo-orthodoxy had to overthrow liberalism because of its failure to understand existence adequately and to interpret Christianity appropriately, so too is neo-orthodoxy affirmed, negated, and transformed by the emergence of political theology. The problems of existential meaninglessness and despair needed the response of neo-orthodoxy; the problems of pluralism, relativism, and ideology critique require a theology that is both "public" and "critical," one that is both "open" and "transformative." In this cultural situation, modernity is both shattered and transformed; political theology must share with its own situation the spirit of rupture and revolution. Indeed, as we shall see, it is in the revolution of modern theology that political theology continues the agenda of its theological parents.

POLITICAL THEOLOGY: STAGE ONE

Political theology originates as a critique of neo-orthodoxy's individualism and modernity's ambiguities. Political theology becomes a form of ideology critique through its attention to the ideological function of religion, the daily conformity of the bourgeoisie, and the victims of suffering in modernity. Moreover, the nature of the critique defines two distinguishable stages of political theology.[27] In the first stage political theology emerges as a corrective to neo-orthodoxy—correcting the problems of individualism and existentialism through the interpretation of a God who creates and redeems history from the future. In the second stage political theology becomes an interruption of history, a critique of the very foundations of the subject, of freedom, and of reason through the history of suffering.

To begin the first stage—in which political theology is formulated as a critical corrective—Johann Baptist Metz sounds the charge to neo-orthodoxy:

> The religious consciousness formed by this theology attributes but a shadowy existence to the socio-political reality. The categories most prominent in this theology are mainly the categories of the intimate, the private, the apolitical sphere. . . . The category of encounter is predomi-

nant; the proper religious way of speaking is the interpersonal address; the dimension of proper religious experience is the apex of free subjectivity of the individual or the indisposable, the silent center of the I-Thou relation.[28]

Political theologians argue that neo-orthodoxy simply went along with the ethos of the day by allowing Christianity to be used as an escape for the middle-class subject. Religion was reduced to a matter of personal opinion and taste, which had little public import and no critical impetus. By its obsessive concentration on the abstract, privatized individual, neo-orthodoxy, in the assessment of political theology, failed to recognize that anxiety, despair, and loneliness were social problems in a bourgeois society. In contrast, for the political theologians the human subject whom theology addresses is always and only a social subject, who realizes meaning, value, and truth through concrete historical particularities. Furthermore, according to this critique, neo-orthodoxy also misread the Bible and misinterpreted Christian tradition. Neo-orthodoxy's method of demythologization—reading "through" the myths to occasion the religious encounter—rendered the biblical texts formless and timeless, and thus protected the privatized religiosity of the bourgeoisie. Political theology judges neo-orthodoxy as another form of Christianity's accommodation to modernity—avoiding the critical and practical challenges of the Enlightenment, ignoring the real human subject, and denying the critical import of Christianity.

In this first stage of political theology, the antidote to neo-orthodoxy is provided by eschatology. From the eschatological center of Christian faith, political theologians argue that history is characterized by an orientation to the future.[29] The importance of eschatology demands a critical role for Christianity in society and requires a new understanding of and method for theological reflection. Eschatology is the most dominant theme of the first stage, and includes at least three distinguishable emphases.

First, the theme of eschatology suggests a particular interpretation of the contemporary situation: oriented to new forms of social and political structures, the contemporary situation is one of ferment and change, characterized by ideology critique, pluralism, and relativism. History is oriented to the new, the future: time itself has an implicit orientation to the new, the not-yet. Humanity does not live by the repetition of the past (the classical view) or by the representation of the present (the modern view), but by the mediation of past and present through the future. The present is always relative, always penultimate to that which is to be in the future.

In this understanding of history as oriented to the future, political theologians were influenced by the philosopher Ernst Bloch.[30] Bloch's philosophy can be summarized in his slogan: the subject is not yet the predicate (S is not yet P).[31] For Bloch the human being, the natural world, and history all have the fundamental character of not-yet being: nature moves toward the future; history experiments; the human hopes.[32] For humanity's utopian desires, Bloch searched daydreams, visions, stories, myths, and folklore, all of which provide the material for a critique of the present situation and the impetus for revolution. Because the stories of religion have so often expressed humanity's future yearnings, Bloch defined religion as that which reveals the telos of reality. Therefore, Bloch concluded, God is a projection of what humanity is, the desire for the future.

Political theology found much to agree with in Bloch's understanding that history, nature, and the human person are all oriented to the new; but, for the political theologians, this lure of the future comes solely from God. The second emphasis of eschatology is an explicitly religious foundation for the "natural" orientation to the new in history. The promises given by God and revealed through the Bible create history; history is the time between the bestowal of the promises of God and their fulfillment by God.[33] Indeed, God is interpreted as "wholly transforming," present in history from the future, constantly realizing God's promises. Metz offers the notion of the eschatological proviso as the relation of nonidentity between God and history, the not-yet between the future and the present.[34] The eschatological proviso signifies that every present manifestation is partial and incomplete.

If eschatology provides a more adequate way to understand human existence, and a way far more appropriate to Christian tradition, it also offers political theology a different, more critical, function for the Christian church in society. From its own eschatological center in the resurrected Lord, the church criticizes every penultimate fulfillment of history. For Metz the church as a critical institution of freedom exists under the eschatological proviso to criticize the relative nature of all systems and structures.[35] So, too, for Moltmann the role of the church in society is to proclaim the critique and transformation of history by God.[36] Calling into question the present nature of society, the church pronounces the eschatological newness of history and demonstrates the relative accomplishments and failures of the present order.[37]

Moltmann and Metz argue that political theology must correct neo-orthodoxy by bringing the eschatological center of the Christian message into dialogue with the particular concerns of the present situation. For both theologians this correction changes the method and nature, as well as the content, of theology. Political theology involves, in this final theme of the first stage, an inquiry into a new relation between theory and praxis in theology. The new turn to praxis in theology necessitates that theology cannot merely reflect on doctrines or on abstract categories of existence but, rather, must begin its reflection within the concrete sociopolitical situation.

It should be observed that, throughout this first stage, the term "political theology" is a troublesome term, a name reminding many critics of the very ambiguous results of other political theologies. In ancient Greece and Rome, "political theology" referred to state religion, often considered the most important type of religion since the purpose of the state was to worship God.[38] In the age of Enlightenment "political theology" existed as a form of civil religion, providing social cohesiveness.[39] But far more bothersome than the ancient state religion or the modern civil religion was Carl Schmitt's attempt to formulate a "political theology" as the religious foundation for Nazi Germany.[40] Though Metz and Moltmann are aware of the highly ambiguous history of this term, they have no intent or desire to formulate any such type of "political religion." The primary purpose of their political theology is to be critical and transformative, not functional and legitimizing. Political theology, in the intent of these theologians, is not a theology of politics; it is a reflection and critique of the sociopolitical constitution of human life and the Christian tradition.[41]

In sum, the first phase of political theology can be characterized by the critique of neo-orthodoxy through the eschatological center of Christian faith. In this stage, political theology corrects the privatizing tendency of neo-orthodoxy by adding social history to the representation of the human subject. But in making itself a *corrective*, the first stage of political theology stumbles on its own notable internal problems. The notion of "political" is ambiguous and vague; political theologians are better at demanding that the political be considered rather than at clarifying how it is to be analyzed.[42] The intense emphasis on the future as the location for meaning, truth, and value leaves little validity to present experience. Political theology, with its privileged position in the eschatological proviso, threatens to become purely negative dialectics, with little transformative content. Despite the ambiguous contribution made by its searing ideology critique, the first stage of political theology continues the basic tendency in the paradigms of both neo-orthodox theology and liberal theology. Theology is, as it was in both neo-orthodoxy and liberalism, a theoretical reflection on the meaning of life in light of the contemporary situation and the Christian tradition. Liberalism explained the meaning of history as the meaning of religion; neo-orthodoxy proclaimed that Christianity offered a meaning beyond history; political theology moves the meaning of history to the future. Liberalism whispered, in its religious consciousness, a weak affirmation of progress; neo-orthodoxy heralded a personal, formless decision of faith; political theology, in its first stage, utters an ongoing negative ideology critique as religious praxis. Political theology has only corrected the fashion and not the form of modern theology's agenda to understand and give meaning to the human subject through a reinterpretation of Christian tradition.

POLITICAL THEOLOGY: STAGE TWO

If the first phase of political theology is designated by the key word "eschatology," then the second phase can be designated by the term "suffering": the suffering of a God on a cross, the suffering of the dead who shall not be forgotten, the suffering of the aged and the lonely, the suffering of the poor, the victims, the suffering of Christians and non-Christians, and the suffering that is both history and hope. The theme of suffering is, of course, present in the first stage of political theology. The eschatological mission of the church places it in a position of critique against the injustices of society so that the church, in its criticisms of society, is already on the side of the oppressed. The glorious resurrection of Christ occurs through his agonized suffering on the cross. In the second stage, however, suffering does not "function" to mediate meaning, be it a critical-social meaning for the subject in the future or an individual-interior meaning for the subject outside of history. Suffering "interrupts" modernity and modern theology, demanding transformation and conversion in history. Suffering brings forward a different subject of history; it reveals history as the history of suffering; it identifies Christ with the history of freedom. Deepening the critique of modernity and theology, suffering relocates anthropology, Christianity, and theology. The themes of this second stage are suffering, solidarity, and the praxis of theology.

Suffering, according to the political theologians, names our present situation, existing in interrelated "circles of death"—poverty, institutional rule by force, racial and cultural alienation, industrial pollution, senselessness and meaninglessness, and psychological agony.[43] The struggle for the transformation of the circles of death replaces the existentialist decision of faith as theology's major issue. No longer a mere corrective to neo-orthodoxy, political theology's purpose addresses the problem of massive public suffering that lies beyond any attempt at mere understanding—this problem of massive public suffering demands transformation. Suffering is the specific, sensuous suffering of groups and individuals; it forces the central categories of history, anthropology, and theology to be concrete. But suffering is more than the mere addition of new categories for improved understanding; it is the rupturing of the human subject: the revelation of a new human subject, who in memory and hope makes a claim yet to be realized in history.[44] With this human subject, the history of freedom becomes the history of suffering, for, as Walter Benjamin observed, history must now be read against the grain with those who suffer.[45]

In focusing on suffering as a lens to interrupt and interpret anthropology, political theology moves to a different kind of critique of modernity. The first stage was characterized by a critique of the *functional* ideology of modernity. The second stage is marked by a critique and transformation of the *epistemic* and *genetic* nature of modern consciousness.[46] The epistemic nature considers the very status of consciousness—the way we structure experience—as false and distorted. Consciousness may be false because value judgments are presented in it as empirical facts, because it maintains that a social phenomenon is really a natural phenomenon, or because it believes that the interest of one particular group is the interest of the whole society. The genetic nature of ideology critique uncovers how such false consciousness came into being, the origin of objectifying or masking ideologies. These problems are not, as in the first stage, simply functional, securing the operational character of beliefs and values, but constitutive, creating the very nature and structure of consciousness itself. What must now be criticized is the subtle and complex nature of consciousness, in other words, of not only the meaning but the very constitution of the human subject.

For such a critique of modernity's human subject, the second stage of political theology turns to those who suffer, and those who have already suffered, in history. Suffering is understood through concrete events, situations, and historical relations. The ultimate symbol of suffering becomes the image of the loss of memory and thus the loss of identity. In this second stage political theology fears, in the words of Metz, "the silent disappearance of the subject and the death of the individual in the anonymous compulsions and structures of a world that is constructed of unfeeling rationality and consequently allows identity, memory and consciousness of the human soul to become 'extinct.' "[47] As this history of suffering makes us question the very foundations of modernity, so it makes us question the epistemic and genetic principles of human consciousness.

This new form of ideology critique parallels the work of the Frankfurt School of critical theory, especially the work of such persons as Max Horkheimer, Theodor Adorno, Herbert Marcuse, and Walter Benjamin.[48] In its early years at the Institute for Social Research, the Frankfurt School continued the basic thrust of the German Idealist tradition by discovering ways in which reason could be critically realized in society. The Frankfurt School contributed no formal method, denying any attempt to arrive at a generalized view of freedom, history, and reason. Theodor Adorno's *Negative Dialectics* exemplifies the position of the early Frankfurt School; in this book, critical theory as nonidentity thinking moves in the distance between the object and the concept, the material world and the idea.[49]

As in the Frankfurt School, political theology reflects on the very nature and structure of Western consciousness—a consciousness that must be criticized and transformed in order to stop the rampage of history called "modernity." As a reflective theory, political theology seeks to serve the emancipatory interest of humanity, as this interest is represented by those who suffer history. With its attention to suffering, political theology creates a reflective theory for emancipation and enlightenment modeled after neither the natural sciences nor the hermeneutical disciplines. Hence political theology continues the anthropocentric turn of modernity through a radically different anthropology of the human subject, a new interpretation of Christianity, and a reformation in the very nature of theology itself.

As suffering reveals the distortions of anthropology, so it provides the constructive reformulation of anthropology and Christianity through solidarity with those who suffer. Solidarity is the most fundamental category of anthropology both ontologically, in terms of the underlying structures of being, and ontically, in terms of actual sensuous being. Solidarity implies not only that our lives are intertwined with the living, but also that we are intrinsically connected to the dead. Intersubjectivity is the primary character of individual life and life as a whole; there are no purely individual categories for meaning, for freedom, or even for reason. Solidarity is the basis for pluralism, relativism, and ideology critique but through a praxis of dialogue, discernment, and action.

Solidarity is mediated through memory and hope; the radical eschatology of the first stage becomes incarnate, in the second stage, through the dangerous memory of Christ. Political theology claims that, through its own dangerous memory of suffering, Christianity is the representation of human subjects in the history of suffering. The cross of Christ, for Moltmann, reveals the nature of freedom to be a solidarity with the past and an anticipation of the future.[50] God is not an abstract correlate for trust in existence; God is not merely an inescapable mystery beyond the horizons of thought. God is the liberator of history, choosing to be on the side of the oppressed, on the side of those who suffer history. The solidarity of human history and of Christian witness finds its ultimate referent in God's solidarity with the despised of the earth.

This solidarity with those who suffer is the gift of grace and, correlatively, the nature and role of Christian witness. Far beyond any easy religious consciousness reflective of historical process or any radical encounter with a totally other God, Christian experience is now a praxis of solidarity with those who suffer. In the first phase of political theology, Christian witness existed as a purely negative critique of the society. Now, in its second phase, Christianity is a "messianic" religion, testifying to the realization of a new human subject in history and proclaiming a new reformation in the church.[51] This messianic religion is a concrete praxis, not merely a belief system or an existential decision, but a concrete form of discipleship in imitation of Christ.[52] Christian witness takes sides, makes commitments, and works for liberation. In solidarity with those who suffer, Christian witness interrupts history—rupturing the structure of consciousness, the systems of oppression, and the massive denials of human hope.

In this second stage, therefore, political theology is itself a form of praxis. More correctly stated, political theology is a reflective element in the larger context of Christian praxis. Political theology articulates the Christian witness through the dangerous memories of Christ and those who suffer; it interprets these dangerous memories as providing a basis for critique and a vision of transformation. Such memories break into our unquestioning acceptance of the way things are and call our lives into question. Such memories provide the basis for critical reason, a basis reflected in the form of the iconoclasm of the cross (Moltmann) or dogmas as dangerous memories (Metz). Indeed, eschatology is now disclosed through memory as the freedom yet to be realized—a freedom that criticizes every oppressive form of societal praxis but also illuminates possible ways of transformation.

The dangerous memories of the Christian faith are expressed in the form of narratives. Metz claims that theology articulates the dangerous memories of the Christian faith and, hence, has essentially a narrative structure. The primary task of theology is telling, interpreting, and understanding the narratives that constitute Christianity. Metz does not want to exclude the role of theoretical argument in theology; theory has a secondary value, that of protecting, explaining, and criticizing the narratives of Christian praxis. Thus the nature of political theology, as a theology, seems quite different from other forms of theology. Political theology is not a correlation of abstract meanings taken from theoretical explanations; it is not a verification or falsification about specific linguistic claims. Political theology may include these tasks as secondary arguments, but it is first and foremost a reflective method interpreting narratives and recalling memories for the sake of human freedom. If it can be called a "theory," it is a practical theory of freedom, based on the anticipatory freedom of the human subject seeking identity through memory and hope in human history.

Yet even in this radical reformulation—in the shift from a theoretical mediation of subject and tradition to a practical formation of subject and tradition—political theology inherits the agenda of modern theology. For the agenda of modern theology represents the freedom of the human subject as a *Christian* fact, be it the liberal freedom of escaping the myths of tradition to be engaged in the progress of historical forces or the neo-orthodox freedom of shrugging off the myths to arrive at an encounter with God. Political theology also focuses on this special aspect of human life as the contact point with Christianity, though now it is the freedom of suffering and the freedom to suffer. In this joining of freedom and Christianity, modern theology reinterprets the tradition, a reinterpretation, so the theologians claim, demanded by the tradition itself. Political theology thus follows its predecessors in good stead when it offers a "new way of Christianity," demanded, of course, by the dangerous memory of Christ. But political theology radically departs from modern theology in the mediational role of theology; political theologians believe that in order to mediate existence and tradition, existence and tradition must be transformed. Understanding gives way to rupture; interpretation gives way to revolution; the point of theology is formation, transformation, conversion, change.

Be it the interruption of those inside or the revolution of those outside, the contexts of Latin American liberation theology and German political theology point to a radical change and rupture in the context and process of theology. Indeed, the testimonies recorded thus far suggest far more than a theological reorientation; they demonstrate a radical shift in the understanding of human existence and in the very experiencing of Christian faith. To explore the claims of radical change and rupture, to continue the journey with the poor and with those who suffer, and to trace further the discontinuity/continuity of modern theology, we must turn to representative figures in liberation theology.

3

Gustavo Gutiérrez:
A Theology for Historical Amnesia

The name most frequently associated with Latin American liberation theology is that of the Peruvian priest and theologian Gustavo Gutiérrez. Gutiérrez's now very famous *A Theology of Liberation,* first published in 1971, continues to be the basic text of liberation theology both in its challenge to modern first-world theologies as well as in its constructive formulation of a theology for the Latin American context. In this text and in his more recent writings, Gutiérrez never wavers from one central claim: that the irruption of the poor qualitatively changes history, Christianity, and theology. But this change, which is a real break and contradiction from what has previously existed, is also a conversion; the "new event of the poor," the "new praxis of Christian faith," and the "new way of doing theology" are, in themselves, conversions of other events, other experiences, and other methods. Perhaps more than any other theologian, Gutiérrez testifies to the experience of God in the journey of the poor.

Gutiérrez's work illustrates the paradigm shift of liberation theology: it offers a new understanding of human existence, a new interpretation of Christianity, and a new form of theological reflection. Indeed, the structure of liberation theology can be discovered by attending to Gutiérrez's three most basic claims: first, the claim that there is a new subject of history; second, the claim that there is a new experience of Christianity; and third, the claim that there is a new form of and purpose for theological reflection.

Any reflection on Gutiérrez's work must begin its interpretation where he begins—with the poor in their historical situation. The irruption of the poor in liberating praxis, the subject matter of Gutiérrez's first claim, is the fundamental fact in Latin America, a fact demanding that history be experienced and understood from its underside, from the destiny of those who have been excluded from the making and interpreting of history. Gutiérrez introduces his second claim by relating liberating praxis to a new way of being Christian, a way of faith that is a praxis of solidarity with the poor. With both the Christian message and the historical situation irrupted and made new, Gutiérrez considers his third claim of a new way of doing theology. In this new paradigm, theology comes as a second act, as a form of critical reflection on Christian praxis.

Gustavo Gutiérrez has a distinct style that is itself an "irruption," a constant counterposing of contradictions: contradictions between the poor and the rich, between the nonperson and the person, between the victors of history and those absent from history. Gutiérrez forces the differences, the dissimilarities, and the oppositions within experience, Christianity, and theology to the point of rupture. To understand Gutiérrez is to follow the rhetorical repression of our experience by the journey of the poor; for, in Gutiérrez's theology, only by seeing through the eyes of the poor—by rupturing history along with the absent ones—can the contradictions be opened for close inspection, elaborated for accurate understanding, and made public for social transformation. These radical contradictions, according to Gutiérrez, irrupt into the present as possibilities for transformation in social systems, religious practices, theological methods, and ways of being human. The rhetoric of contradiction in Gutiérrez's writing matches the distinctive contribution of his thought; his rhetoric of liberation mandates the paradigm shift of liberation theology.

THE POWER OF THE POOR

The most recent years of Latin America history have been characterized by the discovery of the real-life world of the "other," of the poor and the exploited and their compelling needs. In a social order fashioned economically, politically, and ideologically by a few for their own benefit, the "other side" has begun to make its voice heard. The lower classes of the populace, forced to live on the margins of society and oppressed since time immemorial, are beginning to speak for themselves more and more rather than relying on intermediaries. They have discovered themselves once again, and they now want the existing system to take note of their disturbing presence. They are less and less willing to be the passive objects of demagogic manipulation and social or charitable welfare in varied disguises. They want to be the active subjects of their own history and to forge a radically different society.[1]

Gustavo Gutiérrez thus describes what is for him the most important event in Latin America: the irruption of the poor in history. The poor irrupt into the prevailing religious and theological systems to become the question of the nonperson. They rupture history constituted as the stream of exploits by the privileged with their memories of suffering kept alive in the expressions of popular religion. These nonpersons, the anonymous poor, break into the present, past, and future with their agonizing memories, their soundless voices, and their visions of hope.[2]

Though the poor are anonymous and outcast, Gutiérrez reminds us, they are a people, a collective people. These people are cast-offs and refuse as a group;

they are, according to Gutiérrez, the "product, or by-product of an economic and social system fashioned by a few for their own benefit."[3] The poor are oppressed and exploited for the benefit of "persons," the rich victors who, thus far, have made and interpreted history. Gutiérrez, relying on the contradiction between the poor and the rich, argues that the "nonpersons," the poor, gain their identity over against the "persons," the rich; the identity of the poor is their nonidentity, an identity that is gained through their suffering. For Gutiérrez the contradiction between the poor and the rich is the fundamental basis for any analysis of the human situation, a basis that defines the terms and orders the issues for any theological reflection on human existence. To be poor is the representative human experience; only by standing with the poor and by focusing our interpretive lens through the poor may we, too, adequately experience and interpret history. The first step is taken: we stand with the poor in the underside of history; from here we seek to understand human existence.

Gutiérrez argues that the irruption of the poor means that history cannot be reinterpreted by adding in the stories of the poor or corrected by developing charitable social policies; rather, history must be reread and remade from the perspective of the poor.[4] But this struggle to remake and reread history depends upon the process and interpretation of history in the nineteenth and twentieth centuries, a process Gutiérrez characterizes as "man's" attempt "to transform swiftly and in a controlled manner the world in which he lives."[5] The rupture breaks into that which gave it birth, the transformation re-creates and converts the chaos of the old into the possibilities of the new. In order to stand with the poor, we must, in turn, understand the rich; in order to envision new possibilities for the future we must look to the events and interpretations of the past.

Now, with the poor, Gutiérrez seeks to understand the massive contradictions of the past and present through an interpretation of modernity. Modernity, beginning in the fifteenth century with the emergence of the experimental sciences, is formed by the intentional manipulation and control of nature, society, and the self: "thus man gradually takes hold of the reins of his own destiny."[6] Modernity's process of historical transformations is characterized by the dual traits of individualism and rationalism; traits which, in modernity, are interpreted as "natural" characteristics. Capitalism grows as the "natural economic system" because it depends on individual interests and rights; society develops as a social contract among free, autonomous individuals. Knowledge, important in all the realms of modernity, is "rational knowledge," allowing the humanistic study of humankind, the development of technology, and the manipulation of the environment.

Modernity recognized, Gutiérrez explains, that traditional religion supported neither individualism nor rationalism; traditional religion, concluded modernity, imposed superstitious "eternal truths" on individuals, preventing the free use of human reason.[7] In Gutiérrez's reading, though nearly all of Catholicism responded by ignoring—as best it was able—the challenges of modernity, liberal Protestants embraced modernity with an "enlightened" version of Christianity. Gutiérrez contends that liberal Protestantism, playing by the rules of modernity, located the "religious" within the limits of individual reason. With this embrace, Christianity affirmed modernity through its understanding of God as the invisible force behind the modern process of development.

But, Gutiérrez argues, the process of modernity becomes successful only through its dependency upon massive contradictions. The irruption of the poor exposes this process as one of massive contradictions—contradictions in economics, industry, politics, and philosophy. The industrial and economic revolutions of modernity are made possible by the displacement of large numbers of unemployed or seasonally employed persons. The international project of development serves the interests of rich nations at the expense of poor countries. Philosophy, as the reflection on human existence, selects its questions and offers its answers in relation to the rich person, and not the poor nonperson.[8] In short, though modernity offers a new perspective and existence in history, its success depends upon massive contradictions—contradictions that give rise to the irruption of the poor.

This reading of history through the irruption of the poor and the contradictory process of modernity yields two fundamental categories for Gutiérrez: (1) historical praxis and (2) liberating praxis. In these two categories is crystallized Gutiérrez's philosophy of history: history is the arena of new ways of becoming human. Though distorted by its own massive contradictions, historical praxis reveals the quest for a new way of being human in history—a way that discovers and expresses humanity's *historical* nature. "In this historical praxis there is more than a new consciousness of the meaning of economic activity and political action: there is also a new way of being man and woman in history."[9] Historical praxis is intensified, ruptured, and transformed by the process of the poor becoming human agents; a process Gutiérrez calls "liberating praxis."

Liberating praxis, Gutiérrez's second fundamental category of historical interpretation, is the intensification and the interruption of historical praxis as it forces the transformation of history to be reread and remade from the place of the poor. As a radical critique, the category of liberating praxis entails a hermeneutics of distrust on modernity's claim to represent all humanity. But as a conversion of the promises and vision of modernity, liberating praxis favors a hermeneutics of liberation in the making and shaping of history through the irruption of the poor. In the hermeneutics of distrust, the poor are the privileged place to examine the misuse of freedom in the demonic maturity of modernity; in the hermeneutics of liberation, the irruption of the poor leads to a new liberation in history.

> But the existence of the poor is not fated fact; it is not neutral on the political level or innocent of ethical implications. Poor people are by-products of the system under which we live and for which we are

responsible. Poor people are ones who have been shunted to the sidelines of our socio-cultural world. Poor people are those who are oppressed and exploited, who are deprived of the fruits of their labor and stripped of their life and reality as human beings. Poor people are members of the proletarian class. That is why the poverty of the poor is not a summons to alleviate their plight with acts of generosity but rather a compelling obligation to fashion an entirely different social order.[10]

What undergirds the centrality of historical praxis and liberating praxis is Gutiérrez's insistence that politics is the primary dimension for understanding human existence. Though we can debate the liberating praxis versus historical praxis, it is obvious that, for Gutiérrez we must begin with some interpretation of the historical situation to understand human existence. By "politics" Gutiérrez means, in the broadest sense, the determination of human history. Under the reign of historical praxis, politics consists of the control of the many by the freedom of the few. In the new vision of liberating praxis, however, politics is a far more inclusive category, open to all humans and composed of all human activities.[11] Politics, in liberating praxis, conditions the whole of life and life as a whole; thus, for Gutiérrez, politics names human existence both in its entirety and in its multidimensional character. In one sense, then, politics means simply historical possibility, while in a related sense politics refers to the reality of power in which all persons participate in the creation of history. Thus liberating praxis is political in a universal sense as the historical condition of all life and life in its entirety, and it is political in a more restrictive sense as the struggle for transformation through the irruption of the poor. Be it in the dominating oppressiveness of politics in historical praxis or in the liberating creativity of politics in liberating praxis, human existence must be understood through its political character.

Gutiérrez thus completes his first claim about the irruption of the poor, a claim that can be entertained only within the journey of the poor. Lest we miss the full impact of this interpretation, we must pay close attention to Gutiérrez's language of contradiction throughout his argument. The irruption of the poor discloses the contradictions of modernity between the rich and the poor, between the "persons" and the "nonpersons"; the poor present an understanding of history that modernity conceals—the history of the "other." Today the poor and oppressed are calling forth memories that expose the freedom of modernity as domination and reveal the reason of modernity as irrational repression.[12] At stake is history itself, or more explicitly, how we experience and interpret history. Between the paradigm of historical praxis and liberating praxis, there is no easy correlation in understanding or any quick fix of correction. Historical praxis and liberating praxis exist in contradiction, a contradiction that, if we follow Gutiérrez's arguments, ruptures history in the present day. And thus we turn to Gutiérrez's second claim, that in the midst of this rupture a new experience of God is occurring, an experience of God that both irrupts and converts Christianity.

FAITH: POVERTY, SOLIDARITY, AND PROTEST

In the midst of the poor and despised of the earth, Gutiérrez experiences God.[13] According to Gutiérrez, the experience and expression of Christianity in the liberating praxis of the poor is a *kairos*, a special time during which God appears in history in new ways, "in the midst of many and varied forms of suffering something new is being born in Latin America. This is what prompts talk of a *kairos,* a favorable time—a moment when the Lord knocks on the doors of the ecclesial community that lives in Latin America and asks it to open so that he may come and dine there (Rev. 3:20)."[14] The experience of God in the liberating praxis of the poor constitutes Gutiérrez's second claim and, within the paradigm of liberation theology, leads to a formulation of a new way of Christianity.

In a manner parallel to the contradiction between historical praxis and liberating praxis, this experience of God with the poor intensifies, ruptures, and transforms previous ways, or paradigms, of Christianity. In particular, at least for Gutiérrez, this new "liberating" Christianity breaks into the New Christendom movement; it ruptures New Christendom's political and theological distinction between the spiritual and temporal planes by mediating the spiritual through the temporal in the new way of liberating Christianity.[15] As the misery and injustice in Latin America became more and more apparent, persons accused the New Christendom model of functioning as a mask for the church's support for the status quo. Over and against the theoretical ideals and political realities of the church in the New Christendom movement, theologians began to reflect on the intrinsic relationship between church and world, and Christians started demanding that the church itself be in solidarity with the poor. As Christians participated in the struggle of the poor they began to ask themselves the meaning of this new experience of faith; the New Christendom movement was ruptured and transformed by Christian action and reflection within the liberating praxis of the poor.

As historical praxis is contradicted by liberating praxis, so the *old* way of the New Christendom model is contradicted by the *new* way of Christian love. What contradicts and replaces the New Christendom movement is a journey of Christian love in solidarity with the poor. Christian love is the active solidarity with the neighbor who is "other"; Christian love as solidarity with the poor is the religious equivalent of the irruption of the poor in liberating praxis.[16]

The joining of liberating praxis and Christian love is the center of Gutiérrez's theology. For Gutiérrez's first claim of a new subject in liberating praxis, and his third claim of a new way of doing theology, both have their identity in relation to this second claim of Christianity as a praxis of solidarity, of love for the neighbor. Christian praxis represents, forms, and directs liberating praxis as a new way of being human; it demands, informs, and provides, as we shall see, a new way of doing theology. Gutiérrez's primary desire is neither to record history nor to construct theological method; his real hope is to give a new language for faith, a new way of talking about God from the experience of the poor. More than anything else, Gutiérrez is impelled to interpret the new spirituality of Christian praxis, a spirituality marked both by the gratuitousness of God and the following of Christ through a way of solidarity with the "other," the poor. "The other is our way for reaching God, but our relationship with God is a precondition for encounter and true communion with the other. It is not possible to separate these two movements, which are perhaps really only a single movement: Jesus Christ, who is God and man, is our way to the Father but he is also our way to recognition of others as brothers and sisters."[17]

Gutiérrez's main task in this second dimension of his work is to interpret the new experience of God with the poor that arises out of the confluence of liberating praxis and Christian existence. Appropriately, Gutiérrez first turns to the Bible to search for a language to speak of this religious experience. The Bible, according to Gutiérrez, is a witness to the Word of God made human— the incarnation of God in human history. The Bible reveals a process of the universalization and internalization of the presence of God in history; God's presence is universalized as it extends to all persons and is internalized as it becomes incarnate in humanity.[18]

Gutiérrez contends that the universal and internal presence of God in human relationships must, in light of the present experience of liberating praxis, lead to a Christian praxis marked by the continual conversion to other human beings, especially to the poor. Gutiérrez threads together a reading of the Bible with his interpretation of the present situation: the new Christian praxis is an active appropriation of the Bible's witness to the incarnation of God in solidarity with the poor. What is significant in this weaving together of biblical themes and Christian experience is the meaning of faith: faith is not merely *expressed* in historical action; rather, it is *constituted* through historical encounter. As Gutiérrez reversed the usual location for understanding human experience, so now does he invert the interpretation of faith into a historical activity. To explore this new location of faith, Gutiérrez continues his reinterpretation of Christianity through three notions: liberation and salvation; eschatology and politics; and the church as the sacrament of God in history.

Liberation and Salvation

If faith is now itself a historical activity in the liberating praxis of the poor, then, we must ask ourselves, in what way is this salvation? Gutiérrez contends that salvation, throughout much of the Christian tradition, has been understood quantitatively, that is, as the numbers of persons saved. Now, however, salvation must be understood *qualitatively,* namely, as the fulfillment of humanity. Sin, once understood as those acts impeding the attainment of spiritual salvation in the afterlife, must now be understood as a historical reality, "an obstacle to life's reaching the fullness we call salvation."[19] For Gutiérrez, sin is the state of fundamental alienation from God and humanity, expressing itself in oppression, poverty, and injustice. Though sin is the basis of all alienation, it is never contained in any one form of alienation, for, according to Gutiérrez, "sin demands a radical liberation, which in turn necessarily implies a practical liberation."[20] In relation to sin, salvation contains a radical-practical mediation as the redemption of creation mediated through partial fulfillments in history. Salvation is total, complete, absolute: it can never be identified or reduced to one specific instance of fulfillment, correction, or transformation.

Gutiérrez draws upon two biblical symbols to express the language of salvation in the new way of Christianity. The first symbol is that of the exodus and relates creation and salvation through liberation: creation is transformed in the liberation from slavery into freedom. The exodus event symbolizes the nature and goal of human participation in creation: "the liberation from Egypt, linked to and ever coinciding with creation, adds an element of capital importance: the need and place for man's active participation in the building of society."[21] The exodus portrays redemption as the fulfillment of creation through re-creation and as the fulfillment of creation through transformation of concrete situations. God's salvific work unites with God's creative work and is linked to human participation in the transformation of history.

The second symbol expressive of Christian praxis is the symbol of promise, revealing the dynamic character of salvation as a process, as both "already," experienced in the present, and as "not-yet," hoped for in the future. The Bible, Gutiérrez argues, is the book of the promise: "the promise is gradually revealed in all its universality and concrete expression: it is *already* fulfilled in historical events, but *not yet* completely; it incessantly projects itself into the future, creating a permanent mobility."[22] Through this symbol, faith is oriented toward the future; God creates, liberates, and redeems in a history that is oriented toward the future. In the symbol of promise Gutiérrez brings together God's providential activity and humanity's orientation toward the future; in promise, eschatology and providence meet.

The symbols of promise and the exodus represent salvation as mediated in history, thus securing history's importance as the realm of religious and temporal activity. The exodus symbolizes the continual transformation of history as re-creation, and promise symbolizes history as dynamic and oriented toward the future. These two symbols provoke, as well, the qualitative vision of salvation, that "salvation embraces all men and whole men."[23] Salvation is the fulfillment of history, of nature, of humanity, and of the cosmos and, as such, salvation is inherently involved in the struggle for a just society. To the question of how salvation relates to faith as a liberating, historical activity, Gutiérrez can answer: "the work of salvation is a reality which occurs in history. The work gives to the historical becoming of mankind its profound unity and its deepest meaning."[24]

Though liberation is intrinsic to salvation, no one historical act of liberation can ever be completely identified with the fullness of salvation. Gutiérrez relates liberating acts in history to the fullness of salvation through what he labels the three levels of liberation: (1) particular or political liberations, (2) the liberation of humanity throughout history, and (3) liberation from sin into the freedom of solidarity with humanity and God.[25] These three levels of liberation provide Gutiérrez with a way to mediate the identity-in-difference between particular events of liberation and liberating salvation. Liberation then, by definition, entails particular events, the nature and purpose of history, and the fullness of salvation.

The growth of the Kingdom is a process which occurs historically *in* liberation, insofar as liberation means a greater fulfillment of man. Liberation is a precondition for the new society, but this is not all it is. While liberation is implemented in liberating historical events, it also denounces their limitations and ambiguities, proclaims their fulfillment and impels them effectively towards total communion. This is not an identification. Without liberating historical events, there would be no growth of the Kingdom. But the process of liberation will not have conquered the very roots of oppression and the exploitation of man by man without the coming of the Kingdom, which is above all a gift.[26]

In sum, the praxis of Christian faith is understood through salvation in the ultimate sense of gift, in the historical sense of the continual transformation of the new humanity, and in a particular sense as liberation in concrete situations. The historical relationship of salvation and liberation necessitates that Christian faith must live toward a future, a future of a new way of being in history for all persons.

Eschatology and Politics

The next question might well ask how we *experience* faith as the mediate relation between salvation and liberation. It should , of course, be clear to us by now *where* we experience faith—in the journey of the poor in liberating praxis; this question asks Gutiérrez to give us a language for speaking of the nature of this experience. Gutiérrez's answer is, on first blush, quite simple: the mediation of salvation and liberation in history is experienced by Christians as hope. Faith, expressed through liberation and salvation as a participation in history toward the future, is experienced through the continual creation of new possibilities in history. For Gutiérrez hope is appropriately represented as eschatology; in reference to eschatology, hope is experienced in relation to the possibilities of the concrete present but also in relation to the ultimate vision of the gospel. "The life and preaching of Jesus postulate the unceasing search for a new kind of man in a qualitatively different society."[27] Because this hope is grounded through particular historical situations and through an ultimate vision of history, hope makes faith political in working for the transformations of existing situations. The political nature of faith expresses itself in utopian thought through the relation of present possibilities and an ultimate vision. Characterized in its relationship to historical reality, its verification in praxis, and its rational nature, utopia denounces the present order and announces a new society, a new way of being. Utopia, for Gutiérrez, is the concrete imagination of political action.[28] Gutiérrez draws upon the category of utopia to make the important link of faith and political action, so that neither faith nor political action are sublated into one another or substituted one for the other. Just as liberation and salvation must have a relation of identity-indifference, so too must faith and political action be joined together without being reduced to one or the other. Only within the utopian quest can faith and political action work together for a new humanity and a new society.

As the permanent creation of humanity, utopia is the "place of encounter between political liberation and the communion of all men with God."[29] Within the utopian vision, human activity is in communion with God and oriented to the new creation of humanity. Utopia, for Gutiérrez, is a human work as well as an expression of faith. By relating Christian hope to politics through utopia, Gutiérrez wants to protect the autonomy of the political and thus to prevent any false hope of the possibility of a Christian state. Gutiérrez makes sure that particular acts of liberation are related but not identified with salvation and that, likewise, salvation is not understood as the sum of history's liberating acts. Salvation and liberation, God and humanity, grace and freedom are always related through the nature of history as the continual quest for new ways of being human. Eschatology as hope symbolizes the political nature of Christian faith. Thus the nature of faith is to hope, and the goal of faith is the creation of new ways of being in history. As politics names the basic dimension of human existence—human existence in its entirety and as the struggle for transformation—so utopia expresses faith's relation to history. Again Gutiérrez provides us with a rather radical reorientation for the experience of faith: we experience faith in our participation in the continual quest of history, which is, of course, a political-utopian quest.

The Church as the Sacrament of God in History

The exploration of faith as the encounter of God in the poor can be queried from a somewhat different, ecclesiological angle: What is the purpose of the church in this new way of Christianity? The traditional understanding of the relationship between the church and the world, argues Gutiérrez, either subsumed the world into the church or distinctly separated the two. But neither option is appropriate to the nature of Christian faith, at least as that faith is reinterpreted by Gutiérrez. Vatican II, Gutiérrez thinks, contributed a new notion of the church, defining the church as a sacrament, a visible sign of God's encounter with history. Gutiérrez uses this definition of the sacramental nature of church to argue that the church does not exist for itself but for others: by existing for others, the church manifests the salvific activity of God in the world. "To call the Church the 'visible sacrament of this saving unity' (*Lumen gentium*, no. 9) is to define it in relation to the plan of salvation, whose fulfillment in history the Church reveals and signifies to men. . . . The church can be understood only in relation to the reality which it announces to men. Its existence is not 'for itself,' but rather 'for others.' "[30] As a sacrament that makes visible God's grace, the church denounces sin and announces God's love. In the present situation of Latin America this denunciation of sin takes the form of a radical critique of the present order: the church denounces injustice, oppression, poverty, and all occasions of sin. But, in the midst of this denunciation, the church announces the love of God in communion with humanity. In the present situation of Latin America, the church does this concretely through its commitment to liberation and its effective solidarity with the poor. The image of the church as sacrament means that the church exists as both means and sign of God's gratuitous activity in the liberating history of the world.

The gratuitous activity of God in the sacrament of the church has been experienced by Gutiérrez through his own pastoral activity in basic Christian communities. These communities exemplify the spirituality of gratuitousness that Gutiérrez attempts to give voice to in his interpretation of Christianity. In expressing both judgment and love, basic Christian communities rupture and transform the church in Latin America.[31] Basic Christian communities, Gutiérrez argues, are an irruption of the poor into the structure (hierarchy) and the purpose (an institution securing salvation) of the church. Yet in this irruption they are a conversion of the church as a sacrament, a sacrament uniting God's work of salvation in history with faith as a praxis of solidarity with the poor.

The church manifests God's grace through its own spirituality of poverty:

> Poverty is an act of love and liberation. It has a redemptive value. If the ultimate cause of man's exploitation and alienation is selfishness, the deepest reason for voluntary poverty is love of neighbor. Christian poverty has meaning only as a commitment of solidarity with the poor, with those who suffer misery and injustice. The commitment is to witness to the evil which has resulted from sin and is a breach of communion. It is not a question of idealizing poverty, but rather of taking it on as it is—an evil—to protest against it and to struggle to abolish it.[32]

Evangelical poverty, as the new form of Christian spirituality, combines the biblical notion of spiritual poverty as one's relationship to God with the scandalous condition of material poverty in liberating praxis. Through this evangelical poverty, the church manifests God's continual incarnation in history in the journey of the poor.

Gutiérrez attempts to give voice to what he experiences, hears, and lives in the irruption of the poor in Latin America. This second claim of Gutiérrez's work continues the call for irruption and conversion—a breaking into that is also a transformation, a displacement that is also a new creation. The new way of Christianity—a way that cannot be understood in older forms of interpretation—represents, guides, forms, and transforms the liberating praxis of the poor. Within this liberating praxis, Christian faith works for concrete changes, envisions the utopia of history, and is redeemed in the fullness of God's salvific activity. In Gutiérrez's interpretation, Christianity is a radically new way of following Christ, of encountering God, of being the church; this new way, as we shall see, demands a new form of theological reflection.

THEOLOGY AS THE VOICE OF THE VOICELESS

Gutiérrez's first two claims, the claim for a new subject in liberating praxis and the claim for a new experience of Christianity, lead directly to his third claim, the claim of a new way of doing theology. As with the first two claims, the third claim occurs as a radical break: theology is ruptured as the poor speak of God; and through this process of rupture, theology is converted into a critical theory of human freedom. Within this third claim we now see the paradigm shift of liberation expressed in the nature of theological reflection, composed of new categories, concepts, and metaphors, and constituted through new forms of reflection.

As historical praxis is transformed by liberating praxis, so is modern theology transformed by liberation theology. As the praxis of solidarity with the poor, Christian faith demands a new understanding and method of theology, that is, a "new way of doing theology."[33] Gutiérrez's claim in theology depends on and parallels his claims about the historical situation and the present reality of Christianity. Theology is a "new way" in its commitment to the poor, in its concern for the relationship of power and knowledge, in its critical role within reflection and action, and in its method of relating historical situations, utopian thought, and redemption. Gutiérrez recognizes this new way as a "Copernican turn" in theology.[34]

Liberation theology is formulated, as is any theology, in relation to the proclamation of the gospel. Hence, argues Gutiérrez, Latin American liberation theology must reflect on the proclamation of God in Latin America; liberation theology finds its questions, its issues, and certainly its language, in the encounter of God through solidarity with the poor. For the poor this proclamation of the gospel is an experience of God's grace as the demand for justice, equality, and freedom. As such, the uniqueness of Latin American liberation theology must be understood in contradiction to what Gutiérrez calls "progressivist theology."

The difference between liberation theology and progressivist theology, according to Gutiérrez, is not only a theoretical disagreement, but a political contradiction, involving the social location and historical purpose of theology. In Gutiérrez's words, "the yawning chasm that divides these two theological perspectives, that of progressivist theology and that of liberation theology, mirrors a rift in the real world, where persons live and die—not in the world of ideas."[35] As a theoretical response to the concerns of the Enlightenment, progressivist theology asked the question of reason and belief: How could a modern person "believe" in traditional religion and still have the free use of individual reason? Relying upon critical reason to reinterpret and reform Christianity, progressivist theology explored the notion of a religious dimension within individual existence. This religious dimension allowed, progressivist theology maintained, an ultimate or existential meaning in human life;

progressivist theology guaranteed this dimension through a special relationship to God as the giver of ultimate meaning. Schleiermacher led the way for this liberal theology by "demonstrating the essential religious dimension of every human being."[36] Struggling for its own survival in the modern world, progressivist theology accepted the limits of the modern bourgeois nonbeliever as the foundation of its own existence. At its best, Gutiérrez judges, progressivist theology incorporated the critical reason of the Enlightenment to interpret Christianity. At its worst, progressivist theology reduced Christianity to an abstract "essence" that formally correlated with what every person has by nature, a religious dimension. And so, concludes Gutiérrez, progressivist theology became prone to "generic affirmations and a false universalism."[37]

Liberation theology, based in the joining of liberating praxis and Christian praxis, has a different concern and subject than those of progressivist theology. Progressivist theology contemplated how one could be a mature believer; liberation theology works for the historical possibilities of becoming a person.[38] Liberation theology begins not with the secularity of the first world but, rather, with the oppression of the third world. Against the reduction of Christianity to a formal representation of the religious dimension, liberation theology formulates faith as a praxis of solidarity with the poor.

If Christian faith is a praxis of solidarity with the poor, then theology is, for Gutiérrez, a way of understanding this experience and expression of faith. Gutiérrez favors the classical definition of theology as faith seeking understanding: to think, to understand, to interpret is but a part of the Christian journey. In Gutiérrez's words:

> Theology, in this context, will be a critical reflection on the historical praxis when confronted with the Word of the Lord lived and accepted in faith; this faith comes to us through multiple and, at times, ambiguous historical mediations which we make and discover every day. Theology will be a reflection in and on faith as a liberating praxis. The understanding of faith will proceed from an option and a commitment. This understanding will start with a real and effective solidarity with discriminated races, despised cultures, and exploited classes and from their very world and atmosphere. This reflection starts from a commitment to create a just, fraternal society, and must contribute to make it more meaningful, radical, and universal. This theological process becomes truth when it is embodied in the process of liberation.[39]

But, of course, theology takes on quite a new location when faith exists as a praxis of solidarity with the poor; this theology will live in a world of violence and hope, reflection and action, spirituality and politics. From the location of theology in faith's praxis of solidarity with the poor, there are, for Gutiérrez, two important insights of liberation theology. The first is that liberation theology is a *critical reflection* and as such is a second act; it follows commitment and involvement in Christian praxis. The second insight of liberation theology is the privileged option for the poor. These two insights comprise the sum total of Gutiérrez's rupture and conversion of theology; together these two insights allow a new nature of and purpose for theological reflection.[40] The first and more formal insight concerns the nature of theology as a "critical reflection." Gutiérrez boldly asserts that theology is not prior to faith or outside faith, but within faith; as critical reflection, theology is an act of faith.[41] The critical reflection of and on faith is thus a continual process of analysis, explanation, conversation, and understanding. Theology is never a final, finished statement, but always a provisional and ongoing process because of its situated perspective in history and because of its limited nature as a knowledge of God. Theology as critical reflection mandates, for Gutiérrez, that theology is itself part of liberating praxis, contributing to the rupture and conversion of history.

The nature of this critical reflection has what Gutiérrez calls a "practical" character; knowledge is not ahistorical, abstract, or technical but "practical," grounded in concrete history with the norms, values, and traditions of human communities.[42] Practical knowledge grows out of the memories, desires, and hopes of community—knowledge recalls and remembers, it understands and projects. As a practical knowledge, critical reflection has a long history in figures such as Aristotle, Marx, Augustine, and Ignatius of Loyola; in all these figures, as in Gutiérrez, knowledge is an intrinsic part of how humans make history.

Both as critical reflection and as practical knowledge, theology has particular functions within the Christian community. Functioning to mediate salvation as the meaning and depth of the human project, theology helps to form the relationship between Christian faith and the liberating activity. Theology as critical reflection relies upon the resources of the social sciences and of Christian tradition to aid Christian praxis, bringing together an analysis of the situation and the resources of the tradition to guide pastoral activity. Theology as "critical reflection" has three identifiable tasks for Gutiérrez: (1) it is the theory of a definite praxis (related to particular situations), (2) it is a critique of church and society in light of the Word of God, and (3) it is the projection of future possibilities related to the present situation. Thus theology includes moments of analysis, appropriation, interpretation, imagination, and transformation. Theology interprets, interrupts, and transforms. Criticizing systems of oppression and injustice, it proclaims the Word of God through specific strategies of change, models of transformation, and projections of new possibilities.

Theology as a form of critical reflection is a practical knowledge within a concrete historical situation; it is essentially open, open to change, to rupture, and even to conversion and transformation. Theology is an ongoing process of reflection, dialoguing with contemporary categories, reformulating concepts in light of the situation and the Christian message, addressing new and changing situations. But theology has a nonreducible character in relation to the community's place within the larger political system and within the community's own history and structure—theology does not simply repeat political ideology or dogmatic teachings. In one of his rare points of formal theological method, Gutiérrez maintains that theology must always use the forms of current rationality in any given historical period to reflect on Christian praxis.[43]

Theology's incarnation through current forms of rationality includes, in the contemporary period, its dialogue with Marxism, just as in earlier times theology's incarnation conversed with Aristotelian philosophy. But liberation theology is always a critical partner in this dialogue, criticizing and revising Marxist concepts in light of Christian tradition. Gutiérrez demands that theology never simply adopt the categories of any current period, but always criticize, appropriate, reject, and transform the categories of current reflection in light of Christian tradition and Christian praxis. Thus, for instance, liberation theology must be critical of Marx's affirmation of the revolution of the proletariat as the fulfillment of the future. The fulfillment of the future, in liberation theology, ultimately lies in the redemption of history by God. But liberation theology can and must relate its option for the poor with Marx's emphasis on class conflict in the analysis of the present situation in Latin America. Gutiérrez seems, at times, to abuse this criterion by adopting rather than critically adapting Marxist categories. Indeed, the inevitability of class conflict, a Marxist concept, sometimes threatens to overtake Gutiérrez's notion of the privileged option for the poor.[44] Internal to Gutiérrez's own theological method, however, is the demand that categories, concepts, and methods of reflection must be critically appropriated, in light of Christian tradition and praxis, into theology.

Gutiérrez expands the nature of theology as critical reflection and practical knowledge by suggesting that theology is continually remade in terms of its own truth. Theology does not prove eternal truths that are to be applied subsequently to history; it does not merely reflect on existential truth that is poetically disclosed through history. Rather, liberation theology helps create truth, it determines truth, for "theological reasoning is uttered upon a truth that is a way, upon a Word who has pitched his tent in the midst of history."[45] Thus truth, for this theologian, may be judged only in light of the possibilities for human fulfillment in history. There is, of course, a danger in Gutiérrez's pragmatic approach to truth; truth may be reduced to the success of a revolutionary project.[46] If truth is, in this manner, identified with the historical success of a particular project, Gutiérrez will deny the mediate relation between liberation and salvation that he has carefully established. According to the mediate relation of liberation and salvation, truth must have different criteria depending on the level of liberation, for "truth" is itself historical. In Gutiérrez's first level of liberation—changes in particular situations—the truth of theology involves the adequacy of both analysis and strategy for change. In the second level of liberation as the historical project of humanity, truth is mediated in the relationship between a particular situation and an ultimate religious vision through a critical theory of emancipation and through models of transformation. In the third level of liberation as faith in total redemption, truth is disclosed through the mutually critical appropriation of religious tradition and present experience. Truth is not purified in objectivism, but neither is it reduced to mere relativism; truth judges and is judged through its own participation in history. Though Gutiérrez himself sometimes appears to sublate truth into the success of a revolutionary project, the truth of theology, based on Gutiérrez's own theological criteria, must be judged in the process of determining, deciding, discerning, and speaking of God in the historical situation.

Gutiérrez's second insight about the nature of theological reflection is his insistence on what he calls "the privileged option for the poor." Gutiérrez demands that theology must necessarily choose a particular position of solidarity with the poor based on the experience and expression of faith in liberating praxis. Gutiérrez establishes the option for the poor in liberation theology through three interdependent routes. First, he analyzes the rupture and transformation of historical praxis by liberating praxis, an analysis that argues the practical necessity of the preference for the poor and the critical imperative of ideology critique in liberating praxis. Second, he interprets the Christian tradition as an "analogy of love" through which God and humanity join in communion through a praxis of solidarity with the poor. The poor are the addressees and the bearers of the gospel, privileged not because of human choice, but because of God's choice. Third, the nonperson, according to Gutiérrez, represents the project of humanity—the quest for the new in self, society, and history. The poor represent universal solidarity with all of humanity in the historical project of the quest for new ways of becoming human. To be in solidarity with the poor is not an option to be particular, but an option to be universal.

The option for the poor necessitates that theology is itself an active form of solidarity with the poor. If theology is the language of God, then based on Gutiérrez's option for the poor, theology can authentically speak of God only as it is with and of the poor. In this way, theology as a form of solidarity helps the poor to understand their faith, as Gutiérrez has observed: "even the poor have a right to think. The right to think is a corollary of the human right to be, and to assert the right to think is only to assert the right to exist."[47] The witness of poverty in Christian praxis is expressed through the purpose of theology to let the poor speak. In this manner, theology retrieves its classical definition of faith seeking understanding. Faith is the praxis of solidarity with the poor; understanding is a practical and critical reflection bringing to awareness the consciousness of the poor, criticizing oppressive systems, and guiding action for transformation. The poor "reclaim their faith" from systems that make them poor and despised and from ideological distortions that bless and secure their poverty.

It is the option for the poor that uniquely characterizes Gutiérrez's theology of liberation as a new theological paradigm. The first characteristic, theology as critical reflection, parallels much of the contemporary theological and philosophical conversation on the nature of and necessity for practical reflection. Obviously its centrality may not be dismissed: the theology of liberation will be a critical, practical reflection, involved with guiding and interpreting praxis. But the option for the poor suggests to us that how we experience faith and how we interpret history may influence and even dictate the nature of our theology. Gutiérrez's methodological claim is clear: we cannot separate the formal elements of theological method from the substantive claims of Christian witness. The option for the poor, in the nature of theological reflection, is therefore not first of all an ethical claim, though of course this theological insight has ethical implications. Rather, the option for the poor is Gutiérrez's hermeneutical strategy, a wager that we shall understand differently as we risk encountering God in the poor. As such, the option for the poor is the methodological parallel to the rupture of the poor in liberating praxis and the spirituality of poverty in the new way of Christianity. This wager, with its referent in the irruption of the poor, forces theology to be a liberating hermeneutics, an ongoing interpretation of Christian faith as itself a praxis of solidarity with the poor.

CONCLUSION

Through the claims for a new subject of liberating praxis, a new Christianity, and a new way of doing theology, Gutiérrez places us in a new paradigm of liberation theology. By identifying a new subject in a new history, he shocks us into viewing reality through a new and different framework. At the center of this framework is a new way of Christianity, with new interpretations, relations, and metaphors of the experience of faith. Within this framework, Gutiérrez suggests a new process of reflection, including a new nature of and purpose for theology. What is striking in Gutiérrez's thought is the constant interplay of the terms "contradiction," "irruption," and "new way"; these terms indicate that Gutiérrez is directing our attention to a radically different way of experiencing and interpreting both human existence and Christian faith. The way to which Gutiérrez directs us is the way of the poor, a way that theology must now tread.

From the underside, Gutiérrez does not puzzle with the modern theological obsession of whether or not religion has a place in the making of history. In fact, he never questions that religion has a purpose, but questions only the political intent of Christianity's purpose. Gutiérrez's main concern is not to demonstrate a new paradigm of theology; his concern is to provide a language for this new experience of history and Christianity. The interpretation of Christianity's purpose and vision through the notions of salvation and liberation, of hope and politics, of the church and the spirituality of poverty is a reasoned elucidation of what Gutiérrez experiences in the basic Christian communities of Latin America. In this way Gutiérrez is a practical, systematic theologian interpreting Christian symbols, concepts, rituals, and acts. His approach to religious language is not the "unpacking" of theological method but the weaving together of lived experience.

His theology has methodological implications, but it is not a treatise on method as such. Indeed, for Gutiérrez theological method may well be more the conversation and conversion that we are rather than the specific theories of interpretation and change that we employ. As we have indicated at several points, Gutiérrez often transgresses the internal coherence of his own theology; for example, identifying truth with historical success in spite of the mediate relationship between liberation and salvation. Indeed, Gutiérrez's contribution does not consist of new models or structures for theological method, though his redefinition of the nature of theology certainly suggests some methodological implications.

If one wants to compare Gutiérrez's work in genre and self-understanding one might do well to locate his work neither in theological ethics nor in theological method but, rather, to place his writings in systematic theology with a work such as Augustine's *Confessions*. The *Confessions* is not a work that begins or ends with theological method; rather, it is a theological journey on the historical path of faith. Like Augustine, Gutiérrez uses theology to understand faith traveling on its journey to God. For Gutiérrez, as for Augustine, the fundamental fact of theology is confession as first and foremost an act of praise. Theology, for both Gutiérrez and Augustine, is part of the process of a journey to God, which is, at the same time, a process of history, an active contemplation both in and of time.

4

Johann Baptist Metz: The Subject of Suffering

The political theology of Johann Baptist Metz is a "theological conversion," an attempt, within the paradigm of liberation theology, to formulate the conditions of possibility for the human subject, Christianity, and theology through the memory of suffering. As Gutiérrez demonstrates that modernity's "person" is developed on the bent backs of dependent "nonpersons," so Metz reveals that this "person" is defined by a dominating subjecthood that subjugates history and nature. If Gutiérrez proclaims the irruption of the poor in Latin America, then Metz pleads for a conversion of bourgeois consciousness. "The direct struggle of the poor and oppressed people there must be matched here by a struggle and resistance against ourselves, against the ingrained ideals of always having more, of always having to increase our influence."[1] As Gutiérrez interprets faith to represent the depth and unity of liberating praxis, so Metz reforms Christianity to represent the claims of those who suffer and the dangerous memory of Jesus Christ.[2] Metz follows a different route into the paradigm of liberation theology—the route of an internal critique of bourgeois society—but this route is also a call for transformation and conversion, a demand for a new way of being and doing in history.

Metz's fundamental contribution to the paradigm shift of liberation theology is his reformulation of anthropology and its relationship to Christianity. Metz's work makes a formal contribution to liberation theology by exploring the conditions of possibility for a new, social anthropology; his work makes a material contribution by criticizing the present reality of the bourgeois subject and finding within Christianity the memory and hope of a new subject of freedom. Metz's work develops in three stages as his anthropology becomes more historical both in the formal conditions of human subjectivity and in the material interpretation of the contemporary situation; in each stage, Christianity accepts an increasingly active role in representing the subject. These stages are not separate; themes appear, reappear, and are transformed. But the distinction of three stages carves out spaces where Metz intensifies his social anthropology and the role of Christianity in the world. In Metz's work modern theology deconstructs itself when it takes seriously the social conditions for the reality and identity of the free human subject.

64

Metz structures each stage through a careful consideration of the historical conditions of the human subject and the subject's relationship to Christianity: *(a)* he examines the historical consciousness of the subject, *(b)* he relates the historical consciousness of the subject to God through an interpretation of Christian symbols, and *(c)* he identifies the explicit witness of Christianity. The first stage of Metz's work accepts the world's secularity by letting the world go its own way. In the second stage, Christianity constantly criticizes the ambiguities of the world in light of the eschatological proviso of God. In the third stage, Metz uncovers the distorted consciousness of the bourgeois subject and finds, in the dangerous memory of Christ, the representation of a new subject, the subject of suffering. Against modernity's attempt to suffocate the subject through systems of subjugation and domination, Metz now argues that the human as *subject* is located in suffering—the suffering of both the living and the dead. These subjects have an identity gained through the memories of suffering, memories decisively represented in the memory of the passion, death, and resurrection of Christ.

FREEDOM AS AUTONOMY AND FUTURE

Secularization

In the first stage of Metz's work the historical consciousness of the modern subject is defined by secularity, the radical autonomy of human history.[3] Secularity presents Christianity with a major choice: either Christianity ignores the situation of secularity and continues its descent into mythology, or it accepts secularity as a challenge, "to give a positive interpretation of this permanent and growing worldliness of the world in light of Catholic theology."[4] The recognition of this challenge must take seriously the full autonomy of the world's freedom; it is this challenge that Metz accepts for his work.

Metz thus begins with the assumption that history is fundamentally secular, an assumption he calls the "worldliness of the world." Secularization frees the world from the theopolitical control of the church; it moves human existence from the reign of the magical and mythical to the reality of the factual and historical. Secularization marks the shift from a cosmocentric universe to an anthropocentric universe, in which humanity experiences the world not as nature but as history, open to transformation and control. Humanity works together to make history and in this way experiences human community: "the experience of the world and behavior in relation to it take place, rather, within the framework of human community, and this not simply in the 'private' sense of the I-thou relationship, but in the 'political' sense of social togetherness."[5]

In the secular process of making history, humanity develops a historical consciousness of freedom. The historical consciousness of freedom—the experience of autonomy, maturity, and responsibility in history—provides Metz with a contact point for the experience of God in the modern world. Before identifying this experience of God, Metz must "interpret" secularity in light of Christian symbols. This detour into the Christian foundations of secularity allows Metz to claim that the experience of autonomy is, in a sense, the experience of God. In his interpretation of secularity, Metz turns modernity on its head through the symbols of creation and incarnation: the autonomy of modernity depends on creation; the freedom of history continues the incarnation. First, the reality of secularity necessitates, in Metz's opinion, that the world is a creation of a Creator. Creation, in Metz's interpretation, expresses the distance between God and humanity: only when God as the transcendent Creator distances creation from Godself is there the possibility for autonomous freedom. Second, secularity is the manifestation of the incarnation. In the incarnation God accepted the world in Jesus Christ, and this acceptance is the condition for the radical freedom of history in the world.[6] The incarnation is God's acceptance of the world as radically different from Godself.

Metz's conclusion is a bold one: secularity is not opposed to God, or God to secularity. Secularity, correctly understood, is an unthematic, or anonymous, act of faith in history; as such, secular history is an advent of Christ.[7] Whether or not persons name their experience of secularity as Christian, God is always present through the freedom of historical consciousness, as Metz observes: "God is not the source concurring with human freedom but the freedom that allows human freedom to be in the concrete. His freedom holds sway as the liberating basis of freedom's subjectivity. Through his previous call and urging, which can be present to man only anonymously, as moral duty, the unconditional dictate of conscience, etc., man is called to be his free self and liberated."[8] Continuing the gift of the incarnation in the autonomous history of the world, Christianity does not reign over or oppose the progress of the world; Christianity accepts the radical freedom of historical consciousness and leaves "the world in its secularity."[9]

Secularity, in this first stage, is, therefore, the referent for understanding the human subject and Christianity. The historical consciousness of the human subject is characterized by secular freedom: the autonomy and responsibility to make history. This secular freedom, according to Metz, depends on the acceptance of the world by God in Jesus Christ; secularity, in other words, continues the incarnation. The human subject always experiences, anonymously, God through the radical freedom of historical consciousness.

What is important about the location of the human subject in the context of secularity is the social anthropology that Metz develops, an anthropology characterized by corporeality, intersubjectivity, and historical freedom. For Metz the human subject is "in the world," fully corporeal in nature and history. Metz's human subject is characterized by an intersubjectivity that is both social and political. Freedom is constituted through the ongoing activity of making history. As in much of modern theology Metz connects his anthropology to God via the nature of human freedom; unlike most of modern theology, this freedom is defined, even in the first stage of Metz's work, in a sociohistorical manner, identified with the making of human history.

Yet Metz's social anthropology is connected to Christianity in only a formal fashion, since secularity is the anonymous continuation of the incarnation. Metz's solution to the danger of secularity (the danger of leaving Christianity behind in history's journey toward complete autonomy) surrenders any real content of Christian symbols by replacing the symbol of the incarnation with the process of secularity. The role of Christianity in this first stage is purely formal—Christianity silently lets the world go its way—and thus Christianity has no real contribution to make to the human subject or in the world. Metz has located a social subject, but at the cost of denying any substantive content to Christianity while uncritically blessing the progress of Western history.

Eschatology

In the second stage of his work, Metz's analysis of the historical situation is characterized by two factors: (1) the primacy of the future, and (2) an increased emphasis on the ambiguities within modern history. Metz now argues that history is oriented toward a future—a future that exists in a relationship of nonidentity with the present. A quality of striving for the new *(novum)* marks the technological, political, and social revolutions of the modern era. This pragmatic, future-oriented history is constitutive of social and personal life; it is existential because it is social. As Metz's material reading of the historical situation changes from being characterized by secularity to being characterized by the primacy of the future, the historical consciousness of the subject is now oriented toward the future, and the freedom of the human subject is a freedom to anticipate and work toward new possibilities.

Within this new interpretation of the historical situation, Metz worries about the dangerous ambiguities of the present. Metz speaks of the negative experience of the modern era, in which freedom, peace, and justice are threatened. No longer lauded as an ever increasing progress, secularity is wrenched out of the dialectic of God's acceptance. History may be oriented toward the future but, according to Metz, it is also true that "the danger of new wars is too close. The irrationalities of our action in the social and political fields are too manifest. There is still with us the possibility that 'collective darkness' will descend upon us."[10] The strength of history is its orientation to the future; the problem of history (and history now has its problems) lies in the ambiguities of the present.

As secularity was grounded in creation and incarnation in Metz's first stage, so now does the future orientation of history depend on God: "the orientation of the modern era to the future and the understanding of the world as history, which results from this orientation is based upon the biblical belief in the promises of God."[11] God is the future not just as the telos, the inherent goal toward which history progresses, but, for Metz, as the radically new. God's future is not-yet, a free future of God. In the orientation toward the future, the human subject freely transcends the self toward God; not through the autonomous freedom of secularity but through the orientation to the radically new does the human subject experience the lure of the future, the lure of God. As in the first stage, the historical consciousness of freedom is grounded in God and represented through Christian symbols.

But in this stage there is a distance between God and the freedom of the present, a distance Metz represents by what he calls "the eschatological proviso." This not-yet future of God allows, though it does not necessitate, ambiguities to exist in history. The present is not the future, the redeemed, the new; as a provisional time, history is not yet perfected—the time of war, irrationality, and darkness. Grounded in God, the future relates dialectically to the present, giving Christianity the role of criticizing those ambiguities and provisionalities that threaten the human subject.

What motivates hope and the goal toward which it moves, in my theological opinion, is not the still hidden man, the *homo absconditus,* but the free future of God. This is an understanding of history and the future in which the future becomes visible, not just as what has been accomplished, what has been struggled for historically, but also as forbearance, forgiveness, and reconciliation. This seems to me to be decisive also in the history of humanity for the understanding of hope. For me as a theologian, the future as a whole stands under the eschatological proviso of God. It cannot *in its totality* become the content of the social and political endeavors of the individual or of single groups, lest it succumb to mystification or totalitarianism.[12]

God is the fulfillment of history and yet God is neither totally within history nor totally apart from history, but always dialectically related to history from the future. As the relationship of nonidentity between the future and the present, the eschatological proviso symbolizes that the final end or meaning of history will never be realized in any one particular situation. The eschatological proviso relativizes all systems and radicalizes the importance of historical activity in relation to God.[13]

As an explicit witness to the eschatological proviso, Christianity carries a critical and vocal role in society; it represents the eschatological proviso against the provisionality of all systems and structures in society. The church exists in society, according to Metz, as an institution of critical freedom: "the Church protects the individual man, living here and now, from being considered exclusively as matter and means for the building of a completely rationalized technical future."[14] The church must speak on behalf of the human as subject; it must uncover irrationality in its many diverse forms; it must refute the ideologization of one class, race, or society.

In this second stage of Metz's work, eschatology both qualifies and replaces the historical activity of secularity. It replaces secularity as the formal referent for the freedom of the human subject with the orientation to the future. But eschatology qualifies historical activity as ambiguous. Though ambiguity is present in the first stage, only in the second stage do the ambiguities of history pose a real threat to human existence. The orientation toward the future and the ambiguities of the present are answered by Christianity: the eschatological proviso grounds the orientation toward the future and criticizes present ambiguities. Eschatology allows the subject to experience God in the free orientation to the future; the eschatological proviso requires the church to proclaim God over and against the provisionalities of the present. Said differently: the hidden God of eschatology is both anonymously experienced in the lure of the future and thematically expressed in the church's critique of present ambiguities.

To further Christianity's critical-eschatological role, Metz calls for a new "political" theology. A political theology, maintains Metz, both corrects personalist, transcendental, and existentialist theologies, and expresses the eschatological message of Christianity in the present historical situation. As a corrective to earlier theologies, political theology offers a more adequate understanding of the sociopolitical nature of the human subject. Existentialist theology claimed to address the individual, but refused to reflect on the real historical nature of the subject. Relegating reason and freedom to individual experience, existentialist theology could not reflect critically on reason in society, and hence delivered "faith up to modern ideologies in the area of societal and political theory."[15] Political theology, on the other hand, begins with the fundamental relationship of reason and society in order to reflect on the social conditions of the human subject. By thus attending to human praxis, political theology addresses the human subject both in the intrinsic orientation to the future and in the critique of the ambiguities of history.

In this second stage, Metz uses the term "praxis" to suggest that theology should be grounded and constituted in concrete history. As the basis of reflection, praxis includes the following: *(a)* the political conditions of freedom and knowledge (a Kantian emphasis); *(b)* a philosophy of history giving rise to new forms of knowledge (a Hegelian emphasis); and *(c)* the relations of interest, power, and knowledge (a Marxist emphasis).[16] Within this rather free-flowing definition of praxis, Metz argues for the necessity of ideology critique as intrinsic to the nature and task of theology. Theology is not a secular ideology but a *theologia negativa* from the future and hence a critique of all ideologies in the present.

To develop this second stage of his theology, Metz repeats his basic structure of human subject, religious foundation, and Christian expression. The human subject is, in the second stage, characterized by an orientation toward the future and is threatened by historical ambiguities in the present. God grounds the future orientation of the human subject and, from God's place in the future, renders every particular situation as provisional and in need of transformation. There are two experiences of God: one experience is the anonymous experience of God in the transcendence or orientation toward the future; the other experience of God is the constant critique of the world by the church.

The relationship of these two experiences suggests the transitional nature of this stage of Metz's theology. In this stage Metz struggles with two problems.

The first problem expresses the cognitive challenge of the Enlightenment: How do we understand the human subject and the relationship of the human subject to Christ? The second problem revolves not around understanding but around transformation, a problem that Jon Sobrino calls the second challenge of the Enlightenment: How do we transform history?[17] Now, we might ask, how does Metz join the first problem to the second? Metz's answer would be at the point of the eschatological proviso; unfortunately, however, the proviso is so vague and ambiguous as to render any relationship between an *understanding of the subject* and the *transformation of history* nearly inexplicable. To understand the human subject, the eschatological proviso becomes a referent for the orientation toward the future. To change the ambiguities of the present, the eschatological proviso criticizes everything as provisional and calls for the radical transformation of society. But Metz never links this critique of the present situation and the call for transformation with his understanding of the human subject. The second problem of the Enlightenment, for Metz, is an external problem of society; the first problem of the Enlightenment is the internal problem of understanding the human subject. In Metz's next stage, these two problems will join in a radical critique of historical consciousness and modern society. But in this stage, the vagueness of the eschatological proviso allows the understanding of the subject to be formal and transcendental while it forces Christianity's critique of society to be wholly negative in content and merely functional in intent.[18]

Another expression of the transitional nature of this second stage is the puzzling nature of Metz's call for a political theology. He defines this new theology as, on the one hand, a corrective to previous theologies and, on the other hand, an expression of the eschatological message of Christianity. This problem might be stated in the following fashion: once the eschatological proviso is fully proclaimed in society, one has more than a mere "corrective" to existentialist, personalist, and transcendentalist theologies. For the problem of such theologies, at least according to Metz, is their inadequate *understanding* of the human subject; the solution of the eschatological message demands a radical transformation of the ambiguities in history. The solution, in a sense, swallows the problem! As a corrective to existentialist theologies, political theology enlarges its understanding of the human subject; as a manifestation of the eschatological proviso, theology becomes a form of ideology critique— and one such ideology is, of course, existentialist theology. As an ideology critique, therefore, political theology negates and transforms that to which it is a corrective.

The struggle for Metz is now twofold: (1) how to relate the formal conditions of the human subject in praxis with the material reading of the present situation and the Christian message, and (2) how to bring the challenge of understanding together with the challenge of transformation. Despite the transitional nature of this second stage, Metz opens up new possibilities for theology. In this second stage, Metz realizes that once the historical nature of the subject is brought into the nature of theology, theology is bound to turn to praxis for its foundation. Furthermore, with the addition of ideology critique to theology, even more change is promised as theology explores its new role as a radical critic and as a critical theory of freedom. If both the nature and the task of theology change, theology itself may soon be transformed.[19]

DECONSTRUCTING THE SUBJECT

Boy! Metz, sure wouldn't like this title!

The third stage of Metz's work begins with a far more critical, even pessimistic reading of the present situation; in this reading the understanding of the subject becomes interrupted and transformed. Metz moves from applying a functional ideology critique (criticizing ambiguities in a situation) to employing genetic and epistemic ideology critiques (uncovering the distortions of principles of knowledge, belief, and action through their origin and their operation). More importantly, Metz's basic structure—the consciousness of the human subject, the relation of this subject to God, and Christianity's explicit witness in the world—undergoes a radical transformation, making his theology neither a corrective to previous theologies nor a *theologia negativa* but a new practical, fundamental theology of the human subject. In this stage Metz shifts to a new paradigm of theology as he asks new questions, formulates new categories, retrieves forgotten Christian symbols, and finds a new goal for theological reflection.

Far from the secularity based in the Christian message, Metz argues that a "new" subject, a rational autonomous subject, appears in the Enlightenment.[20] This subject is not, as in the past, established through cultural traditions or political systems; this subject is determined by the pervasive principle of exchange. The marketplace—the primary location for the principle of exchange—adjudicates all norms and values of human life by supply and demand, by replacement and substitution. In modernity anything can be bought or sold; nothing—including values, traditions, and relationships—can stand in the way of the exponential consumption of the market system.

The principle of exchange proscribes the limits and foundations of the middle-class subject. This principle determines the "public" life of the person through production, trade, and consumption; cultural values are marginalized by isolating them into a realm appropriately labeled as "the private." Private values pacify the repressed needs of the subject and thus, Metz fears, appease the critical instincts of freedom: these "private" values must make no public demands and impose no external necessities. Individuals, reaching the age of maturity, may "decide" whether or not they "appreciate" art, whether or not to "believe" in God, and whether or not to continue the ethnic and cultural traditions of their families. Religion may be marketable, but only as it serves the human subject in some private, remainder aspects of life such as death and guilt outside the purview of modernity. Tradition, everyone knows, is superstitious and irrational—the very concept of following a tradition is antithetical to the modern ideology of the free and autonomous use of reason. The middle-class subject will, in sum, "subordinate everything, including his own love of the past and of tradition, to the rules of the exchange game."²¹

Within modernity, Metz contends, reason is defined solely as a technical, calculating reason that conforms life to the laws of profit and success. This "planning" reason results in a praxis of control over nature and history for the interests of the principle of exchange. Reason and freedom, the promises of modernity, combine to cement a destiny of domination: "at the beginning of what we call the "Modern Age," the limits of which we are now reaching with ever increasing clarity, there unfolds—embryonically and overlaid with many religious and cultural symbols—this anthropology of domination."²² Subjugation is the real "act" of the Enlightenment freedom, an act that controls the destruction of nature, the bureaucratization of human relationships, the manipulation of history; an act that, according to Metz, "has long since permeated the psychic foundations of our total sociocultural life."²³ The subject that Metz has located and represented by Christian symbols in the first two stages now stands in danger of disappearing: "the purely technologically and economically planned production of man's future would seem to foreshadow the very disappearance of man as the being who has nourished himself on the historical substance of his freedom."²⁴

This middle-class subject, according to Metz, lives in the context of two forms of historical consciousness: evolutionary logic and historical materialism. Since the second form is but a manifestation of the first, an analysis of evolutionary logic suffices to display how modernity has constructed the consciousness of the middle-class subject.²⁵ Promising emancipation through increased control over nature and history, evolutionary logic has "evolved" into an irrational ideology suffocating human history in a blanket of timelessness. The timelessness of evolutionary logic stands as the symbol for the distortion of historical consciousness in, to use the famous phrase of Horkheimer and Adorno, the dialectic of the Enlightenment. In this consciousness of timelessness, there is no future or past, while the present is one of time as a continuous, empty process.²⁶ The critical problem of this timelessness, which becomes for Metz the central problem for theology, is how evolution alters and even destroys the historical consciousness of the human subject. "The modern world, with its technical civilization, is not simply a rational universe. Its myth is evolution. The silent interest of its rationality is the fiction of time as empty infinity, which is free of surprises and within which everyone and everything is enclosed without grace."²⁷

Evolutionary consciousness—the myth of timelessness—is expressed in the Enlightenment prejudice against tradition, in the functionality of bourgeois religion, in the apathy of the middle-class subject, and in the inability of individuals to mourn or feel guilty. This logic of evolution with its suffocating timelessness threatens to destroy the human subject, and with it the history of freedom. Metz has, at last, located the fully concrete historical subject only to discover that the very conditions of possibility—both the formal conditions of intersubjectivity, freedom, and corporeality as well as the material characteristics such as apathy, the public-private distinction, and bourgeois consumerism

—threaten the very survival of the subject. Throughout his three stages Metz has expanded the implications of a social anthropology only to realize that anthropology is itself being destroyed by that which gave it birth—modernity and its "quest" for freedom. Evolutionary logic, then, replaces "real" historical consciousness, forgetting the intersubjectivity of the human existence—life as constituted in relation to other subjects, with history, and with nature. In place of intersubjectivity, the domination and subjugation of modernity makes the subject "incapable of seeing himself and judging himself through the eyes of his victims."[28] Evolutionary logic denies corporeality, a corporeality composed of sufferings, of memories, of hopes, as well as of desires, longings, and needs. It smothers the passions of human life, replacing the pains and ecstasy of time-filled existence with the control and management of timeless reality.

The destruction of historical consciousness through evolutionary logic results in the forgetfulness of history—the inability to question who we are and what we do. Auschwitz symbolizes, for Metz, modernity's barbarity—both the horror that Auschwitz could occur and the horror that its occurrence could be so easily forgotten: "yet in the meantime, has not a massive forgetfulness long since taken over? The dead of Auschwitz should have brought upon us a total transformation; nothing should have been allowed to remain as it was, neither among our people nor in our churches, above all, not in the churches."[29] Evolutionary logic allows us not only to be dominating and subjugating, but to forget our past acts for the sake of our future conquests. The problem of this "form" of historical consciousness is that it denies history and destroys freedom. We can, concludes Metz, no longer hope to arrive at a better understanding of the human subject; the conditions for understanding are themselves distorted and disrupted through the insidious myth of evolutionary logic.

Metz directs the fires of his critique of evolutionary logic at modern Christianity: bourgeois religion is the mirror image of evolutionary logic. Metz's explanation of modern religion parallels the explanation of progressive religion by Gutiérrez: modern religion creates a religious dimension that hovers within the limits of pure reason. This religious dimension serves as a foundation for a new natural religion, a religion of reason, that no longer needs religious authorities or superstitious beliefs. Though supposedly a religion of "all men," Metz regards modern Christianity as elitist because it appeals to and serves only the middle-class subject. Modern Christianity, Metz concludes, functions to support the middle-class subject and to mollify the critical impetus of the Christian message and the anticipatory struggles of the human subject. The evolutionary logic of the middle-class subject is simply reflected back in the cloudy mirror of bourgeois Christianity.

Metz's new reading of the present situation concentrates, as before, on the historical consciousness of the human subject. But in this third stage of Metz's development, the historical consciousness must no longer be merely understood, but must now be radically transformed. Thus, Metz concludes, there can be no easy corrective; the attempts to fix the problems of modernity result in more and more control. Nor can there simply be constant critique, for critique too easily appeases the timelessness of evolutionary logic. The solutions of the second stage no longer hold any hope: what is needed now is the transformation of the subject. Only radical therapy, a revolution in consciousness, a dramatic conversion in history can save the subject from the logic of forgetfulness. Metz breaks into a new paradigm with this quest for a new subject, a new way of Christianity, and a new purpose for theological reflection.

THE SUBJECT OF SUFFERING

Metz, giving up on the middle-class subject, now turns his gaze on a new subject—the subject of suffering—located in a different history of freedom. Influenced by Walter Benjamin, Metz argues that history is not the total sum of the actions and the interpretations of the victors but, rather, the reality of the sufferings of human victims.[30] History is not, as the Enlightenment told us, a "natural" progression of time; the history of suffering as the history of freedom provides a new way to understand and interrupt the timelessness of the Enlightenment:

The substratum of history, then, is not nature as evolution or a process without reference to the subject. The natural history of man is to some extent the history of his suffering. . . . The essential dynamics of history consist of the memory of suffering as a negative consciousness of future freedom and as a stimulus to overcome suffering within the framework of that freedom. The history of freedom is therefore—subject to the assumed alienation of man and nature—only possible as a history of suffering.[31]

Within this different history, a new, or more correctly, a forgotten subject is discovered—suffering reveals the human subject as one with a past and a future. Metz discovers that, within the iron cage of modernity, the freedom to be a human subject is the freedom to suffer.[32] For Metz, it is the memory of suffering—the ability to remember and the memories of suffering—that provides the possibility for the concrete historical identity of the human subject. The freedom to suffer includes "the freedom to suffer the suffering of others" and it includes the freedom to become old, to contemplate, and even to die.[33] To ignore this freedom, observes Metz, is to lose the identity of the human subject, since the freedom to suffer is also the freedom to hope—to live in a time-filled history recalling the past and anticipating the future.

Out of the dialectic of freedom in suffering and hope, Metz constructs the new categories of historical consciousness: memory, narrative, and solidarity. Memory constitutes human identity, for "identity is formed when memories are aroused."[34] The human subject is formed by memories, which give rise to practical knowledge and concrete anticipations. These memories constitute the human subject through narrative, and hence reason has a practical, historical, and personal structure. Memories are recalled in narratives, which give our lives a timefulness, a beginning and an end, an experience of history. Narratives form, inform, and transform individuals and communities through traditions, shared values, and concrete solidarities. Solidarity is the timefulness of belonging to our memories and our future, the timefulness of suffering with and for others, the timefulness of freedom as human intersubjectivity. Memory, narrative, and solidarity are, for Metz, the new categories of historical consciousness.[35]

Metz continues the basic structure of his theology by exploring the conditions for human consciousness as dependent upon God and expressed in Christianity. But the foundational relationship between God and the human subject is somewhat obscured or hidden in this stage; Metz says only that God is a practical idea, that God is the condition whereby the human has an identity in history. The argument that Metz previously used—in which the experience of freedom is an anonymous experience of God—no longer fits Metz's practical, fundamental theology.[36] For the former argument depended on a decidedly transcendentalist turn—an argument of the universal apriori type—which Metz has now criticized as being one more expression of middle-class ideology, "an elitist idealistic gnoseology."[37] The historical consciousness of the suffering subject cannot have a universal, anonymous experience of God—this subject is grounded by concrete memories, specific narratives, and historical events. It may be that Metz cannot retrieve or invent a new, transformed transcendental argument; he does suggest a more limited claim with hermeneutical backing, a claim of God and the human subject as revealed through the Christian tradition: "the history of biblical religion is a history of the way in which a people and the individuals belonging to that people became subjects in the presence of their God."[38] The Christian narratives in the Old and New Testaments, asserts Metz, all refer to the formation of the human subject in relation to God. Metz adds that the relation of God and the identity of the human subject might be demonstrated from the history of religions. Yet even with these weak assertions, Metz seems left without his usual foundational experience of God to which historical consciousness "anonymously" or "naturally" relates. How is God a practical idea? Do we experience God in danger, in suffering, in freedom? Is God wholly Deus Absconditus?

On the more thematic relationship of Christianity and the subject—more specifically, how Christianity represents the freedom of the human subject— Metz offers a powerful and radically new interpretation of Christianity as the identification of suffering with hope in Jesus Christ. Through the passion, death, and resurrection of Jesus Christ, Christianity provides a tradition of dangerous memories—memories of suffering with a future orientation. Suffering functions in Christianity in much the same way that it functions in the human subject through the categories of memory, narrative, and solidarity.[39] Against the Enlightenment separation of freedom from tradition, Christianity represents freedom as a tradition, a tradition of memories and hopes; as Metz argues, "knowledge of freedom, even in its critical form, or, rather, particularly in its critical form, participates in religion as recollection."[40] Freedom is no longer opposed to the tradition of Christianity but is now dependent upon it.

Christianity represents human freedom as a definite memory; it "declares itself as the *memoria passionis, mortis et resurrectionis Jesu Christi.* At the midpoint of this faith is a specific *memoria passionis*, on which is grounded the promise of future freedom for all."[41] The memory of Jesus is the memory of his resurrection by way of his crucifixion. The resurrection-crucifixion of Jesus represents the dead, "who have a meaning which is as of yet unrealized."[42] Through this memory we experience history as a history of the dead and of those who suffer. The resurrection-crucifixion is a forward memory that calls us to criticize and interrupt the present sociopolitical situation on behalf of those who suffer. This is not a critique from a vague eschatological proviso: Jesus Christ represents the memories of suffering as anticipatory memories that place a claim on history; in Metz's words: "What emerges from the memory of suffering is a knowledge of the future that does not point to empty anticipation, but looks actively for more human ways of life in the light of our experience of the new creation of man in Christ."[43]

Against the middle-class subject, Metz discloses the real subjects of history in suffering. Against the Enlightenment pseudo-promise of freedom from tradition, Metz offers a freedom of tradition and solidarity, of hope and suffering. In this freedom there are no separate realms of public and private; the values of religion, tradition, and art all provoke dangerous memories and future hopes. Christianity represents the subject of suffering, as one who cannot be forgotten in history, as one whose time is still to come. Christianity's nature and role is to represent the full freedom of the human subject, the freedom to remember and to hope, the freedom to make a claim on history.

The dangerous memory of Christ as the representation of the full freedom of the human subject differentiates, for Metz, redemption from modern theories of human emancipation. Redemption, according to Metz, must include the whole history of human suffering, including guilt, finitude, and death.[44] Metz argues that in many modern theories of emancipation the subject is abstract and irrational; guilt is ignored or projected onto scapegoats; the identity of the subject is canceled into banality. Such attempts at perfect or complete emancipation fail, Metz warns us, because they do not treat humanity in its full historical identity; they do not examine the nature of human subjectivity, the thrust of remembering and of hoping beyond any historical realization.

According to Metz, redemption is not a theory or a belief but fundamentally a praxis of following Christ. Following Christ is not the application of dogma or contemplation of a theory, but a way, a journey, an imitation of Christ.[45] The New Testament narratives do not impress upon us a belief in Christ; they provoke and perform a way of following Christ. These narratives "form" the Christian, they make the Christian understand, experience, and imitate Christ. Christology—the logos of Christ—is a practical knowledge, a praxis of following Christ.

This new praxis of following Christ, as an expression of the relationship between redemption and the human subject, is an interruption, an interruption of the middle-class subject, of bourgeois religion, and of modern theology. But this interruption is, at the same time, a conversion to a new way of being and doing in history. Unlike Metz's first two stages, Christianity does not accept the world or prophetically critique the world; now Christianity converts, transforms, and changes the world. Christianity now testifies to and participates in an anthropological revolution.

> For this revolution is not, in fact, concerned with liberating us from our poverty and misery, but rather from our wealth and our totally excessive prosperity. It is not a liberation from what we lack, but from our consumerism in which we are ultimately consuming our very selves. It is not a liberation from our state of oppression, but from the untransformed praxis of our own wishes and desires. It is not a liberation from our powerlessness, but from our own form of predominance. It frees us, not from the state of being dominated but from that of dominating; not from our sufferings but from our apathy; not from our guilt but from our innocence, or rather from that delusion of innocence which the life of domination has long since spread through our souls.[46]

The anthropological revolution centers around a new historical consciousness of timefulness, of imminent expectation. Represented by the notion of apocalypticism, Metz's notion of imminent expectation becomes the antidote to evolutionary logic: if the despair of evolutionary logic was the forgetfulness of time (the continual denial of memory and hope) the promise of apocalypticism is the catastrophic nature of time (the continual quest of the past and the future). Against the evolutionary logic of timelessness, Christianity now contributes a time of imminent expectation.

In the dangerous memories of suffering, time is lived apocalyptically—as discontinuous, as rupturing. Apocalyptic time necessitates that human meaning is never reduced to a one-time event in the past or in the future, or sublated into a worldview of progress. The apocalyptic consciousness of the anthropological revolution forces history itself to be called into question: suffering calls the future, the past, and the present into question. As the antidote to the poison of evolutionary logic, apocalyptic time is the placement of Metz's major concerns—freedom, subjectivity, and Christianity—into the concrete history of suffering.[47] Apocalyptic time includes freedom, subjectivity, and Christianity within the transforming memory of suffering, a memory that displays the religious quest: "to whom does the world belong? To whom do its suffering and time belong?"[48]

With this time of imminent expectation, messianic Christianity is a praxis of hope in solidarity; for Metz, "the faith of Christians is a praxis in history and society that is to be understood as hope in solidarity in the God of Jesus as a God of the living and the dead who calls all men to be subjects in his presence."[49] The centrality of the term "praxis" in this new definition of Christianity has three implications in Metz's thought. First, Christianity, like any other tradition, is constituted historically—it exists within human praxis. Second, Christianity testifies to the freedom of the human subject not only to act, but also to suffer actively—it is a praxis of freedom. Third, Christianity has a specific content to its praxis drawn from Christian tradition and lived in apocalyptic expectation—it is a praxis of the imitation of Christ. Christian faith is a sociohistorical activity representing human freedom through the active imitation of Jesus Christ.

In the first stage of Metz's work Christians imitated Christ by accepting the world, and in the second stage they imitated Christ by criticizing the world. Now, in the third stage of Metz's work, Christians imitate Christ through the acceptance of suffering and through a praxis of interruption and conversion. This praxis of imitation is not just a matter of believing but a life of enactment, combining narrative and action in radical discipleship. Christian faith is no longer captive to understanding the world and letting it go its way; it is no longer isolated to criticizing the world and pointing out God's freedom. Thus Metz arrives at a new paradigm of Christianity: Christian faith now interrupts and transforms the world; it manifests God's grace, which is, according to Metz, a way of living differently.

A PRACTICAL, FUNDAMENTAL THEOLOGY

In this interruption and reformation of Christianity, theology takes on new forms, new tasks, and new relations to Christianity. Just as Gutiérrez realized that a new way of doing theology was required given the liberating praxis of the poor and the new way of Christianity, so Metz deems it essential to formulate a new practical, fundamental theology based on the praxis of Christianity and the praxis of human suffering. Metz continues, albeit in a radically different manner, his insistence in the second stage that theology be based in praxis. By this insistence, Metz now intends that theology become a praxis, a practical activity that relates to the anthropological revolution of historical consciousness and the messianic religion of Christian witness.

In order to understand the relationship between theology and praxis we must turn to the categories of historical consciousness and to the enactment of these categories through Christian witness. These categories—solidarity, memory, and narrative—reorient the nature and purpose of theology. Both the foundation as well as the aim of human life and Christian praxis, according to Metz, is captured in the phrase "solidarity with the living and the dead." The nature of theology must be in concurrence with this foundation and aim of life: theology is not, therefore, a methodological reflection on a general religious dimension in human experience, but the narration, through practical reason, of solidarity with those who suffer.[50] Solidarity, as the foundation and aim of life and as the witness of Christianity, forms the nature and purpose of theology.

Invoking the mystical and political nature of theology, solidarity forces memory and narrative to be practical, social, and concrete. Theology is mystical in its universal connectedness with the living and the dead; it is political in its particular narrative memory. Theology is thus a praxis of solidarity with the suffering, a praxis specifically enacting the memories of suffering (and thus provoking the apocalyptic historical consciousness) through the retrievals of Christian tradition and the history of freedom. Narrative allows, in a way theory does not, for the relationship of salvation and history. Narrative engages salvation in theology without subordinating it or making it unhistorical.

Narrative, as the structure of theology, has two interrelated tasks for Metz. First, it is performative and practical as it forms and informs the human subject through dangerous memories. This is its hermeneutical task, forming and transforming the lives of subjects through the recollection and interpretation of the memories of suffering. Second, it is critical insofar as these memories call into question the prevailing sociopolitical structures.[51] "It is here, however, that the idea of narrative plays a part in hermeneutics, insofar as it determines praxis on the basis of dangerous stories which call the social conditioning of human activity into question and which are directed against a kind of history in which, under certain structures and systems, the subject, who can never be accurately calculated by anyone, is made to disappear."[52]

But how, we must ask, does this make theology *political*?[53] To answer this question we must consider the basic claim of Metz's work. Metz claims that the human subject, Christianity, and even theology itself must be interrupted and transformed. Indeed, Metz goes so far as to define religion as interruption and to call for an "anthropological" revolution and a new reformation. In both revolution and reformation, the distortions of modernity—subjugation, domination, timelessness—must be transformed. In a sense, then, we might argue, as Metz says, that theology is political because it deals with an entire transformation of all that we are and all that we know. We can turn to Metz's basic structure to investigate how and what this political revolution-reformation will contain. If Metz claims that a transformation is needed and that theology, minimally, contributes to this transformation, then the new structure of theology should guide us in our transformative activity. Here, strangely enough, "politics" becomes a decidedly vague term. For Metz's structure allows us to transform the fundamental categories of anthropology and Christianity but, once transformed, the categories are not directly connected to concrete praxis. We must, Metz argues, find a new historical consciousness of time that allows the subject to suffer. This historical consciousness is testified to in Christianity, and through its apocalyptic witness Christianity becomes a praxis of solidarity with those who suffer. But though this transforms our understanding, will it transform our history? Or, to approach the problem from the point of Christian witness, is narrative enough to heal therapeutically the distortions of evolutionary logic? While narratives certainly form, inform, and even transform us, can they restructure the social system of the first world or even the ecclesiastical structures of the church? How do we move from a transformed consciousness to a changed world? Can Christianity be more than a barefoot apocalyptic witness to a new way of doing and being? How does political theology really enter the fight of history—as social, economic, moral history?[54]

CONCLUSION

By following the development of Metz's thought through three distinct stages, we have traveled along a route of the intensification and the critique of modern theology. Metz begins by taking the challenge of secularity seriously and trying to understand the human subject and Christianity in light of this challenge. Thus Metz understands the human subject historically—both within a particular experience of history (a material understanding) and as being able to experience history (a formal understanding). And as Metz puts the subject into history, following the anthropocentrism of the Enlightenment, his understanding of the subject grows more and more radical. By the third stage of his theology, Metz realizes that the historical situation is distorted and disrupted, and that it will not be enough simply to understand the human subject. The survival of the subject is threatened; only radical conversion can offer any hope for saving the human subject. In Metz's works, as modern theology places the subject in history, its own understanding of the subject—dependent on universal, a priori ideas—becomes deconstructed. Theology must now live with a much more fragile subject, a subject who realizes its freedom in the midst of concrete, sensuous history.

As we have indicated, Metz's own conversion is perhaps not yet complete. His brilliant material reading of the bourgeois subject and the subject of suffering is met by a formal reading of new categories of solidarity, memory, and narrative for historical consciousness. These new categories, represented in Christianity, counter the timelessness of evolutionary logic with the imminent expectation in Christian apocalypticism. Yet the new categories of historical consciousness suggest two problems: first, how is God related to the experience of freedom through suffering and hope? and second, how do these categories give rise to real social change? Perhaps the structure of Metz's thought (a rather modern structure of theology) must be not only interrupted, but ruptured and transformed by a far more practical argument for the experience of God and by transformative models of new social relations.

Metz, like Gutiérrez, illustrates the paradigm shift in liberation theology. His call for an anthropological revolution and a new reformation in Christianity all demand a new frame of reference, a new way of acting. The language of interruption and conversion demonstrates, as well, that Metz has moved beyond any notion of simply correcting the paradigm of modern theology. Within the new paradigm of liberation theology, Metz helps us to envision a new human subject; his genetic and epistemic ideology critique aids us in uncovering the distortions within our categories, concepts, ways of experiencing. Metz forces us to understand that what is needed is not just more generosity on the part of the bourgeoisie, not just increased production or better understanding, but a total conversion of who we are and how we live in history.

Metz's other contribution to liberation theology, a quite significant contribution in this writer's judgment, lies within his methodological and material insistence on the importance of tradition. Contra to the Enlightenment, Metz argues, human freedom rests on cultural tradition, and new possibilities for the future arise out of the continual reinterpretation of the past. Where modern theology once ran from Christian tradition to become reasonable and relevant to the human subject, Metz now urges theology to recall its tradition in order to testify to the freedom of the human subject. While modern theology turned classical theology on its head, Metz suggests turning modern theology inside out. According to Metz, political theology represents the subject through tradition, memory, spirituality, and apocalypticism. But political theology, for Metz, recalls its tradition only through a radical enactment of narratives, a solidarity of suffering, and a mystical-political imitation of Christ.

5

José Míguez Bonino: The Conversion to the World

The paradigm shift to liberation theology occurs, as Gutiérrez and Metz have demonstrated, as a break, a rupture, an upheaval in the way we experience and understand Christianity. For both Gutiérrez and Metz this rupture also leads to a transformation: the breaking of the old leads to the birth of the new. The process of break and transformation, upheaval and conversion in the works of Gutiérrez and Metz serves to reinterpret history and anthropology through suffering and to relocate Christianity and theological reflection in praxis. The next two theologians, José Míguez Bonino and Jürgen Moltmann, concentrate on particular theological issues *within* the new paradigm of liberation theology. Jürgen Moltmann, considered in the following chapter, interprets the narrative of God through the identification of hope and suffering in the midst of the agonies of the world. José Míguez Bonino, the subject of this chapter, constructs a hermeneutics of liberation once theology "undergoes a conversion to the world."

> I think the basic task, not only theologically, and not only Protestant, may be defined as the need for a "conversion to the world": Latin America is seeking the road to self-understanding and self-realization in all areas. It is not the task of Christianity to define the ways or to direct the process. But it is definitely its responsibility modestly to contribute to it through a theological reflection on the meaning of life, development, crisis, change, revelation, justice, freedom, peace, man and society—all the elements and structures of the situation and to do so not in the abstract but in the living conjunction of the message and experience of the Church and the given facts of the situation.[1]

Theology in Latin America, Míguez Bonino claims, is in a new position: a position of violence and death, of revolutionary consciousness, of reflection on praxis, of responsibility for social location. This new position raises important questions for the interpretive activity of theology: how does theology

82

interpret God's Word in this situation? How does theology avoid simply being determined by the situation and thus becoming one more false ideology? How does theology use the Bible as a guide to Christian praxis? Such questions compose the nature of theological hermeneutics—the logos of the Theos interpreted through Christian Scriptures and historical situations. Míguez Bonino argues that these questions of theology must now be asked within a sociopolitical context; the interpretations of theology are adequate and appropriate only as they are mediated through historical situations: "individual and interpersonal conditions and relations are shaped and find significance in a *polis*, a total, organized and intentional social formation. A meaningful Christian faith, therefore, has to be mediated through historical and political participation."[2] Given the basic assumptions of the priority of praxis in liberation theology, the tasks of hermeneutics are greatly enlarged; hermeneutics now includes interpreting text and context, incorporating ideology critique, identifying strategies for change, and proclaiming the Word of God not only in the midst of the world but through the activities of the Christian community. Standing at the origin of the paradigm shift, Míguez Bonino orients us toward a new, practical activity of hermeneutics, providing us with guidelines and provoking Christian faith through the interplay of the Christian Scriptures and historical situations. Within the paradigm of liberation theology, Míguez Bonino contributes a hermeneutics of the world and the Word.

Míguez Bonino's hermeneutics of world and Word is formulated through two basic principles of interpretation. In the formulation of each principle Míguez Bonino argues the necessity for this type of hermeneutics—the basis on which liberation theology interprets world and Word—as well as some general guidelines for interpretation. The first principle addresses theology as a hermeneutics of the world arguing for the importance of understanding the context of interpretation; in Míguez Bonino's words this principle "is the determination of the historical conditions and possibilities of our present situation, as discovered through rational analysis."[3] An adequate hermeneutics of the world includes matters of ideology critique and the use of the social sciences. The second principle formulates a hermeneutics of the Word by clarifying the demands and use of Scripture in liberation theology; this principle determines that theology is "concerned with the reading of the direction of the biblical text, particularly of the witness of the basic, germinal events of the faith."[4] Through the constant interplay of these two principles, liberation theology brings together the Word and the world. The interplay of Word and world in liberation theology can be traced through Míguez Bonino's interpretation of violence in the Latin American context.

A HERMENEUTICS OF THE WORLD

Míguez Bonino's first hermeneutical principle formulates a foundation for and strategy of interpretation within the social location of theology. The hermeneutics of the world is necessary, according to Míguez Bonino, because religion, like all other forms of human activity, lives in the sociopolitical sphere. Due to this primary location, every theory of interpretation must take into account the sociopolitical mediation and constitution of religion. Míguez Bonino's first principle argues for the sociopolitical nature of theological interpretation and considers the inclusion of ideology critique, the advocacy of a theological position, and the use of socioscientific analysis.

Theology, according to Míguez Bonino, lives in the double reference of text and situation. Within this double reference, theology understands the sociopolitical constitution of human life as the full sphere of human responsibility and freedom. If theology is to reveal the logos of the Theos in this time and place, it must do so by addressing human responsibility and freedom within the polis. The social location of theology, according to Míguez Bonino, includes:

(a) recognizing that theology operates under the conditioning of the political realm with its conflicts and its own kind of rationality; (b) incorporating socio-political instruments and categories in our theological reflection, realizing that the political sphere is the realm of structures, ideologies, and power; (c) abandoning the assumption that theology can prescind from politics and be non-temporal while at the same time taking on and articulating some concrete option: in our case, the struggle for liberation.[5]

For Míguez Bonino there is no value-free statement in hermeneutics, no purely abstract or scientific proof of the correctness of one way of life. Rather, every interpretation involves, at least implicitly, some indication of how it is to be a human subject in the world—knowledge reflects and guides praxis, praxis constitutes and is formed by knowledge. The hermeneutics of theology are not abstract descriptions of situations; theology reflects on that in which it participates. Since theology elaborates, by its systematic content and its participation in history, a way of being in the world, it cannot abstract itself from the polis, the realm of human decision-making and community.

Interpretation theory is, for Míguez Bonino, a reflective theory, and thus interpreters must be conscious of their class, their culture, their tradition, and their functions in society. Relying upon arguments from the sociology of knowledge and from a revision of Bultmann's hermeneutics, Míguez Bonino highlights the importance of the preunderstanding of the theologian as interpreter. The sociology of knowledge emphasizes the shared knowledge of the interpreter; knowledge is always socially produced and constituted. The categories, concepts, and cognitive operations of the interpreter are social knowledge, both in the sense of arising out of particular traditions and in the sense of participating within a particular polis. Míguez Bonino wants to "deepen" Bultmann's theological hermeneutics by emphasizing the preunderstanding the interpreter brings to a text, "not in the abstract philosophical analysis of existence but in the concrete conditions of men who belong to a certain time, people, and class, who are engaged in certain courses of action, even of

Christian action, and who reflect and read the texts within and out of these conditions."[6] Both positions agree that the interpreter's own categories, frameworks, and methods of reasoning depend, to a great extent, on the culture and period in which they live. Thus, Míguez Bonino argues, every interpreter lives in a situation that in some way supports, reflects, legitimizes, or criticizes a certain way of being in the world.[7]

In sum, the sociopolitical nature of a hermeneutics of the world depends upon the location of theology and the theologian within praxis. Consequently, any interpretation theory of religion must be aware of its own social location in the political sphere; it must critically reflect on its own position, its history, and its social interest. Given the sociopolitical nature of interpretation theory, Míguez Bonino offers three general guidelines for a hermeneutics of the world: (1) the inclusion of ideology and ideology critique in theology, (2) the positioning of theology within the social location, and (3) the use of social sciences in theology.

1) *The inclusion of ideology and ideology critique in theology*: The social location of interpretation theory requires attention to the ideological frameworks within different forms of praxis and, hence, within theology itself.[8] Míguez Bonino employs the term "ideology" in a much more positive sense than many liberation theologians; Míguez Bonino defines ideology as the general worldview—the unified picture of reality—within a particular praxis.[9] With this broad definition of ideology as worldview, Míguez Bonino argues that every interpretation has some form of ideology as the unified elements of an understanding of the world. The ideological nature of theology is intrinsic to the historical character of theology. By this Míguez Bonino intends nothing more than the relation of theology to the worldview of its situation; ideology supplies the general content to the knowledge of a period. Yet ideology cannot be simply assumed, for, precisely as with the worldview of a period, it must be examined and analyzed; the fundamental assumptions we have about our world must, in theology, always be questioned. In Míguez Bonino's words: "any course of action which keeps a certain coherence implies a unified perspective on reality, an explicit or implicit project. Ideology, in this sense, has also a positive meaning; it is the instrument through which our Christian obedience gains coherence and unity. It is so, though, provided that it be always brought to consciousness and critically examined both in terms of the gospel and of the scientific analysis of reality."[10]

Because theology always relates to various forms of ideology, interpretation theory must include a strong moment of suspicion in analyzing every ideology.[11] Ideology can be false; it can mask the real interests and intents of power structures in society. Míguez Bonino limits his hermeneutics to the use of a functional ideology critique that uncovers a position used to mask the special interests of a select group of people. Míguez Bonino suggests, for instance, that Latin American liberation theologians must be suspicious of all theologies coming from the first world and ask what kind of praxis the theology supports, reflects, or legitimizes. Questions of interests, location, and commitment reveal the effects as well as the intent of a theological position. Míguez Bonino incorporates the role of ideology critique in theology as an implication of the social location; ideology critique is necessary because of the sociopolitical mediation of all of theology.

2) *The positioning of theology within the social location*: Theology, according to Míguez Bonino, must reflect on its social location, for otherwise it is merely determined by the particular class, status, and interest of the theologian. This internal reflection on the social location of theology provides for the possibility that theologians may "position" their theology through a discernment of God's action in a particular historical situation: "we are *situated* in reality to be sure—historically, geographically, culturally, and most of all groupwise and classwise—but we can also *position* ourselves differently in relation to the situation."[12] Theologians, as interpreters, are not just mirror images of particular interests, but constructive interpreters; they participate in the situation through analysis, criticism, and interpretation. Liberation theologians cannot argue, as did their modern predecessors, the true, correct or transcendental position for all times and places; given Míguez Bonino's insistence on praxis as the basis of interpretation theory, theology has no universal vantage point for all times and places. But liberation theologians can make practical theological interpretations employing various forms of analysis and theories of transformation to argue the adequacy of their position.

3) *The use of social sciences in theology*: The social location of theology also requires that new categories, concepts, and other theories from the social sciences be used in theological hermeneutics. Míguez Bonino believes that the use of social sciences represents a new phenomenon in theology. Since the second century, theology has relied upon philosophical language and theoretical principles of rationality to construct its interpretations and to argue the adequacy of theological interpretations. The truth of theology, Míguez Bonino contends, was traditionally located in its *conceptual* relationship to various philosophies; untruth was regarded as error—something that could be conceptually cleared up, corrected, or reinterpreted. But now the philosophical enterprise itself has been called into question; there is no pure concept through which to interpret history. Indeed, philosophy has become more praxis-oriented, using its theoretical arguments to aid in the ongoing interpretation of human existence. It is, Míguez Bonino argues, the interpretation of praxis that demands new categories and concepts:

Finally, both the criticism and the introduction of the criterion of historical verifiability introduces into the hermeneutical task new areas and instruments. We are not concerned with establishing through deduction the consequences of conceptual truths but with analyzing a historical praxis which claims to be Christian. This critical analysis includes a number of operations, which are totally unknown to classical theology. . . . The area of research is the total society in which these agents are performing; economic, political, and cultural facts are as

relevant to a knowledge of this praxis as the exegesis of their pronounce-
ments and publications.[13]

For Míguez Bonino, once theology becomes an interpretation of praxis, it
must forge ahead with these new tools and conversation partners. For Míguez
Bonino, these social tools allow theology to analyze and interpret the world, as
philosophy allows theology to analyze and interpret ideas. The social categories make theology concrete, both in its ability to understand the situation and
in its ability to speak to the situation. Social categories and concepts offer new
ways to translate religious symbols and ideas. Reconciliation, for instance,
when used with oppressed groups struggling for their rights, now includes a
historical and political meaning through the uses of social categories.

In this first principle of interpretation theory—his hermeneutics of the
world—Míguez Bonino broadens theological hermeneutics to include what he
calls the double reference, the context of praxis as well as the text of faith.
Míguez Bonino's hermeneutics of the world depends on a dialectical relationship between knowledge and praxis: knowledge grows out of praxis, but is
never reduced to mere action. Because of the dialectical relationship between
knowledge and praxis, the interpretation theory of liberation theology will
always be context-dependent.[14] The specific form of interpretation theory will
depend, to a certain extent, upon the particular situation: a hermeneutics of the
world might rely heavily on economic analysis in one situation, upon ideology
critique in a second situation, and upon educational theory in a third situation.
With this turn from a universal method to context-dependent methods, interpretation theory within the paradigm of liberation theology becomes a form of
practical reason, a deliberation of possibilities within praxis. As practical
reason, theology interprets the world always in dialogue with the Word.[15] The
faith upon which theology reflects is a faith in God active in the world calling
all Christians to follow God's Word. Therefore any interpretation theory must
consider the Word as well as the world.

A HERMENEUTICS OF THE WORD

For faith to be located and positioned in a particular situation, theology
must not only analyze the social context, but must also attend to the claims of
the tradition, and especially to Christian Scriptures. What Míguez Bonino
ponders in his hermeneutics of the Word is a twofold question: How is the Bible
a revelation of God's activity in history? and, How do we discern the actions of
God within our own situation? This second principle of interpretation, for
Míguez Bonino, appeals to the Scriptures as authoritative for Christian praxis
by the "reading of the direction of the biblical text, particularly of the witness
of the basic, germinal events of the faith."[16] This hermeneutical principle
grounds the historical activity of Christians through the status of the Bible as a
witness to God's action in history and includes hermeneutical guidelines for the
obedience of Christian praxis.

The sociopolitical praxis of Christianity is both demanded by as well as guided by the Bible. This implies that Christians act in history not simply because of their own social location, but also because of the nature of their Christian faith. The nature of this faith, for Míguez Bonino, portrays a God acting in history: Christians act because God acts. Míguez Bonino develops the nature of his hermeneutics of the Word out of his theological convictions about the agency of God in history. The theological treatment of the Scriptures proceeds through three steps: (1) an understanding of God's action in history, (2) an interpretation of the relationship of the kingdom to history, and (3) the discernment of the kingdom as the work of the church in this intermediate time.

Because of the Bible's privileged status as a revelatory document within Christianity, theology must always include a hermeneutics of the Word, a reading of God's action through history as testified to in the Scriptures. The Bible contains narrative accounts of God's action in history, which we, according to Míguez Bonino, must interpret through analogy. Míguez Bonino warns against the constant temptation to assume that God acts today in history as God acted in various biblical narratives. Indeed, the plurality of modes of God's action within the biblical accounts makes any literal interpretation impossible. The Bible, therefore, reveals the uniqueness of history in light of God's action.[17] History is composed of events, actions, new possibilities; history disallows rigid norms or literal rules in the interpretation of God's action.

From this general argument for an analogical interpretation of the Scriptures, Míguez Bonino draws three theological observations: (1) God acts in history for all, (2) God uses different forms, methods, manners, and ways of acting within any one given historical time period and throughout all history, and (3) there is a certain constancy to God's action in history.[18] "The action of God, therefore, cannot be interpreted as a series of examples of the same behavior, it must be interpreted in its dynamic."[19] Interpreters must not make a distinction between earthly and spiritual realms (for God acts only in history) and should not attempt to draw universal principles out of the biblical witness (for God acts in multiple ways). What is important for Míguez Bonino is that the Bible reveals God's action in history as a dynamic process.

Though the ways and forms of God's actions may be diverse and multiple, there is a constancy in the action of God—the constancy of God transforming history into the kingdom. The kingdom of God serves as a focal referent for interpreting the diversity and the constancy of how God acts in history. The Bible reveals the kingdom as always related to history, a relationship that Míguez Bonino believes is often misunderstood in theology. This theologian is especially critical of what he calls the dualistic and monistic formulations of the relationship between the kingdom and history. The dualistic formulation, represented by thinkers like Augustine and Moltmann, relates the kingdom of God to a special history of faith, distinguishing this special history from concrete human history. Míguez Bonino argues that such an understanding of the relationship of the kingdom of God to a special history of faith is extremely problematic; the definition of history, in the social location of theology, implies the interrelatedness of all activities. Furthermore, this dualist solution denies the basic biblical thrust of God's activity within all history, beginning with creation and concluding with the fulfillment of the world. The monist solution, represented by classical theologians such as Irenaeus and Origen as well as by some contemporary liberation theologians, tends to reduce God's kingdom to human history.[20] This position denies a distinct mission within Christianity and mollifies any nonidentity between Christian tradition and the cultural situation. The difficulty, Míguez Bonino observes, lies in maintaining the importance and necessity of both the kingdom and history in their relationship of unity-in-difference.

Míguez Bonino's solution to the difficulty is to think of the unity-in-difference between the kingdom and history as similar to the Pauline relationship of the unity-in-difference between the earthly body and the resurrected body. This relationship between the earthly body and the resurrected body affirms the continuity and the discontinuity of historical life: the resurrected body is the transformation of historical life. "The transformation does not 'disfigure' or 'denaturalize' bodily life; instead it fulfills and perfects it, eliminating its frailty and corruptibility."[21] The relationship between history and the kingdom can also be understood as analogous to the Pauline conception of works. For Paul, works receive their value not from their relationship to the present but from their anticipation and representation of the future. The key factor in understanding the unity-in-difference in both Pauline notions is the future orientation—the yet-to-be-fulfilled import—of historical events. History is transformed into the kingdom, and events receive their value in light of the kingdom transforming history. The kingdom is not the simple telos or progress of history, but neither is it a total replacement of human history. The kingdom transforms, cures, makes new the full corporeality of history. Míguez Bonino explains this relationship of unity-in-difference: "thus the kingdom of God is not the negation of history but rather the elimination of its frailty, corruptibility, and ambiguity. Going a bit more deeply, we can say it is the elimination of history's sinfulness so that the authentic import of communitarian life may be realized. In the same way, then, historical 'works' take on permanence insofar as they anticipate this full realization."[22] Míguez Bonino's strategy is to provide basic metaphors for avoiding the reduction of the kingdom to history or the isolation of the kingdom to one particular part of history. It can certainly be argued that the metaphors of body-soul and works-faith are hardly commensurate with that of history-kingdom. But the metaphors do serve to underline a twofold theme of Míguez Bonino's hermeneutics: the kingdom cannot be sublated into history, and knowledge cannot be sublated into praxis.

Thus history, according to Míguez Bonino, is an intermediate time, and theological hermeneutics has the task of making sense of this time of transformation. Hermeneutics is, for Míguez Bonino, a decidedly religious activity, the discernment of the kingdom of God in history by the community of church. In this time of transformation, discernment is, of course, always provisional and ambiguous. The role of the church is to participate in this transformation, especially in the "naming and making manifest the eschatological reality it awaits."[23]

In this manner, Míguez Bonino provides the biblical foundations for an interpretation theory that is centered in the historical appropriation of the gospel. If in the first principle, the hermeneutics of the world, interpretation is always a sociopolitical activity, in this second principle, the hermeneutics of the Word, interpretation is always a religious task. The Bible reveals God's action, and through the interpretation of the Scriptures, Christians discern the present activity of God. The event-character of the Bible provides the material for drawing analogical comparisons between God's activity in the originary witness and God's present activity, and demands that this analogical comparison must be undertaken together with a hermeneutics of the Word. The analogical interpretation theory with the paradigm of liberation theology implies two general guidelines for interpretation: (1) the Bible must be explained through its own particularity; (2) the Bible must be understood through the use of biblical themes.

1) *The Bible must be explained through its own particularity*: We must recall for a moment Míguez Bonino's analysis of the Bible as a collection of narratives about specific events that, in one manner or another, refer to the kingdom of God transforming history. Within these narratives, facts or principles cannot be separated from specific events; narratives must be understood in their particular contexts and as written texts. Míguez Bonino argues that the nature of the kerygma itself demands the critical rereading of the text, the history of the context, and the history of the effects of the text. All the means available—historical studies, literary studies, linguistic studies, sociological analyses—are helpful in interpreting the texts. Only by understanding the particularity of the text, this liberation theologian argues, does the text open up for a present reading.[24] Míguez Bonino calls this the "double location" of the text. Though the text cannot be literally transposed onto a contemporary situation, it can be interpreted through the particularity of its own situation.[25] Only as we see and understand the social location of a text, its past interpretations, and the present readings of it can we arrive at a hermeneutical circulation "between the text in its historicity and our own historical reading of it in obedience."[26]

2) *The Bible must be understood through the use of biblical themes*: Míguez Bonino's answer to the complex problem of the relationship of biblical texts and the present situation, given the ambiguity and provisionality of all interpretations, is through the use of biblical themes.

When we ask ourselves if it is possible for us, in this limited and tentative way, to glimpse the meaning of God's action in history, we can discern a direction in the action of God apparent in the Scriptures, namely the redemption of human life in its totality (individual and communal, spiritual and physical, present and future). That redemption is described in terms drawn from everyday human experience which, although they have a special significance in their biblical context, permit of a certain analogous projection in secular history (insofar as God's action opens the way for, and makes possible a human action). A projection of these terms (basically: reconciliation, justice, peace, liberation) and the biblical paradigm in which they are used, allows the believer to orient himself in his search in and through faith, for his course of conduct in the *civita terrena*.[27]

The development of biblical themes is composed, for Míguez Bonino, of three steps: (1) relying on the fundamental "direction" or unity of the Scriptures as the vision of the redemption of life, which is always the transformation of history, (2) locating terms or themes that work within specific narrated events to provide paradigms of God's action, and (3) using these paradigms analogously within a present historical situation to discern God's activity. Míguez Bonino's *Ama y haz lo que quieras* illustrates the notion of biblical themes and paradigms; it argues for the theme of love as the primary hermeneutical paradigm in the Bible.[28] The theme of love in the Bible revolves around Jesus as showing a new way of being human. Jesus represents this new way of being human as a model, as a picture of human origin and future, and as a leader of humanity. In Jesus, as the ultimate paradigm of love, the creative and redemptive activity of God is uniquely realized in history. Jesus represents both the way of Christian love and the horizon of the love of God: in Jesus, love is both gift and task.

Together these principles aid the interpreter in exploring the analogical relationship between the Scriptures and present Christian praxis. This analogy of interpretation, according to Míguez Bonino, depends on the obedience of faith, which demands a back-and-forth movement from text to situation and situation to text. For Míguez Bonino, the obedience of faith finds its referent in the action of God in history. God acts in certain, constant ways but through various different methods and means. Likewise, the obedience of faith requires the use of different means and methods to testify to and work for the kingdom's transformation of history.

Interpretation depends on and constitutes praxis itself—a praxis of obedience. Interpretation and the larger discipline of theology rest not on mere theoretical correlations of text and situation but on the lived relationship of God and the community discerned in the text and the situation. The activity of the Christian community is, in part, an interpretive activity—using the themes of the Scripture to discern the present action of God and using the experience of God's love to understand the action of God in the Bible. Interpretation as a praxis of obedience underlies Míguez Bonino's insistence that, within liberation theology, "there is, therefore, no knowledge except in action itself, in the process of transforming the world through participation in history."[29]

DISCERNING THE LOGIC OF DEATH

With the hermeneutics of Word and world in hand, we can examine Míguez Bonino's theological interpretation of violence. In this reading, Míguez Bonino's hermeneutical foundations and principles are employed in a consideration of the situation of violence; Míguez Bonino's interpretation of violence attends both to the social location of all reflection and to a critical rereading of the tradition. Such an interpretation of violence can serve, as well, to render explicit the hermeneutics of Word and world in critical evaluation.

Following his hermeneutical principle that interpretation starts in its own social location, Míguez Bonino suggests that the context of Latin America is characterized by violence, by the systematic destruction of human persons. As Míguez Bonino describes the situation: "we are faced with a total system of death, a threat to all life and to the whole of life."[30] Both the present social location and the Bible suggest that humans are always engaged in what Míguez Bonino calls the "play of violence." It does no good, contends Míguez Bonino, to begin with the theoretical questions of whether or not one should participate in violence: "we are always—Christians or not—actually in the field of action in violence—repressive, subversive, systematic, insurrectional, evident, hidden. Actively, I say, because our militancy or lack of it—our daily use of the instrumentalities of the society in which we live out our ethical decision or renunciations—make us actors in the game."[31] If this ever present game of violence seems a shocking revelation, it does, at least, make us recognize the need for a careful analysis of the social situation within hermeneutics: idealism can lead either to complete avoidance of analysis or to an ideological distortion in the interpretation of violence. There is no such thing as an abstract concept of violence—violence has to do with the suffering and perishing of human lives.[32] The theologian's task is neither to produce an abstract meditation on violence nor to proclaim a general rule for all times and places, but to interpret God's activity and the praxis of faith in this situation. Reflecting on our participation in the social location of theology, we ask the practical question: What is violence?

There are, suggests Míguez Bonino, two current ideologies or "global perspectives" on violence.[33] The first, the "priestly" perspective, is based on the belief of a rational universe and seeks to maintain order in the universe as the will of God. In this perspective violence is understood as irrationality—violence disrupts the rational universe. The second perspective is based upon the belief of the universe as a project of liberty. In this "prophetic" perspective the human is the creator, destroying the old for the new in the quest of progress. Violence, in this prophetic perspective, is understood through a dialectical philosophy of history in which the negation of old realities makes room for new possibilities. But both these perspectives, or ideologies, originate in abstract conceptions of violence and attempt to apply abstractions to historical situations. Naturally the theological interpreter must be critical of such abstractions, for the perspectives may well function to conceal hidden interests, denying the systemic nature of violence already present in the situation.

To counter the ideological function of these perspectives, Míguez Bonino turns to what he calls the "general biblical perspective": "the biblical world is always an announcement-mandate referring to a concrete human situation that needs to be corrected or transformed in accordance with this world."[34] In the Bible violence is spoken of only within specific, narrated events; sometimes violence is forbidden by God, but other times it is allowed or even ordered by God. Míguez Bonino concludes that in the Bible violence is always located within the general theme of transformation; this theme invokes the vision of freedom by disclosing persons as responsible and free before God. In general, peace rather than war is preferable, preservation rather than destruction is encouraged. A hermeneutics of the Word must criticize the priestly perspective of violence, since a rational universe is possible only in terms of an ultimate vision of what life ought to be. The prophetic perspective of a fully liberated universe, on the other hand, is found in the biblical summons to transformation. Míguez Bonino contends that the prophetic perspective has, therefore, a certain "priority" or preference over the priestly, but only for what he calls "a mode of action" and not as an abstract principle of interpretation.

Having argued that violence is always understood in particular situations, and that the interpreter cannot decide ahead of time on a perspective of violence, Míguez Bonino continues his hermeneutics of violence by exploring the relations between Marxist and Christian interpretations of violence. To understand his reading of violence in the relationship between Marxism and Christianity, we must consider briefly Míguez Bonino's critical appropriation of Marxism for Christian hermeneutics. Any dialogue between Christianity and Marxism depends, according to Míguez Bonino, on the fact that in Latin America the relationship between Marxists and Christians occurs through a "growing and overt common participation in a revolutionary project, the basic lines of which are undoubtedly based on a Marxist analysis."[35]

But in understanding this relationship there is an obvious problem for the interpreters of religion: Marx's critique of religion as an opiate of the people. Without directly addressing the complexity of the development in Marx's thought, Míguez Bonino identifies two elements in Marx's critique of religion. First, Marx universalizes religion as a false ideology that cloaks the interests of the dominant class: "the religious element is seen always as an ideological screen, as a false consciousness of a real human need."[36] Second, Marx's ideology critique of religion is inherently connected to his criticism of the entirety of bourgeois society: "the criticism of religion is valuable insofar as it is a criticism of bourgeois society which unveils its dynamics and provides the revolutionary proletariat with adequate theoretical instruments for carrying out its historical mission of destroying and overcoming the society."[37] What interests Míguez Bonino is the second element of Marx's critique of bourgeois society and its ideology. The value in Marx's critique is the suspicion and demonstration of how religion functioned to cover the interests of the state and of the rich in that specific society.

But this moment of suspicion of religion, according to Míguez Bonino, is not at all alien to Christianity; an appropriate hermeneutics of the Word demands a critique of religion: "the Bible does not merely support the contention that religion becomes an excuse for injustice. It announces God's active purpose to overturn and destroy such idolatrous manipulations of his gifts."[38] This is, Míguez Bonino argues, a major demand of the Christian faith against all idolatry. But the Christian faith departs from Marx's inference, in the first element of Marx's critique of religion, that religion is necessarily a mystification of the human subject. Míguez Bonino accuses Marx of universalizing a specific interpretation of a situation. Behind the Marxist universalization of religion lies, Míguez Bonino observes, the belief that no extraneous mediation is needed for human fulfillment: Marxism assumes that humanity can and must liberate itself. Christianity, however, claims that such a mediation is, in fact, necessary and available; God, Christianity affirms, redeems history, providing the very possibility for historical liberation. And so, Míguez Bonino concludes, the critique of religion is internal to both Marxism and Christianity but is grounded on different beliefs. "To put it briefly: in the Bible it is God who de-mystifies man; for Marx it is man who de-mystifies God. In the process, both are very suspicious and critical of religion, but from radically different perspectives."[39]

Though Marx's critique of religion may be an obvious point to begin the conversation, Christianity also relates to Marxism through a shared telos of human fulfillment, a telos usually identified with Western humanism. Míguez Bonino identifies two general schools of Marxism: scientific Marxism and humanist Marxism.[40] Scientific Marxism assumes that human fulfillment will come about only through revolutionary change in the modes of production in society. More attentive to the important role of culture, humanist Marxism locates Marx in the context of a long humanist tradition; as Míguez Bonino explains in agreement, "in the context of the long heritage of man's aspirations and struggles for a more human and just organization of individual and social life."[41] In the broad tradition of humanism, Marx contributes a philosophy of history based on the reproductive relations of human society and a social anthropology of class struggle. This revisionist interpretation of Marxism allows Christianity to have an affinity to certain broad themes and select categories within Marxism.

It is the social anthropology of Marxism that Míguez Bonino relates to Christianity in his interpretation of violence. In the concept of class conflict, Marx suggests two significant notions—the human as worker and the priority of the oppressed. Marx portrayed the human as worker, "as the being who appropriates, transforms, and humanizes the world through his work and who himself comes to his own identity, becomes man through this same work. If this is so, it is only to be expected that the forms of relationships and organizations in which man works will be the privileged means for understanding human life and society and that changes in one area will be closely related to changes in the other."[42] Theological anthropology describes the human in terms of the person's relationships to self, others, and God. But, Míguez Bonino observes, an adequate anthropology requires both descriptions of humanity. Indeed the Bible, contends Míguez Bonino, portrays the relation of humans to others, self, and God as mediated through work. Conversations about anthropology with Christians help to deter Marxists from a mechanistic materialism, and conversations with Marxists help to deter Christians from idealism.

The second notion that Christians and Marxists share in the interpretation of violence is the priority of the poor. In the Bible poverty is seen as scandalous: it contradicts God's purpose, it robs persons of their subjectivity, and it destroys human solidarity. In light of the biblical vision of the kingdom of God, Christians take sides with the poor as the place for the obedience of faith. This privileged option for the poor, according to Míguez Bonino, is at the level of prophetic judgment—denouncing the unfair conditions of a social situation. Marx's category of the "proletariat" is, in humanist Marxism, on a similar level—the level of empirical observation and ethical judgment. Both Marx's category and the Christian option require, in the revolutionary theory of liberation theology, two further steps: an analysis of the causes and systems of the injustice, and a strategy for transforming the situation.[43] And so, Míguez Bonino affirms, Christians can appropriate Marx's category as both Christians and Marxists seek to analyze and change the systems of oppression.

Though Christians can work with Marxist categories, they are guided in their interpretation of violence by the biblical theme of love. In interpreting this theme, Christians will seek, Míguez Bonino contends, to follow the paradigm of Jesus. Jesus as a paradigm does not mean love without justice; Jesus' own love included condemnation, criticism, rejection, and resistance. Indeed Jesus represents a new way of being in the world of violence—Jesus was on the side of the poor and the oppressed; he was condemned as a messianic ruler. From this representation of Jesus, Míguez Bonino says that Christians have a calling to renounce "self-defense and the struggle for power and to offer themselves, with the oppressed, and on behalf of all, as signs of God's incoming age of liberation and justice."[44] The temptations of Jesus suggest that God's action in history is not to place divine omnipotence in control but to identify with the victims of violence.

From this paradigm of Jesus follow two implications for the Christian community. First, there is no specifically Christian struggle, since Jesus rejected a Christian reign or political system. The Christian struggle is to identify with the other, the victim of violence. As God has revealed divine action in history by transforming the oppressed into free human subjects, so Christians take their identification with the victims of violence as their location in the world. Second, in this all-too-human struggle, the Christian community has no special techniques or shortcuts but must use the same tools, forms of analyses, and strategies as others who participate in the struggle for human freedom. Míguez Bonino believes that in light of the biblical vision of the kingdom and paradigm of Jesus, and in light of the specific situation in Latin America, nonviolent action is the most appropriate and adequate perspective.[45] The goal of revolution is necessarily the removal of violence, hence nonviolent action is the closest approximation to the goal of any true revolution. Furthermore, nonviolence depends on solidarity, respect for the human person, and the internalization of the liberation project. Violent revolution far too often threatens to become counterrevolutionary by replacing one situation of oppression with another. But if absolute violence cannot be condoned, neither can pacifism. For pacifism may be too costly:

> Certainly Christians in the struggle for liberation will witness to their faith—as well as to the ultimate goal of revolution—by insisting on counting carefully the cost of violence, by fighting against all ideologization of destruction and the destructive spirit of hate and revenge, by attempting to humanize the struggle, by keeping in mind that beyond victory there must be reconciliation and construction. But they cannot block through Christian scruples the road clearly indicated by a lucid assessment of the situation. Even less can they play the game of reaction lending support to those who are profiting from present violence or weakening through sentimental pseudo-Christian slogans (however well-meaning) the will among the oppressed to fight for their liberation.[46]

Míguez Bonino's interpretation of violence should illustrate his basic assumptions of (1) the social location of theological reflection, including the use of social scientific theories to analyze the situation, and (2) the critical rereading of Christian tradition through the use of biblical themes and paradigms in light of the referent of the kingdom of God. Yet one immediately wonders if, given the passionate pleas not only to start in a specific situation but to analyze a specific situation, Míguez Bonino's interpretation of violence is more a general reading of the reality of violence than a careful structural analysis of a particular situation of violence. Given Míguez Bonino's insistence on the foundation and implications of social location for theological hermeneutics, is it enough to describe, as self-evident as the description might be, the structure of life as always a game of violence? Must not a name be given to this violence, and shall not the structures and systems of death be uncovered? Unless the situation of violence is analyzed in a more concrete manner, theological hermeneutics remains in generalities—though now in practical generalities.[47]

A similar question can be posed within the relation of Marxism to Christianity in Míguez Bonino's work. Obviously the status of Míguez Bonino's work on Marxism is that of an apology—a defense of the critical appropriation of Marxism by Christianity. Míguez Bonino insists that this is a *critical* appropriation—the iconoclastic symbols of God and kingdom will judge any Marxist attempt to deify humanity. But Míguez Bonino rests his argument for a dialogue between Marxism and Christianity on the nature of Marxism as a form of humanism. Certainly, if Marxism is but one expression of the telos of human fulfillment, Christianity can easily converse with the system, as it has with other expressions of Western humanism. But what then happens to the claims for Marxism as a specific form of social analysis? As a form of Western humanism, Marxism is a philosophy of history, an interpretation of the nature and purpose of life. Though it might imply the use of certain social tools, it does not necessitate any specific social theory for interpretation.[48] As Míguez Bonino realizes, the concept of class conflict entails an anthropology of change as the oppressed agitate for greater opportunities for fulfillment. But, again according to Míguez Bonino, class conflict is not a specific social theory; class conflict is not, in itself, a tool for analysis or a specific strategy for change. Likewise, the notion of the human as worker may imply that in any given situation we must analyze the relations of social structures and individual freedom; but it does not yield the tools to do such an analysis. Where, then, does a hermeneutics of the world introduce a specific analysis of the situation? How do Christians choose among the variety of sociopolitical analyses, even among the variety of dialectical sociopolitical analyses? In sum: Míguez Bonino's use of Marxism contributes to the demand for the use of social theories in theology, but it does not provide socioanalytical theories or criteria for the use of such theories.

The lack of specific arguments to back his theological assumptions also occurs in Míguez Bonino's hermeneutics of the Word. In light of his understanding of the Bible as a collection of narrated events governed by the referent of the kingdom of God, Míguez Bonino contends that violence is referred to within the Bible only within the larger context of making possible freedom and responsibility. Thus the Bible condones or condemns violence as it hinders or promotes freedom. But as persuasive as Míguez Bonino's assertions are, they lack any specific arguments for their own validation. Míguez Bonino, be it in interpreting violence or in arguing for his unity-in-difference relationship between history and kingdom, does not employ specific historical, sociological, or literary arguments for either the foundations or the principles of his hermeneutics of the Word. Without the use of explanatory methods, theology tempts the danger of reading into the Bible positions in need of justification.

Though Míguez Bonino's interpretation of violence does not fulfill all the requirements of his hermeneutics of Word and world, it does demonstrate that a hermeneutics of violence is inescapable. For Christian theology, according to this interpretation, lives in the situation of death, as Christian praxis identifies with the poor in Latin America. In this violence of death, Christian theology, in the play of world and Word, must discern the activity of God and the acts of humanity. If Míguez Bonino's reading often lacks adequate arguments of analysis and fails to offer strategies for change, it does set the agenda clearly for theology: the agenda of discerning God's activity and guiding Christian praxis in a particular situation—the situation of violence and death.

From Míguez Bonino's interpretation of violence we also learn that hermeneutics is appropriation, that in the activity of interpretation we are changed, transformed, and converted. Indeed this activity of appropriation between Word and world is essential to the nature of faith, for there is no rigid Christian way, no literal rules for Christian life. The way of Christianity, in the paradigm of liberation theology, is the appropriation of Word and world, the bringing together of human life and obedience to God in a transformation of history. Indeed the transformation of history by the kingdom is a model of hermeneutics as appropriation—the total immersion, the radical change, the open questioning, the continuing transformation of history.

CONCLUSION

What, then, happens to theology when it makes a conversion, when it turns back to reality, when it decides to reflect on the meaning and power of God's word in this world of the poor? [49]

This is the central quest and question of Míguez Bonino's theology. Theology sets out to speak of God, of the living, powerful presence of God, in the midst of the wretched of the earth. That theology speaks so visibly about God as an actor in history may seem odd to ears too attuned to God as being the victim of history. Míguez Bonino suggests a new way of talking of God and of history in his hermeneutics of the Word and the world. This way of talking is concrete—talking about specific situations; it is practical—talking about events in space and time; and it is an act of deliberation and judgment—open to change and critique. Hermeneutics as a central theological task loses all claims to universal judgments as it becomes a conversation, a discernment of the ongoing activity of history and of God. As a conversation, theology as an activity of appropriation becomes central. For Míguez Bonino, theology is the continual formation, reformation, and transformation of theology's conversion to the world.

Within the paradigm of liberation theology, Míguez Bonino stresses the central importance of hermeneutics—of interpreting both world and Word. As compared to modern theology, this hermeneutics takes a radical turn to social context, including ideology critique and social theory. Indeed the turn to the social context is based, in part, on its hermeneutics of the Word revealing the obedience of faith. Míguez Bonino sets the agenda for a liberation hermeneutics: orienting interpretation to social analysis, ideology critique, the discernment of praxis, the transformation of history. But Míguez Bonino's theory only begins the agenda: his own interpretations are somewhat vague and general. Arguments as to the primacy of certain symbols or the particular contents of his own favored themes are often lacking. On the internal grounds of his hermeneutical theology, more argument and analysis are needed to verify the adequacy of his interpretation; Míguez Bonino allows and forces the arguments to be located within the interpretive activity of faith itself.

Latin American liberation theology, Míguez Bonino tells us, speaks of God through its own participation in history. There is no one language, no universal method, no one "correct" theory for interpreting the logos of the Theos in the journey of the poor. Theology has thus entered history and must participate in the activity of discernment, judgment, change, and formation that is the activity of Christian obedience. Latin American liberation theology is a new paradigm of interpretation: theological hermeneutics names the world in light of the Scriptures but, likewise, hears the Word in light of a liberating praxis.

6

Jürgen Moltmann: The Language of God as the Language of Suffering

One of the most important theological works of the 1960s was *Theology of Hope* by the German Protestant theologian Jürgen Moltmann. Though eschatology was already an important symbol in modern theology, Moltmann succeeded in making it the focal center of theology. Through that center Moltmann issued a searing critique of theology, the church, and society; from that center he sent forth an eschatological knowledge of God, an exodus church, and a new transformation of society. *Theology of Hope* was followed by *The Crucified God* in which the crucified and resurrected Christ stood with eschatology in the iconoclastic center of theology. If *Theology of Hope* opened the world to the proclaimed nearness of God's future, *The Crucified God* shattered history with the manifest presence of the abandoned Christ in all the forsakenness of this world.

Moltmann's theology is a narrative theology, a re-creation of the interplay between the Christian message and Christian praxis. Through Moltmann's works runs the retrieval of forgotten or misplaced symbols: the center of eschatology, the theology of the cross, the messianic power of the Holy Spirit, the ecclesiology of the left-wing Reformation, and the social doctrine of the Trinity. As a systematic theologian, Moltmann both creates and names Christian praxis with the symbols of the Christian faith.

Moltmann frequently constructs his systematic interpretations by structurally opposing them to the formulations of human religiosity within modern theology. This style of definition through opposition is the continual trace of Moltmann's neo-orthodox theological method: the Word of God always arrives in opposition to human expectations and desires. This theological method of Moltmann's—which we shall refer to as the dialectic of contradiction—does not share liberation theology's orientation toward suffering or toward human praxis. Moltmann's narrative readings, however, of a God who is identified in suffering and hope—what we shall call the dialectic of identification—moves beyond his formal method to provoke a witness to the future of hope in the

100

memory of suffering. Indeed, the odd status of Moltmann's work—substantively treating God and hope, Christ and suffering, the Spirit and freedom, but methodologically locked in the paradigm of neo-orthodoxy—shall direct us, in the rest of this book, to explore liberation theology as both a systematic interpretation of the Christian message and a new theological method.

THE ORIGIN OF MOLTMANN'S POLITICAL THEOLOGY

Jürgen Moltmann wants political theology to exist not as a politicized theology or as a theology of particular politics, but as a theological reflection on contemporary life as political and on Christian mission "in the midst of the public misery of society and struggle against this misery."[1] Moltmann continues: "Political theology is therefore not simply political ethics but reaches further by asking about the political consciousness of theology itself. It does not want to make political questions the central theme of theology or to give political systems and movements religious support. Rather, political theology designates the field, the milieu, the environment and the medium in which Christian theology should be articulated today."[2]

Moltmann begins his political theology not with the rupture of events of suffering or with the interruption of history by the subjects of suffering, but with a bold critique of earlier forms of neo-orthodox theology.[3] Karl Barth, says Moltmann, secured theology in the self-revelation of God but supplanted the God of the Bible with the Greek epiphany of eternal presence.[4] Moltmann's discontent with Barth pertains to Barth's interpretation of God: for Barth, God reveals himself as the Wholly Other, relating to the world in a suprahistorical manner and calling each individual to make a personal decision. The cause for Moltmann's disdain at this point is quite clear: Barth did not read the Bible long enough to realize that his "wholly other" God is not the God of Abraham, Moses, and David. Rudolf Bultmann fares equally poorly under Moltmann's critical pen: Bultmann attempted to prove God by human experience, and thus reduced the Christian faith to a notion of authentic existence.[5] Bultmann, Moltmann claims, offers a religion of the timeless self, pretending that revelation somehow depends upon human experience. Barth eternalizes God, Bultmann eternalizes humankind: but the sin is the same, judges Moltmann, for both privilege a "mysticism of being," an exaltation of present temporality.[6] What upsets Moltmann the most is that these existentialist theologians misinterpret the Christian message and thus reduce Christianity to an epiphany religion—a religion built on human desires and cultural myths. The corrective to the reductions of existentialist theology, argues Moltmann, commences out of the eschatological center of the Christian faith. From this eschatological center comes the self-revelation of a God whose essential nature is the future and who calls persons to an active life of hope in a history made possible by God's promises. Moltmann's corrective to existentialist theologies brings us to the central goal of Moltmann's theology: the retrieval of the narratives and symbols of Christian faith. The origin of Moltmann's call for a political theology is the attempt to arrive at a correct understanding of the Christian message.

Consequently, for Moltmann, *only* as political theology grasps the heart of the Christian message can it comprehend suffering as the main agenda for contemporary theology. The centrality of suffering in contemporary theology depends not on the magnitude of suffering, not on the interruption of the poor, and not on the memory of Auschwitz, but on the gospel itself. Moltmann interprets the present situation through suffering; indeed, for Moltmann the modern world is identified largely with suffering: economic exploitation, political oppression, cultural alienation through racism and sexism, emptiness in personal life, physical suffering, and environmental destruction.[7] People, Moltmann observes, suffer from a deeply "ingrained primal fear" of the death of humankind. This suffering, for Moltmann, is God's own cry, for God suffers in and through human suffering: "he suffers with them, he suffers because of them, he suffers for them. His suffering is his messianic secret."[8] Suffering is both understood and responded to through the prism of the Christian message.

It is important to contrast Moltmann's origin of political theology with those of the other theologians in this book: their call for a theology of liberation—articulated in the language of rupture, break, interruption—depends upon the question of suffering and the foundation of praxis. Within this new paradigm, liberation theologians retrieve and reinterpret the Christian tradition; for Moltmann, on the other hand, it is a new interpretation of the Christian message that forces a paradigm shift. Said somewhat differently: for Moltmann, Christianity interprets suffering, but suffering does not interrupt Christianity.

But Moltmann does remind us that the Christian Scriptures present a radical narrative that must be joined with a radical witness of Christian praxis. Christian praxis, the experience of following Christ in the world, is opposed to the dictates of modern religion and modern theology; it is folly to the world, a contradiction in history. As the interpretation of God's Word, theology has to reveal the radical contradiction between God's Word and human reason, between God's future and human destiny. Only in the interpretation of the radical narrative of God will Christian praxis be formed as a witness to God. Theology, in Moltmann's work, substantively interprets the narratives of God while it formally reveals the contradiction between God and world.

THE ADVENT OF HOPE

The first, and most primary, narrative of God is developed in Moltmann's *Theology of Hope* and centers on the symbol of eschatology. For Moltmann, Christianity—its message and its witness—is eschatology.[9] The definitive event of Christian eschatology is the revelation of God in Jesus Christ.[10] The revelation of Jesus Christ does not portray an epiphany of the eternal present that sanctifies the present in correspondence to the cosmos. Disclosing God as always and only the coming one, the revelation of Christ is, instead, the advent of history, the opening up of the future of freedom. Well within Christian tradition, Moltmann recognizes that the resurrection appearances of Christ affirm the importance of the incarnation. And so, Moltmann concludes, the resurrection becomes the ground for faith's remembrance of the incarnation of Christ. But the resurrection appearances also affirm the reality of Christ in the future, an affirmation that becomes anticipation—the foretaste of what will be.[11] The identity of Christ as the resurrection of the crucified one is, for Moltmann, an identification of the memory and hope of the future. "It is this that forms the ground of the promise of the still outstanding future of Jesus Christ. It is this that is the ground of the hope which carries faith through the trials of the god-forsaken world and of death."[12] Easter and the resurrection appearances are not merely events of the past, they are also events of the future—as yet unfinished.

Moltmann opposes his interpretation of the resurrection-crucifixion of Christ to the dying and rising of the lord of the cultus. Within the epiphany of the eternal present, the lord of the cultus is far removed from history: within the resurrection of this lord, redemption is instantaneous and ahistorical. The resurrection of Christ, Moltmann counters, points beyond itself to the future God, but it points beyond itself only because it has taken history within itself through the crucifixion. Within eschatology, then, there is an internal dialectic of identification between the cross and the resurrection of Christ: in this identification, the promise of God is revealed in its universal significance for humanity.

But Moltmann directs his attention not to the identification between the cross and resurrection within Christ, but to the nature of this event as revelation. In this narrative of God, Moltmann examines the nature of revelation through the structure of God's promises. To understand what Moltmann means by promise, we must first recognize that, whatever it may mean, the promise of God is not inherent in universal history, or above history in salvation history, or within the present in the harmony between humanity and eternal being. The promise of God is the shattering arrival of the future into the present: the promise comes from God who is in the future, "not in us or above us but always and only before us."[13] Revelation depends on God's own faithfulness to divine promises, and therefore the knowledge of God is not God's eternal presence, but God's future, God's presence in history as the not-yet, the new, the claim for fulfillment in history.

The revealing of the divinity of God therefore depends entirely on the real fulfilment of the promise, as *vice versa* the fulfilment of the promise has the ground of its possibility and of its reality in the faithfulness and the divinity of God. To that extent "promise" does not in the first instance have the function of illuminating the existing reality of the world or of human nature, interpreting it, bringing out its truth and using a proper understanding of it to secure man's agreement with it. Rather, it contradicts existing reality and discloses its own process concerning the future of Christ for man and the world. Revelation, recognized as promise and embraced in hope, thus sets an open stage for history, and fills it with missionary enterprise and the responsible exercise of hope, accepting the suffering that is involved in the contradiction of reality, and setting out towards the promised future.[14]

Revelation comes through God's promises, promises that both contradict "natural" human knowledge and open up history for God's future.

Since the knowledge of God arrives only through God's own promises, we cannot rely upon natural knowledge to "reflect" God or to understand the nature of God's revelation. Rather, to receive God's revelation, we must turn to the book of God's promises, the Bible. Moltmann contends that in the Old Testament God is revealed as one who creates a future for Israel in faithfulness to God's promises. For Israel the appearance of God is immediately linked to the giving of a promise. The identity of Israel lies in its remembrance of God's promises and the expectation of their continued fulfillment. This distinguishes Israel's religion from other religions, and forces Israel to eradicate from its midst any elements of an idolatrous epiphany religion. The call to Abraham can be best understood as a promise to be filled, transformed, and filled again; this call appropriately becomes paradigmatic for Israel. The history of Israel is now a journey, a journey of faith and hope toward a future. The continual filling, overfilling, and reinterpreting of God's promises to Israel is what Moltmann calls the "overspill" of God's promise; the overspill guarantees the dynamic nature of revelation, for the fulfillment of any particular promise is not yet the fulfillment of God's future.

Revelation thus travels into history through the promises of God. These promises, God's revelation, are contained in the Bible. The biblical prophets record God's promises as the revelation of God as the Lord of all people—a Lord with the power over life and death.[15] In the apocalyptic literature, God is revealed as Lord over the entire cosmos.[16] The Bible, the book of God's promises, discloses the entirety of creation—suffering and groaning to be remade—as involved in the eschatological history of God.

Revelation arrives through promises and promises are found in the Bible; but what, we might ask, is revelation—what does it do? Promise, as revelation, Moltmann answers, is a declaration of God that creates history.[17] Declaration, in Moltmann's sense, means not a simple descriptive statement but, rather, a creative act—the formation of history itself. As declared through God's promises, history is the time of remembrance and expectation, the recollection of past promises and the anticipation of their future fulfillment. Revelation not only gives us knowledge of God, it also creates history—it opens history for the new. Stated differently: revelation gives history a new future. From this vantage point of revelation, Moltmann criticizes views of history that deny the importance of the new by crystallizing the meaning of life above, beyond, or apart from history. Such views of history—against the biblical promises of revelation—deny the radicality of the future and ignore the unrest and suffering of the present age. Within this narrative of God, historical events are provisional; remarks Moltmann, "they intimate and point forward to something which does not yet exist in its fullness in themselves."[18] The recipients of revelation—those who have ears to hear the promise—live in the time of the not-yet, continually anticipating the coming of the future.

The narrative of God—not just a story about God but the enactment of God in history—can, so far, be construed as Revelation-Promise-History, beginning, so to speak, with the radically creative revelation of God's promise. But we might also want to read this narrative the other way round, and ask about the nature of promise from the experience of history. How do we, in other words, receive or experience the giving, fulfilling, and transforming of God's promise? In this reading, the character of promise names the horizon of experience as anticipatory through a continual process of the overspill of promise. In the overspill of promise, experience transforms memory by projecting new possibilities into the future; experience anticipates this future by transforming the present in its recollection of the past. Moltmann suggests that within the horizon of promise, the experience of history is both the experience of future possibilities and the experience of the totally new: the future is known as *futur* and *zukunft*. *Zukunft*, literally "coming to," forms the present as an anticipation of the future. *Zukunft* names the not-yet of the new, or, in Moltmann's words, "the future does not simply emerge from the present, either as a postulate or a result; the present springs from a future which one must be expectant of in transience."[19] *Futur* names the experience of the relation between being and not-yet being, "the temporal prolongation of being."[20] And the present, with the experience of *futur* and *zukunft*, exists in relationship to the past, for history is the reconciliation of memory with its future. In this reading of the narrative of God, what is essential in the experience of *futur* and *zukunft* is the temporality invoked—time, as displayed in this narrative, is the reconciliation of the past and the future.

Christian experience can also be expressed through the relationship of immanence and transcendence in history.[21] For the Christian, living between God's promises and their fulfillment, history is immanence, the presence of God. Transcendence is the limit of experience both negatively, as that which is not finite, and positively, as finitude's transformation. As the realization of the new, transcendence is not to be reduced to immanence or seen as its contrary but, rather, understood as its fulfillment and at the same time its transformation. As fulfillment, transcendence lures immanence to its potentialities that, as transformation, transcendence negates and gives again in new forms of immanence. For Moltmann, immanence and transcendence exist together, not in contradiction but within a dialectic of identification that reveals history as open.[22]

What Moltmann suggests in the peculiar nature of promise and the relation of transcendence and immanence is the dynamic process of limitation, negation, fulfillment, and transformation of experience in the future. History, for Moltmann, is open both as revealed in the text of promises—the Bible—and in our experience of God's immanence and transcendence. This is a narrative of God, a story of God's being as future, of God's providence as liberating, of God's transcendence as wholly transforming. Moltmann has offered God's narrative as the hope of the future, a hope that creates and discloses the temporality of history. Hope is the futurity of life, the breaking of all possibilities, the advent and the future of history itself.

Having thus arrived at freedom, we can finish this narrative of God: God-Revelation-Promise-History-Experience-Hope. The narrative can, however, be read two ways: as coming from God to humanity; or as being represented by Christianity through the play of text and life. The narrative of God has two central aspects: the formal character and the substantive nature of God's revelation. The first aspect, the formal character—the "how" of revelation and Moltmann's major concern in this narrative—necessitates that God cannot be known through human history but must be revealed through God's promises in unique events.[23] What we know and say of God arises not out of our own longing, experience, or knowledge, but only through God's revelation that both breaks into and creates human history. The formal character of God's narrative is Moltmann's method of a dialectic of contradiction between God and world.

The second aspect, the substantive nature or the "what" of revelation, names God as the creator of possibilities, of hope, of freedom, and of newness in the experience of God's promise-filled history by Christians. In this dialectic of identification, the Christian narrative is the experience of God's revelation through promise, as recorded in the Scriptures of the Christian community. Through these promises God is revealed and experienced as a future God, and eschatology is revealed and received as the center of faith. In this experience and knowledge, *futur* and *zukunft*, immanence and transcendence, always exist together in a dialectic of identification. Another dialectic of identification was suggested by Moltmann in the identification of the cross and resurrection of Jesus Christ: in the next narrative, this dialectic of identification becomes the revelation of God.

THE CROSS AND THE RESURRECTION

If the first narrative of God creates history, then the second narrative of Christ, the subject matter of Moltmann's *The Crucified God*, redeems history through an identification of the cross and the resurrection and of suffering and hope. For Moltmann, the two contrary moments of suffering and hope within history join in a dialectic that is named in the central Christian symbol. It is a dialectic not of contradiction—juxtaposed to identity—but of identification within suffering and hope and within the cross and the resurrection of Christ. As the dialectic of identification suggested in the reception of the first narrative of God (both immanence and transcendence, both *futur* and *zukunft*), this dialectic both discloses and transforms human experience. But unlike the identification of *futur* and *zukunft* and that of immanence and transcendence, which arrive last in the narrative of God, this dialectic of identification occupies the central terms of the narrative of Christ. Nevertheless, as we shall see, the dialectic of contradiction asserts itself in this second narrative, through the quest for a correct concept of God in light of the suffering of the cross.

Moltmann maintains that the dialectic of identification of the cross and the resurrection is a "continuity in radical discontinuity" and that the understanding of this dialectic has been the central problem in most Christological controversies.[24] Christologies have traditionally solved the problem, Moltmann contends, by sublating the cross into the resurrection (Docetism) or by elevating the Easter appearances and life of Jesus (Ebionitism) or by reducing the cross-resurrection to two distinct modes of expression (Modalism). But Moltmann insists that not to keep the problem unresolved, that is, not to accept the dialectic in the relation of cross and resurrection, is to deny the symbolic power and truth of the event. The cross and the resurrection cannot be understood if one is sublated into the other; to deny the dialectic—to reduce the tension of the cross and the resurrection—is once again to base religion on human understanding. The key, for Moltmann, lies in understanding that the resurrection does not *solve* the crucifixion but *intensifies* it so that the crucifixion forces the radicality of the resurrection as the resurrection of the crucified and not just "any" resurrection.

The dialectic of identification reveals in turn a dialectic of suffering and hope in which "the two experiences stand in a radical contradiction to each other, like death and life, nothing and everything, godlessness and the divinity of God. But how can it be possible to identify both experiences in one and the same person without resolving either the one experience or the other and making it of no account?"[25] This dialectic of suffering and hope, of the cross and the resurrection is not the radically negative contradiction between God and world in eschatology, but the mysterious and even ambiguous identification of suffering and hope within time, within the narrative of God and history. Now we know God's hope in suffering, God's light in darkness, and God's name in godforsakenness.

In developing a Christology through a dialectic of identification, we must not make the choice, Moltmann believes, between Jesusology with its reference to the earthly life of Jesus and its stress on historical-critical methods and a high Christology using only theological-philosophical speculations.[26] Rather, history and eschatology must be read together so that history as recollection and history as hope become complementary with hope in the form of recollection. The historical understanding of Jesus is to be read with what Moltmann calls the eschatological-theological understanding of Christ.

Moltmann begins the reciprocal relationship of history and eschatology in Christology by focusing on the death of Jesus.[27] The death of Jesus, Moltmann contends, must be understood as the violent end of Jesus in the context of his life and in the context of the belief in the resurrection.[28] Moltmann recalls the various trials of Jesus in order to understand the death of Jesus in the context of his life. These trials involve being tried as a blasphemer before the Jews, as a rebel before the Roman state, and as the Son abandoned by his Father, God.

The conflict of Jesus with the Jewish law centered on the issue of the righteousness of God in keeping the promises to Israel. Jesus proclaimed a God of eschatological forgiveness and gracious mercy whose love was free from human observation of the law.[29] Hence Jesus put God and himself above the authority of Moses and the law. As Moltmann comments: "in his ministry Jesus placed himself with sovereign authority above the limits of the contemporary understanding of the law. . . ."[30] The Jews judged Jesus according to their law as a blasphemer for placing himself above the law and for forgiving sins, an act the Jews reserved for God alone.

The death of Jesus also must be seen, contends Moltmann, in the context of his conflict with Roman authorities. The freedom that Jesus taught meant the abolishment of the state's religious foundations, since Jesus taught and brought about a rejection of human self-deification in the state.[31] In an age in which religion and politics were inseparable in the very foundations of the state, Jesus was a rebel who threatened the Roman empire.

The political conflict with the Romans and the religious conflict with the Jews explain why Jesus was crucified as a rebel and a blasphemer. There remains, however, the question of the suffering of Jesus on the cross. Other persons, such as Socrates or the Zealot martyrs, died because of political and religious conflicts and passively accepted their fate.[32] But as Moltmann reads this narrative, Jesus did not passively accept his death upon a cross as fate. Quite the contrary, on the cross Jesus cried out in suffering and agony; Jesus died, describes Moltmann, "with the signs and expressions of a profound abandonment by God."[33] To understand this suffering, Moltmann returns to the biblical accounts of the life and ministry of Jesus. According to these accounts, Moltmann isolates the uniqueness of the life of Jesus in his close fellowship with God and in his identification with God in the act of the forgiveness of sins. And having discovered this uniqueness, Moltmann can now interpret the impact, the tragedy, and the uniqueness of the cross: the cross denies, forgets, ruptures this fellowship and identification between Jesus and God. Jesus died on the cross not only as a rebel and a blasphemer, but also as one abandoned by God. The cries of agony by Jesus are the expression of this abandonment by the God he knew and proclaimed, the God of grace and love. What is at stake, in this event, Moltmann argues, is the very deity of God.[34] Psalm 22, the cry of Jesus in his tortured agony, *could be*, Moltmann observes, appropriately rendered, "My God, why hast thou forsaken thyself."[35] Here, on the cross, is God (Jesus Christ) abandoned by God (Jesus Christ's father):

The rejection expressed in his dying cry, and accurately interpreted by the words of Psalm 22, must therefore be understood strictly as something which took place between Jesus and his Father, and in the other direction between his Father and Jesus, the Son—that is, as something which took place between God and God. The abandonment on the cross which separates the Son from the Father is something which takes place within God himself; it is stasis within God—"God against God"—particularly if we are to maintain that Jesus bore witness to and lived out the truth of God.[36]

This is, thus far, only half of a Christology, or we might say only half of this narrative of Christ, for the Gospel texts must also be read from the point of view of eschatology in terms of the belief in the resurrection. Moltmann reconstructs a notion of the resurrection of the dead as the focal point to read the narratives from eschatology. In Jewish apocalyptic teaching the resurrection of the dead is a sign of the end times and the beginning of a new creation. As a sign of a new beginning, the resurrection of the dead does not entail a return to this life but, rather, the annihilation of the powers of death through a creation of new life. In the resurrection of Jesus from the dead, God transforms this "promise" so that "the new world of righteousness and presence of God has already dawned in this one person in the midst of our history of death."[37] The transformation of this symbol to the resurrection of the dead in Jesus recognizes that in this one man, raised before all other persons, a new creation is presented and anticipated. This is a "new eschatological sense of time" that is constitutive for the eschatological faith of Christianity. The future is now, in the present. The way of life in the future—the forgiveness of sins, reconciliation, discipleship—is presented as a possible way of life.

There is, Moltmann maintains, another level to the symbol of resurrection in "apocalyptic" Judaism: resurrection also represents the righteousness of God in light of the suffering of the world. The question of unjust suffering in apocalyptic literature found an answer in the resurrection of the dead as a logical consequence to the righteousness of God.[38] In this meaning of the resurrection, the question of unjust suffering will be answered in the future when God's righteousness will be demonstrated as God assigns some to eternal punishment and some to eternal glory. In the resurrection of Jesus, this notion of resurrection as righteousness and suffering is also transformed. In the crucifixion-resurrection of Jesus the cross represents suffering and the anticipation of judgment, and the resurrection is the demonstration of the righteousness of God that creates right for all. Jesus Christ anticipates the kingdom of God as the one who represents the suffering of the world in the final fulfillment of love. "Thus the cross of Christ modifies the resurrection of Christ under the conditions of the suffering of the world so that it changes from being a purely future event to being an event of liberating love."[39]

This reading of the crucifixion-resurrection from the side of history and from eschatology, Moltmann contends, forces theology to rethink its concept of God.[40] The historical understanding of Jesus calls for a reconceptualization of God in light of the absolute separation within God on the cross. The eschatological understanding of the crucifixion and resurrection demands a notion of God creating history from the future. Now Moltmann sublates the dialectic of identification into the familiar dialectic of contradiction: the cross-resurrection forces God to be understood as the one who raises Jesus from the dead—outside the limits of history, from the future. Moltmann displaces the material dialectic of identification with the formal dialectic of contradiction, replacing the material reading with a conceptual question. To pursue this conceptualization of God forced by the suffering in God and God in suffering, Moltmann retrieves the symbol of the Trinity formulated as an open, history-creating and history-transforming event.

As the doctrine of the God who suffers, the Trinity is a shorthand explanation of the passion-resurrection narratives. The Son suffers dying forsaken by the Father. The Father suffers the death of the Son. The Spirit proceeds from this event as the Spirit that creates love and brings the dead alive. The Trinity is the open symbol of the possibility of new creation, for in the context of the suffering in God—the suffering of the grieving Father, and the suffering of the abandoned Son—the Spirit proceeds from the Father and the Son to anticipate and bring about a new creation.

The Trinity is not a "closed" system, but an "eschatological process open for men on earth, which stems from the cross of Christ."[41] In the open event of the Trinity, all suffering is placed in the context of the radical ground of all suffering, the cross, and answered by the anticipation of the end of history through the eschatological time presented and represented in Christ. The Trinity presents the narrative of the suffering of Christ through the reformulation of the open event of the abandonment of the Son by the Father; the loss of the Father by the Son; and the inner unity of the Spirit. This social conception of the Trinity, Moltmann contends, allows us to arrive at the proper doctrine of God. The Trinity also answers the question of the righteousness of God by the resurrection of Christ as the representation of suffering in the anticipation of the end of history. The sending of the Spirit opens the history of God's love in suffering for the whole world. The sending of the Spirit begins the reverse process of history in the Trinity from Son to Father as Spirit to liberate the world into a new glorified creation and to bring it into unity in the Son to give to the Father.

If eschatology displays the horizon of God's narrative, then together the cross and the resurrection ground the center of this narrative; God is known through suffering as God suffers. But in the resurrection of the crucified one, a new eschatological future for all creation is anticipated. If the first narrative of God creates history, the second narrative redeems history through the anticipation of righteousness and the representation of new life for all. At the center of Christian faith is a belief in the suffering of God identified with the hope of the future. That is why Christian faith has a Trinity, for only the Trinity tells the story of God separated, abandoned, and yet identified with reunion, love, and hope. For Moltmann, the Trinity has a unique status as it *represents* the dialectic of the identification of suffering and hope, of the cross and resurrection and as it *secures* the dialectic of contradiction between God and world.

With the Trinity as the proper understanding of God, Moltmann can place all human suffering within God and can narrate the process of God's history as the reunion of the separated.

> The "bifurcation" in God must contain the whole uproar of history within itself. Men must be able to recognize rejection, the curse, and final nothingness in it. . . . The concrete "history of God" in the death of Jesus on the cross on Golgotha therefore contains within itself all the depths and abysses of human history and therefore can be understood as the history of history. All human history, how ever much it may be determined by guilt and death, is taken up into this "history of God," i.e. into the Trinity, and integrated into the future of the "history of God." There is no suffering which in this history is not God's suffering; no death which has not been God's death in the history of Golgotha.[42]

The privileging of the cross-resurrection has become, for Moltmann, a conceptual inclusion of history into the openness of God. In the concept of the Trinity, the cross is the total measure of suffering; the Trinity occludes all human suffering into one symbol. Though suffering may be the main agenda item for a political theology, it is, in Moltmann, understood only through an appropriate idea of God.

Once again the substantive interpretation of the cross-resurrection must be distinguished from the formal nature of Moltmann's method. The substantive interpretation—the actual reading of the narrative of Christ—holds suffering and hope together as always in relation to the identification of the cross and the resurrection of Jesus Christ. In this dialectic of identification of cross and resurrection, suffering forces the quest of righteousness in a hope that includes all who suffer, both the living and the dead. The narrative of God in the cross and resurrection of Christ forms, informs, and transforms suffering through an identification with hope. In this narrative the suffering of the cross receives its meaning as yet to be fulfilled in the resurrection, and the hope of the resurrection knows its meaning only through its identification with the suffering of the cross. But the formal nature of the cross-resurrection locates the uniqueness of this event in the Trinity, which in turn incorporates the suffering of history in itself. The Trinity joins suffering and hope only in the conception of God abandoning God: the experience of identification exists only in a future redemption when the Spirit unites all creation into God. Though the identification of the cross and the resurrection could name and be named within the human experience of suffering and hope, Moltmann finalizes the relation of suffering and hope by placing it within an adequate conception of God. In sum: the narrative of Christ, the crucified God, substantively discloses the identification of suffering and hope while it formally answers all suffering through a concept of God as the open Trinity.

THE SPIRIT AND THE CHURCH

From the redeeming act of the crucified God, the Spirit is sent forth to bring all of history back into unity with God. In this third narrative, the narrative of the Spirit, God moves through history: uniting the separated, healing the broken, guiding the lost, and leading history toward the final goal of God. This narrative of God reveals neither the horizon of God in eschatology nor the limit-experience of God in cross-resurrection, but the constant movement of God in history. The nature of the Spirit depends, for Moltmann, on the event of Christ as the ultimate promise of God's action in history, incorporating the world's suffering into God. The nature of the Spirit is the ongoing identification of suffering and hope, the resurrection of the crucified, the power that gives love and brings the dead alive. Moltmann's reading of this narrative begins with the nature of the Spirit guiding history toward God. This is the narrative most intimately connected with Christian experience: with this narrative, Christian experience becomes part of the constant play of God in history.

Disclosing and declaring that God is in the world, the narrative of the Spirit uniquely guides the exodus church.[43] The church exists for God in the power of the Spirit: the Spirit creates, baptizes, serves, and proclaims through the church. Through the Spirit the church participates in the reunion of God's creation, and in the Spirit the church testifies to God's love through solidarity with those who suffer. Founded in God's mission of transforming and creating history, Moltmann's exodus church is the herald neither of its own nature and roles nor of society's needs and wants but of God's kingdom and rule.

This narrative of God must be talked about as the presence of the Spirit in the exodus church, a presence that, for Moltmann, is understood only in light of the other narratives of God. Thus the exodus church, according to Moltmann, has an eschatological orientation, pointing toward the open future of God. Precisely because of its openness to God and the future, the exodus church is engaged in following Christ in the world. As the promises of God are decisively revealed in Jesus Christ, so the mission of the church is decisively formed in the service of Christ in the world. "The pro-missio of the kingdom is the ground of the missio of love to the world."[44] The mission of the church testifies to Christ's identification of suffering and hope through the power of the Spirit.

For Moltmann, this mission of the church mandates that the church, as the church of Christ, is found wherever Christ is present. To locate the church, we first have to ask the question of Christ's presence in the world. Moltmann answers by locating Christ's presence in the world in two places—with the apostolate and with the least of the brethren. Christ promised to be present in the apostolic witness, including the proclamation of the Word, the administration of sacraments, the existence of the apostolic, and the fellowship of believers. But Christ also promised to be present with the least of the world; for according to Matthew 25, "if the thesis *ubi Christus, ibi ecclesia* is to be considered a valid one, then this story with its promise of the presence of the Judge of the world is part of the doctrine of the church and the place where it is to be found."[45] This double presence of Christ in history receives its unity only through the presence of Christ in the future, or in Christ's parousia. Christ's presence in the apostolate and in the least of the brethren represents Christ's future as they point to the future judgment, and they anticipate Christ's future as they incarnate the significance of the future in the present. If the promise of God in the first narrative anticipates and represents the future, and if the cross-resurrection of Jesus Christ in the second narrative anticipates and represents new life, so the church of the Spirit in the third narrative of God anticipates and represents the future kingdom.

Central to this ecclesiology is the denial of any social foundation or function of the church. The church does not, in Moltmann's theology, arise out of human longing or human need, but is given—created by God in the unique event of Jesus Christ. "The church's first word is not 'church' but Christ."[46] This unique foundation of the church parallels the formal dialectic of contradiction of God's promise, which is other than human history and knowledge. As God's promise is other than human knowledge, so the church differs radically from any human organization. As eschatology mandated the critique of modern forms of religion, so the unique foundation of Christ necessitates the criticism of society by the church. And, indeed, Moltmann's interpretation of the modern church is one of the most trenchant criticisms of the function of the church in modern society.[47]

Modern society, Moltmann believes, determines its social relations on the needs of labor and consumption; all other needs in this modern world are left to the realm of the private. In modernity the church functions to disburden the individual, taking care of personal and pyschic needs that if left unattended might threaten to disrupt the free society. Religion is, according to Moltmann, a *cultus privatus* in which religious belief, reduced to a mere whim of personal opinion, can be neither demonstrated nor refuted. The theology of *cultus privatus* makes faith personal, but socially irrelevant. In modernity the church also functions to provide some sense of community in a depersonalized and rationalized world. But the church artificially creates this supposedly meaningful community through the collection of homogenous individuals. Moltmann labels such "community" as a Noah's-ark version of the church that attempts to "balance" life for the individuals.[48] The church also functions as an institution that projects security by attending to modes of religious conduct such as church membership rather than vital decisions of faith and life. Moltmann describes how "specialties" and bureaucracy divide the church, reducing theological criticism to perspectival relativism. What Moltmann is after is the distorted mission of the church in modernity: the modern church secures the bourgeois individual, destroys any vestige of critical reflection, and denies the narrative of God declared and experienced in the Spirit.

But, of course, society's church is not the real church; the real church cannot function to secure the bourgeois individual or to protect a social system. Founded in God's future, formed in the crucifixion and resurrection of Christ and empowered by the Spirit, the real church, what Moltmann names the "exodus church," exists as a radical critique of the present. The unique foundation of the church in Christ provides the church with a privileged place, immune from becoming a civil or a political religion. Indeed the church receives, from its foundation in Christ and through its guidance of the Spirit, the function of being a critical institution.[49] Between its horizon of eschatology in the coming of the Christ and its following of Christ in solidarity with the least of the brethren, the church stands against all forms of oppression.

But the church is not only characterized by its location in Christ's presence and its critical function; the church is also characterized by its nature as a congregation. The congregation is a charismatic community, where each person receives the gifts of the Spirit. In the congregation, membership is voluntary; all are called to be in the mission of God's future, and the church is set apart from the world in order to be a part of history's transformation through the Spirit. Moltmann finds his role model for the congregation in the left wing of the reformation, with what he calls "the reformation of life through love."[50]

Relying upon his familiar rhetoric of opposition, Moltmann compares his congregation with the pastoral church of modern society. The pastoral church is composed of homogenous individuals: the congregation is composed of disparate individuals called by God. The congregation is based on God's suffering and God's future in the event of Jesus Christ; the pastoral church is based on self-justification and social need. The pastoral church is legalistic, which makes the Christian life more and more conforming, more and more anxious, more and more closed. The congregation demands a public commitment; the pastoral church accepts only a private commitment.

In the congregation, Christians live a messianic lifestyle.[51] The Christian lives in hope, between the memories and fulfillment of God's promises centered in the resurrection of the crucified Lord. The Christian is justified by Christ and lives towards the future. Indeed, it is this justification of faith that allows a Christian praxis of solidarity with those who suffer and the constant criticism of oppression, injustice, and violence. Faith participates in suffering and prays that suffering will be no more; faith leads to anticipation as Christians empty themselves for God and to political action as Christians give themselves in the struggle for life against death.[52] As a trial of tensions and struggles, the life of faith is also a testimony of joy and hope.

The church, as the narrative of the Spirit, is substantively the ongoing testimony of following Christ both in his apostolate and in the solidarity with the least of the brethren. The church lives a life of anticipation, of resistance, of representation, and of self-giving. As a community critical of the world, the church sacrifices itself for the world in the unifying action of the Spirit. It lives where Christ lives, it functions for God, it exists as a congregation of messianic love. The narrative of the Christian community is its ongoing life—the identification of suffering and hope. But this narrative is connected to Moltmann's formal method—the dialectic of contradiction—through the claim for the church's unique foundation in the event of Christ, untouched by social functioning or human need, completely separated from social foundations or human experience. Viewed from this unique foundation the church is not composed of believers who are also human beings caught in the ambiguities of history, but is "composed," as Moltmann puts it, solely of where Christ is in history. The church is where Christ is, and where Christ is there is the church: Moltmann thus safeguards the church from fully entering history by privileging its foundation in the promise of Christ. This privileging tempts the church to believe that its narrative is the final understanding of human history and that its knowledge is the real comprehension of human suffering.

METHOD, SUFFERING, AND PRAXIS

Within Moltmann's theology we have considered two distinct ways of reading the narratives of God. One reading, what we have called the dialectic of identification, names the Christian testimony as the identification of the cross and the resurrection and of suffering and hope in the substantive nature of Moltmann's theology. The second reading, which we have referred to as the dialectic of contradiction, declares the opposition of God and world within Moltmann's formal theological method. The point of distinguishing these two readings is to demonstrate that, though Moltmann's method lies outside the paradigm of liberation theology, the substantive nature of Moltmann's theology dwells well within the framework of liberation theology.

The practical concern of radical events of suffering can suggest the problems of Moltmann's formal method in relation to liberation theology. Liberation theology revolves around the question of suffering and the quest of human freedom for justice, equality, freedom. Suffering is a question of humanity and, in liberation theology, forces both the relocation of human experience in an anthropology of praxis and the reinterpretation of Christianity in light of a tradition in which God chooses to be on the side of the oppressed.

But in Moltmann's formal method of theology, suffering does not raise the question of humanity, let alone the practical question of human activity. For Moltmann, suffering is, first, the question of the appropriate concept of God. Moltmann can offer, in this way, an answer to the question of suffering by making God the measure and context of all suffering. God's suffering—more ultimate than any human suffering—can be understood and responded to only in faith: faith sees the glory of the triune God in the faces and cries of the oppressed. This conceptual answer, that suffering is in God and that God is the measure of all suffering, in no way locates, measures, or answers massive unjust suffering. Consequently the formal character of Moltmann's theology misses the radical fact of suffering by moving too quickly from the hopeless horrors of millions of innocent victims with no history and no future into a concept of the Trinity. While it is naturally the task of theology to be ever concerned with the concept of God, it is also always the responsibility of theology to do so by giving an adequate account of the present situation. The problem of radical events of suffering in the Holocaust or in Latin America is not only that such suffering is unthinkable in light of God, and vice versa, but also that history and the human subject are practically threatened by such events.

As suffering is abstracted in Moltmann, so Christian praxis becomes a privileged journey of faith. The location of suffering in God results in placing the hermeneutical privilege not with the option for the poor or with those who suffer within the paradigm of liberation theology, but in the faithful, those gathered in God's church. Based on the unique event of Jesus Christ that is untouched by human reason or social function, the church is incapable of correlating other criticisms of injustice with its own radical critique or of appropriating other models of transformation in its own eschatological proclamation.

Moltmann's formal method of a dialectic of contradiction between God and world, revelation and history, and church and society cannot deal with the radical negativity of historical suffering or with the practical activity of human history. Moltmann constantly privileges the dialectic of contradiction as the real interruption of history. Suffering is thus formally a vehicle for God's revelation: God chooses self-revelation in the unlike (history) through the unlike of history (suffering). Moltmann's formal method of a dialectic of contradiction refuses to take history seriously, both in its radical interruption through events of suffering and in its character of human praxis.

Nevertheless the substantive character of Moltmann's readings—the dialectic of identification of suffering and hope and of cross and resurrection—breaks through the narrow confines of his method. If Moltmann fails to let suffering be interruptive and human history to be practical, he succeeds in forcing us to think of God and suffering together in light of a tradition that promises righteousness and justice for all. The peculiar nature of promise as open history names the horizon of human existence as one of anticipatory freedom. The event of cross-resurrection names the identification of suffering and hope in human praxis. The power of the Spirit graces the intersubjectivity of all creation as a gift and as an imperative for human responsibility. If Moltmann's texts can be read against his own formal method, the God whose story is told creates possibilities in the impossible, identifies hope and suffering, testifies through mission, witness, and its own exodus. Moltmann reminds us that theology keeps this story central as both its subject and its substance. But Moltmann also reminds us that the new paradigm of liberation theology is a new way of doing theology, a new way of talking about theology's subject and substance. Moltmann provokes, in this text, an interpretation of liberation theology as not only a theology in which human suffering and God are central, but also a theology in which human suffering and God are related through liberating praxis.

7

Christ Liberating Culture

A new theology emerges out of Latin American liberation theology and out of German political theology. The contexts of these liberation theologies introduce a new question: How does suffering change human praxis and Christian witness? Following a rhetorical style of break and rupture, liberation theologians argue for a new turn to praxis: a new way of understanding human existence through practical activity and of interpreting Christianity through its solidarity with those who suffer. This "newness," which we have referred to as a paradigm shift, affects theology both in its systematic interpretation (the particular way it interprets human existence and Christian witness) and in its methodological procedures (how it orders the investigation of and reflection on human existence and Christian witness). Theological method, the subject matter of the next chapter, attends to the nature and process of investigation and reflection within the paradigm of liberation theology. The systematic interpretation of existence and Christian witness, the topic of this chapter, identifies new anthropological categories and interprets Christian symbols within the paradigm of liberation theology. This interpretation begins where liberation theology begins: with attention to the massive, public events of suffering.[1]

The most fundamental claim of liberation theology is a bold one: massive, public events of suffering rupture both our experiencing and our understanding of history. Liberation theology forces us to view suffering through the eyes of the angel in Walter Benjamin's interpretation of Paul Klee's *Angelus Novus*:

A Klee painting named "Angelus Novus" shows an angel looking as though he is about to move away from something he is fixedly contemplating. His eyes are staring, his mouth is open, his wings are spread. This is how one pictures the angel of history. His face is turned toward the past. Where we perceive a chain of events, he sees one single catastrophe which keeps piling wreckage upon wreckage and hurls it in front of his feet. The angel would like to stay, and awaken the dead, and make whole what has been smashed. But a storm is blowing from Paradise; it has so caught in his wings with such violence that the angel can no longer close them. This storm irresistibly propels him into the future to which his back is turned, while the pile of debris before him grows skyward. This storm is what we call progress.[2]

Though we, mere mortals, cannot perceive the fullness of this horrified angel's vision, we grasp with sudden insight that our modern liberal notions of correction, evolution, and education are no longer possible as final solutions to this catastrophic wreckage. With no hope of eradicating suffering or of explaining history through one large Hegelian sweep, we somberly recognize that the world is not getting better and better. Even if we could in some way affirm that we understand history, or if we could organize some plan to prevent all future suffering, the catastrophic wreckage of our vision remains: the slate of history's sufferings cannot be wiped clean.[3] For, liberation theologians tell us, suffering is our history, our confession, our human freedom, and our human fate: only by realizing its centrality may we, in fact, face our own lives as inhabitants of a particular time and space and as connected to the rest of history.

The demand that we attend to the centrality of suffering catches us off guard; what is most striking about this suffering is the necessity to speak the unspeakable. How does one adequately describe the suffering and torture of the poor in Latin America in a way that does not make the poor an "object" of pity, of theories, of the process of history? How do we understand the Holocaust—what words fit an attempt to exterminate a race of people?[4] How do we contemplate a nuclear genocide of the human species, an apocalyptic destruction that we ourselves create? Suffering, as we have repeatedly indicated, has a nonidentity character in reflection: it cannot be fully expressed in concepts or finally analyzed in theoretical arguments. There is no way to correct or make right the suffering of even one innocent victim, no theory to explain how one human created by God is destroyed by another human.

We must, of course, understand that this is not a subtle new form of negative ontology—that the structure of life is suffering—but that this is a realistic, practical claim of life here and now. Indeed, to the despair of some first-world academic theologians, liberation theologians have shown little concern for philosophical reflection about the structure of existence, preferring for the moment to concentrate on the urgent and startling demands of the present historical situation. This is not, however, to negate the importance of philosophical reflection; significantly, current philosophical discussion is also marked by the issues of polis, praxis, solidarity, and freedom.[5] Though liberation theology and the current "practical" philosophical discussion have yet to engage each other in conversation, the themes and goals of contemporary theology and practical philosophy share much in common. At present the parallel between discussions on both the foundation of praxis and the role of practical reason point to a central fact: suffering demands a response not only of specific acts or theoretical concepts, but also of interpretations, judgments, and transformations centered on human praxis.[6]

It is, therefore, significant that in liberation theology this practical concern of suffering is neither the call for a new ethic nor a sublation of theology into ethics. Suffering, liberation theology claims, ruptures our categories, our experiences, our history; suffering demands a new paradigm for interpreting existence and Christian witness. We must, in this paradigm, address ourselves to a new question, a question that we cannot fit into our old frameworks of experiencing and understanding, a question that is not quieted by our old answers.[7] This question, the question of suffering, functions in liberation theology to demand new interpretations and understandings, new ways of conceiving and answering questions, new ways of ordering questions and concerns.

What is at stake in the arguments of the liberation theologians is the *very character* of human existence and Christianity or, in their language, a radical conversion of anthropology, Christianity, and theology. Liberation theology, however, must not only *demand* an anthropological revolution and a messianic Christianity, but also *provide* new categories for its anthropology of praxis and new interpretations of traditional Christian symbols for its praxis of solidarity with those who suffer.[8] Somewhat rephrased, liberation theology must not only proclaim the passing of an old paradigm and the identification of new needs and questions, but also formulate new constructs within the new paradigm. Final interpretations are, of course, possible only at the end of a theological era and not at its beginning; so we must enter this systematic interpretation, remembering that the theological language we hear in liberation theology is still searching for its full voice. With this condition in mind, then, it is time to consider the constructive formulations of the new paradigm of liberation theology.

HUMAN EXISTENCE: AN ANTHROPOLOGY OF PRAXIS

One of the more interruptive qualities about suffering, so liberation theologians suggest, is that it makes us question our basic assumptions about life; the turn to suffering forces us both to live differently and to understand life differently. Within liberation theology this new form of human existence is often formulated in opposition to the anthropology of modern theology. Liberation theology argues that the subject of modern Western theology is "man," more specifically, the white male of modern Western societies. In privileging this subject, theology not only focuses on a small, albeit powerful, group in history, but also functions ideologically to shield the interests of these few from the demands of the masses. Yet this is not to assume that this "special" subject enjoys a perfect existence, for, as the German political theologians argue, the privilege of power is bought at the cost of isolation, miserliness, and apathy, the effects of which can be readily observed, as Metz points out: "on the one hand, widespread apathy and, on the other, unreflecting hatred; on the one hand, fatalism, and on the other, fanaticism."[9]

If liberation theology is critical of the choice of the subject, it is equally critical of the manner in which modern theology has interpreted the chosen few. Modern theology, goes the accusation, not only conveniently chooses a particular, powerful subject, but then focuses on this subject as an isolated individual, somehow untouched by the political, social, and economic dimensions of life. Individualism leads to the concern for historicity, the lonely individual inwardly dealing with being toward death; a historicity that, as Georg Lukacs noted, is not really distinguishable from ahistoricity.[10] As Gutiérrez points out, the categories of modern theological anthropology are part and parcel of the situatedness of modern theology, a situation in which individualism and rationalism function as the foundation of politics and economics as well as of knowledge.[11]

Freedom, another category of modern anthropology, has been the special concern of theology since modernity threw off the oppressive chains of religion to become "free," and religion in turn blessed this freedom as a religious act. Freedom, in modern theological anthropology, is structured through the dual categories of rationalism (the freedom to examine the conditions of thought) and individualism (the existential freedom to give assent to God). Liberation theology argues that freedom, in modernity, never took seriously the second challenge of the Enlightenment, the challenge to make a better world. Indeed, the Enlightenment act of defiance against traditional authorities and feudal society gave birth to the oppression of the many by the control of the few.

Against the bourgeois subject, liberation theology listens to a new subject who suffers: these are the subjects on the underside, on the margins, in death itself. These subjects are not written about in biographies or schoolbooks; these subjects are not filmed in soap operas or movies of mass culture; these subjects are not studied in the ruminations of a narcissistic society. Though they have no objective records, these subjects have faces, stories, and testimonies. These faces, as the Latin American bishops at Puebla announced, are the subject for liberation theology:

—the faces of young children, struck down by poverty before they are born . . . ;
—the faces of the indigenous peoples, and frequently of the Afro-Americans as well, living marginalized lives in inhuman situations . . . ;
—the faces of the peasants; as a social group, they live in exile almost everywhere on our continent . . . ;
—the faces of marginalized and overcrowded urban dwellers, whose lack

of material goods is matched by the ostentatious display of wealth by other segments of society;

—the faces of old people, who are growing more numerous every day, and who are frequently marginalized in a progress-oriented society that totally disregards people not engaged in production.[12]

These faces include the faces of the "other," the object of modernity's project of extermination in the Holocaust: "in the camps men and women were reduced to a single human mass. They all looked alike—the same filthy rags, shaved heads, stick-thin festering bodies—and the same hurt and need was each other's lot," wrote Terrence Des Pres.[13] These are the faces that must now be brought to the focal center of anthropology and related to new, fundamental categories for understanding human existence.

The center of this new anthropology is, as we have already seen, the subject of suffering, where suffering is related to oppression and injustice in the disasters of history. We shall later examine the argument for the privileging of the oppressed subject based on a reading of Christian tradition, but for now we must understand that this other subject, or the subject as "other," is representative of humanity. That is to say, the choice of the sufferer as the referent to understand human existence is not only for the sake of the mere survival of the overlooked and oppressed, but also for the sake of the practical realization of human existence. Liberation theology depends on this wager: only by understanding the subject of suffering can we hope to understand adequately the present reality of human existence and to transform the polis for the benefit of *all* its members. The argument for the privileging of the oppressed as the central subject in theological anthropology is twofold: (1) attention to the subjects of suffering "ruptures" or breaks into the ideological distortion of privileging the private and individual bourgeois subject as the "universal" or "common" subject, and (2) the position of the subject of suffering locates the most adequate place in which to understand the interrelationships of the present situation. Note that both of these arguments are themselves practical claims, arguing that, in this situation, the subject of suffering has a privileged location both in repositioning theological anthropology to interpret human existence and in giving theological anthropology a new vision of the past, present, and future of history.

As suffering can be said to *relocate* the subject, so praxis can be said to *redefine* anthropology. For, in the arguments of liberation theology, it is only by reconceiving the human subject through praxis that we may respond to suffering. As the referent for a new anthropology, praxis may be defined as human activity, and understood through a retrieval of certain themes in the works of Aristotle and Marx.

The classical understanding of praxis goes back to Aristotle and is connected to the terms "episteme" and "poesis." "Praxis" refers to the sphere of human action in the virtuous life of the citizen in the polis. "Episteme," or theory, studies the eternal order and is the knowledge of the unchanging. "Poesis," or "techne," governs the production of human artifacts. Compared to abstract theory, praxis depends on the changing needs of human community; compared to poesis, praxis anticipates the telos of human realization. Praxis is action, but action within the context of human community, a human community that has the responsiblity for its own political determination. Praxis is not just any action; rather, it is the ongoing activity of a human community responsible for itself.

In the thought of Marx, praxis is the societal foundation of all life and knowledge. Marx argued that all values, norms, structures, and systems are related to the structure of society, thus suggesting the possibility for a "practical" epistemology and the necessity of critical theory. Marx offered the outlines of an anthropology in which the human subject is constituted by and constitutes society. Richard Bernstein describes Marx's anthropology: "Marx had a profound understanding of the ways in which men are what they do, of how their social praxis shapes and is shaped by the complex web of historical institutions and practices within which they function and work."[14] For Marx, praxis meant the possibility and the necessity of transformation within the reproductive nature of human agency and social structures.

The anthropology of liberation theology, in sum, emphasizes practical activity. It draws upon Aristotle's notion of praxis in which human agency is always related to a community and practically oriented. But the anthropology of liberation theology transforms this understanding in light of Marx's conception of praxis stressing the structural relations within society, the realities of ideological and systematic distortion, and the necessity for social and personal transformations. The anthropology of praxis in liberation theology can be examined through the identification of three categories: the political nature, the intersubjective character, and the anticipatory freedom of human existence.

Praxis necessitates that human existence can be understood adequately through attention to the full historical character of existence: covering the broadest horizon of existence, this can be called the political nature of anthropology. The word "political" is used in liberation theology to refer to the activity of life in human community. For some liberation theologians the political nature of anthropology implies attention to specific events in concrete communities. It is not enough to interpret the Holocaust or the poor in general; one must look at a specific group at a specific time in Auschwitz or investigate a particular basic Christian community working for a particular project. For others, it may entail considering existence through the larger lens of social reality by attending to the ongoing interpretations of traditions, to different candidates for cultural criticism and understanding, and to various models of transformation. The political nature of human existence demands a practical interpretation, and "practical" refers not only to applications of theories to specific situations, but also to the practical knowledge of the agents participating in the ongoing production and reproduction of human activity. Whatever the particular stance taken, the goal is to understand human existence in its actual historical constitution, that is, in its political nature.

That human existence must be understood politically has, for liberation theology, many implications. First, it means that theology must understand human existence through broad historical perspectives. To be a human, given the political nature of existence, is to be historical, born of a certain time and place, in a country, within a family and a social system. To be a *historical* human subject is to experience the temporality of having a past, a present, and a future: it is to have a history—to have traditions, memories, experiences, and hopes. It also means that the human is part of a larger history, a history that goes beyond one's personal life and exists through social institutions. The historical nature of the human subject forces us to understand the subject in and through time and space: to understand temporality through the long duration of social institutions, through the ongoing participation of communities and individuals in traditions, and through the existential activity of human experience; and to understand spatiality through particular geographical locations, within particular social relations, and in particular cultural horizons.

Second, the political nature also implies the need for a wide range of theories for interpretation and transformation to understand historical existence. This is not to replace theological anthropology's common conversation partners of philosophy and psychology with sociology and economics; it is, rather, the demand that theology must use a multiplicity of theories to understand human existence in any given situation. The third implication of the political nature is an explicitly normative implication: any visions or models of human fulfillment must be articulated through the polis.[15] Models of fulfillment or strategies of change in anthropology must consider both individual actors and structural relations. Human existence must be understood and transformed through the interdependency of human agency and social structures.

The anthropology of praxis also considers the intersubjective character of human existence, in which life is, at every dimension and level, communal. We think and know the world through language, which is and has a communal structure. Our culture, its values and symbols, belong not to any one individual, but to a tradition and to a community that span generations and include many diverse interpretations. We are dependent upon others globally, nationally, and interpersonally for our needs and desires, our identities and our continuities. Even the "I" of our personal life forms and grows only in relation to others. Beneath and between human existence lies a dependence on an "always already" reality of solidarity in nature.

In part this category of intersubjectivity comes from the fact that the subject of liberation theology is a group of oppressed: the poor, women, ethnic minorities. In part it arises out of the understanding of the radical interrelatedness of human existence. It is, as well, formulated against the lonely individual

"I," and the fear that this "I" has been erected on the backs of others. But we must be clear that the category of intersubjectivity is not a plea for a reductionist form of social theory. Liberation theology, even in its more demonstrative critiques, cannot argue that human existence is simply determined by impersonal social forces. Indeed, the emphasis on conscientization, the pleas for conversion, and the notion of liberation appeal to an awakening of individual and social consciousness as well as to the need for personal and political transformations. In more classical terms, theological anthropology opts neither to convert only the individual in hopes of stacking society with righteous citizens nor to restructure society merely to guarantee better individuals.

Most peculiarly, the category of intersubjectivity in liberation theology means that we must recognize a present solidarity with the dead. If we are connected to the past through our traditions, our institutions, our systems, we are also connected to the past through our solidarity with the dead.[16] Indeed, our connection with history depends not on our own willingness to read the texts of the past, but on an ontological and practical solidarity with those who have lived and died before us. The dead make a claim on us, giving us a vision and a goal for the future as well as a history and an identity from the past. The intersubjective character of human existence necessitates, for liberation theology, that we must reread our history in order to have a future, that we must recreate our freedom out of the possibilities of the past. Intersubjectivity demands that an adequate understanding of human existence will depend on a continual rereading of history, a continual conversation with our ancestors for the sake of ourselves and our children.

Theological anthropology also considers the future in terms of the anticipatory freedom of human existence. Indeed, it is the solidarity of human existence in liberation theology that is the condition for the possibility of freedom. Freedom is the capacity for new action, for transformation, for changing the present status of a community. This understanding is expressed in words of the political philosopher Hannah Arendt: "before it became an attribute of thought or a quality of the will, freedom was understood to be the free man's status, which enabled him to move, to get away from home, to go out into the world and meet other people in deed and word."[17] The anticipatory freedom of human existence identifies the projection of future possibilities, the "going out into the world" as the definitive act of being human. The experience of time, how we live in history and make history, is channeled by liberation theologians through the character of anticipatory freedom: freedom is human activity toward a new future.[18] To be human is to make, to create, and to live out new ways of being human in history.

Anticipatory freedom is, of course, both social and personal, with both an indicative claim—every one and every institution lives toward the future—and an imperative mandate: we must live toward the future. An adequate understanding of human existence requires not only the interpretation of the here and now—the facts of a situation—but also the identification of transformative possibilities for the future. Theories of interpretation must include theories of transformation, or in Marxist terms, every "is" implies some "ought." These theories of transformation, as theories of interpretation, will include a wide variety of disciplines, positions, and resources. Psychology, sociology, education, philosophy, ecology, economics: a diversity of fields will contribute a variety of synchronic and diachronic models to aid in understanding and transforming existence.[19]

Invoking the descriptive adjective of their name, many liberation theologians understand the anticipatory freedom of the human subject to be a location for religious experience. Moltmann's interpretation of hope as *futur* and *zukunft* locates the immediacy of God's mysterious relationship to human spirituality in anticipatory freedom.[20] Gutiérrez suggests, most strongly of all, that utopia mediates liberating activity in the experience of God's redemptive activity. What is significant in these various claims is that the anticipatory freedom of human existence is a new location for the experience of God.[21] God is not just revealed in the Scriptures and witnessed to by the community, but is also *experienced* in a solidarity with the poor that anticipates new ways of being human.[22]

Liberation theology formulates an anthropology of praxis through the categories of the political nature, the intersubjective character, and the anticipatory freedom of human existence. These categories do not compose the totality of an adequate anthropology; other categories and other issues must also contribute to theological anthropology. But these categories do indicate the fundamentals of a new anthropology, suggesting that any understanding of human existence must at least begin in or be in reference to praxis. This anthropology of praxis shares themes in common with some new interpretations of human existence in contemporary philosophy and social theory. As Richard Bernstein's book *Beyond Objectivism and Relativism* indicates, praxis is one of the central themes of contemporary theory with notions of solidarity, freedom, and the polis as constant subthemes.[23] A more guarded observation is made by the political philosopher Fred Dallmayr: "on a still broader scale, it is possible to discern a subtle shift involving a progressive deemphasis of epistemology in favor of pragmatic or practical preoccupation."[24] The new anthropology betrays liberation theology's participation in the global community that needs and desires a practical understanding of human existence. But liberation theology is by no means a mere reflection of the contemporary discussion; its anthropology develops out of and influences a new interpretation of Christian witness. This anthropology of praxis joins with a new reading of Christianity in light of a God who creates, redeems, and liberates history.

CHRIST AND SOLIDARITY

Liberation theology is a new interpretation of Christian tradition; it seeks to recover or to uncover the symbols, the narratives, and the dogmas of Christian tradition forgotten or distorted by modern theology. Christianity, one might argue along with liberation theology, got lost among the arid plains of the Enlightenment and the shifting sands of secularism; with the prophetic desire of returning to tradition via a new form of Christianity, liberation theologians proclaim nothing less than a new way of Christianity.

The irruption of the poor, Gutiérrez argues, has resulted in a new way of Christianity that is qualitatively different from former ways. Metz calls for a messianic Christianity to replace the bourgeois religion masquerading as Christianity in the first world.[25] This newness that Gutiérrez and Metz emphasize entails the way in which Christian faith is experienced and understood. This new way of faith is a relocation of Christianity in activity, with faith being understood not primarily through beliefs, doctrines, or individual feelings but through praxis. Christianity is now understood as the activity of a community: the formation of individuals and communities; the living out of tradition and the projection of future possibilities; and the witness of teaching, mission, evangelism, worship, education, and service. This relocation of Christianity in activity does not deny the reality of personal beliefs or of personal religious experience, but places the personal always in relation to the communal.

Yet Christianity is not just any activity, for the placement of faith in human activity takes on a particular content in light of suffering. It could be said that suffering not only ruptures Christianity by relocating it in the activity of a community, but also reforms Christianity by reinterpreting it as a praxis of solidarity with those who suffer. Or in words reminiscent of Metz: suffering not only interrupts, it converts Christianity into an interruption—an interruption of systems that deny suffering or try to find a total cure for suffering; an interruption of structures that attempt to control rather than transform history; an interruption of theories that deny the dangerous memories and transformative narratives of cultural traditions.[26]

Within this interpretation turned interruption and transformation, liberation theology retrieves and reinterprets Christian symbols. These symbols relate to the root metaphor of liberation with its tensive character: the constant multiplicity of meanings in the term "liberation" gives rise to new and transformative relations. "Liberation" covers particular acts, utopian visions, and the fullness of redemption. The nature of history, the fulfillment of humanity, and the telos of social relations can all be related to the term "liberation." Liberation discloses God's originary act of creation as well as God's continuing activity in history; it names Christ's identification of cross and resurrection, of suffering and hope; it invokes the Spirit's guiding, breaking, rupturing, healing, and transforming movement throughout history.

Two aspects of liberation theology's play of this root metaphor within Christian symbols must be observed. First, because of liberation theology's status as a paradigm shift in theology and because of its incorporation of ideology critique into the nature of theology, symbols are retrieved through a "hermeneutics of suspicion." Liberation theology reinterprets tradition with special attention to the systematic distortions within the tradition and the legitimizing use of symbols in creating false ideologies.[27] Second, because of the transformative orientation of human existence and Christian tradition, symbols are understood not only as disclosing reality, that is, representing the way things are, but also as liberating and transforming reality, namely, anticipating new possibilities and future aspirations.[28]

Although a full reading of Christian symbols in liberation theology is beyond the limits of this book, a brief sketch of the reinterpretation of Christian tradition can be drawn by beginning with the symbol of sin. Traditionally, sin has been understood as the fallenness of all creation, the inability to be or do what God intended—caused, of course, by the willful turning away from God. Sin has been primarily understood as personal: the dark night of the soul, the agony of the individual in doubt, fear, or confusion, and the struggle for control over appetites and desires. It should be no surprise that liberation theology is critical of the privatism and individualism that results when sin is interpreted in personal terms; for liberation theologians sin must be understood as the distortion of human existence in its political nature, its intersubjective character, and its anticipatory orientation toward the future.[29]

Sin results in suffering, the suffering of creation groaning in travail, the suffering of children without any hope. Sin manifests and embraces suffering, the suffering of lost identity, the suffering of freedom without a future, and the suffering of a future without freedom. Sin extracts its price as the victimization of the poor, the suffering of the tortured, the dispossession of the homeless. These are victims of sin not because of moral inferiority or human depravity, but because they bear the brunt and carry the special burden of the world's sin. In the retrieval of this symbol, sin's arena is human praxis and its primary realization is massive global injustice.

Following the traditional correlation of sin with redemption, liberation theology reinterprets redemption to include the realization of the claims on history of all those who suffer, both the living and the dead. Redemption includes the possibility of just structures as well as the entire transfiguration of history. Redemption, referring to the radically new in history and the transformation of the present, is the fulfillment of God's creation, the making new of the distorted, the new creation of history.

If redemption has to do with political reality, then it is mediated or made real in concrete situations of liberation as well as through a utopian vision of history. If redemption conquers sin, then it liberates the oppressed, feeds the poor, breaks through false consciousness, and offers new possibilities for being human in history. For many liberation theologians, the vision of redemption is expressed in the parable of Judgment in Matthew 25, with the feeding of the hungry, the clothing of the naked, and the visiting of the imprisoned. Redemption must be related, though never equated, with liberation; to equate redemption with any one situation of liberation would be to usurp the power of God and deny the openness of human existence. But not to realize the relation of redemption and liberation is to deny the grace of God and the nature of human existence. God's redemptive activity is neither any one historical event nor simply the telos of all historical activity. In its fullness a mystery, redemption is the praxis of God; God acts in history through liberating activity, but God's liberating activity is not yet total redemption.

Biblically, liberation theology unites creation and redemption through the interpretation of God's providential role in history as liberating activity.[30] Within the Old Testament, the exodus and the prophets are frequently favored by liberation theologians to suggest the importance of freedom and the struggle for liberation as central to God's activity in history. As a founding event, the exodus discloses God as a God of people in history, interrelated through familial, religious, social, political, and economic systems. The prophets criticize present social systems in relation to the promises, memories, and traditions of the people and reveal God as one who demands righteousness and justice. In the New Testament, liberation theologians highlight sections such as the Beatitudes, finding within such sections God's identification with those who suffer. Gutiérrez claims that the biblical option for the poor is first a word about God: "the beatitudes in the Gospels—Blessed are the poor—are not, in the first instance, a word about the poor, but about God. 'Blessed are the poor' is a revelation of God."[31]

God's liberating activity in history has, for liberation theologians, a particular incarnation or a "coming into flesh" through Jesus Christ. Jesus Christ announces his mission as a message of grace in history, displaying God's gratuitous activity in the option for those who suffer and the identification of this suffering with Christ's own promise of future life in the resurrection. As sign and presence, Christ is the incarnation of God's solidarity with those who suffer and the promise of freedom and righteousness for all creation in God's still-hidden future.

As in the tradition of the church, there are many images of Christ in liberation theology.[32] Christ is seen as a "moral leader," a political revolutionary, a teacher, and certainly a political rebel. New readings of Christ as a martyr, as a sacrifice, as a bringer of God's grace are offered in the many liberation Christologies. Liberation theologians view Christ in profoundly new ways: Christ judges sin, empties out God's love, rules the cosmos, and suffers as the tortured and scourged of the earth. Popular culture, ancient symbols, and church teachings are transformed into symbols of the liberating Christ. But, for liberation theology, Christ is fundamentally the revelation of God's grace in solidarity with those who suffer.[33] The narrative of Christ discloses the identification of hope and suffering, of cross and resurrection, of God and those who suffer as always together. As the ultimate revelation of God, Jesus mediates the kingdom of God: as for much of the Christian tradition, Jesus comes not to announce himself, but to announce the kingdom.

Through Christ as the revelation of God, Christianity becomes a way of the kingdom in its praxis of solidarity with those who suffer. It is a graced way, for

Jesus Christ reveals the gratuitous gift of God's salvation through love of neighbor. It is the nature and purpose of the church to continue the incarnation as the full embodiment of God's love in the world through the announcement of the kingdom in the midst of suffering, death, and hope. The church continues the witness of the kingdom of God through the power of the Spirit as the sacrament of God's activity.

Through liberation theology's hermeneutics of suspicion, liberation theologians criticize earlier formulations and functions of the symbol of the church. Moltmann, for instance, criticizes the church in the first world as a Noah's ark of individualism, and Metz accuses the bourgeois church of clinging to a paternalistic control of masses.[34] The hermeneutics of retrieval comes, Gutiérrez suggests, through the parable of the Banquet. In this dangerous memory, the master, after the invited guests refuse to attend the feast, goes out into the street to invite the outcasts.[35] The uninvited of history attend, and thus they are the guests of the kingdom. And so the church must be understood and transformed by the uninvited of history; it must become not a church *for* the oppressed but *of* the oppressed. Existing for others as it criticizes unjust social systems, the church speaks out against oppression and works for political and personal transformation; it worships God as it serves the poor and the oppressed by being a place for education, for new relationships, for conscientization, and for exploring new ways of being in the world. This is the witness of the church, a trial for its own martyrdom before God and the world in its solidarity with those who suffer.

The liberation of suffering thus ruptures and transforms Christianity. What is important in this new reading of the Christian tradition is the identification of Christian witness with the liberation of those who suffer. Liberation theology is, in a sense, a new language of God—a language created by the reinterpretation of old symbols in new situations—and the demand that only by this reformation can Christianity maintain its tradition. The new interpretation of Christianity on behalf of liberation theology is an act of loyalty and thanksgiving to a God who creates, redeems, and liberates all of history.

CHRIST AND CULTURE

Having a new anthropology and a new interpretation of Christianity, we can address now the practical relation between Christianity and culture. The relation might be posed through a question that has always puzzled Christians: How should Christianity relate to culture? Throughout the history of the Christian church, Christians have proposed different answers to this question of how Christians live in the world. Traditionally, Christianity has related to the world either by following a model of Christ *against* culture or by following a model of some relation of Christ *and* culture. Another way to interpret the many different answers in the tradition is to focus on the institutional nature of the church: Christianity has lived in the world through the institutions of the sect or the church.[36] In the sect, Christian life is opposed to and withdrawn from the culture; in the church, Christian life discovers some form of identity with the culture. Though the sect has never been completely free from the world and the church never completely identified with the world, neither the option of the sect nor the option of the church operates within the paradigm of liberation theology. For liberation theology's relation to culture is not formulated on the grounds of identity and nonidentity between Christianity and culture, but on the possibilities of identification and liberation; it suggests a new relationship of liberating activity between Christianity and world. Liberation theology proposes a new model to answer our question: a model of Christ liberating culture.

This relationship of liberating activity is dependent upon liberation theology's insistence on suffering as the primary focus for theology and on the creation of new and more just ways of living together as the goal of theology. The crisis of the subject—which is the practical quest for human self-realization—must become, liberation theologians insist, the crisis of Christianity. Furthermore, the practical quest for justice is the particular concern of Christianity as a praxis of solidarity with those who suffer. Obviously, in the reading of the tradition by liberation theologians, Christ liberates culture as the transformative revelation of God's freedom in history; Christianity is the way of following or imitating Christ in liberating activity in the world. The model for the new relation of Christianity and culture is Christ liberating culture, a model that is formed and transformed by suffering, praxis, and liberation.

Liberation theology offers the model of Christ liberating culture as a practical correlation between the quest for human justice and the Christian praxis of solidarity with those who suffer. Within this practical correlation, Christianity represents the anticipatory freedom of the human subject. This practical correlation—that Christianity transformatively represents the human quest for freedom—has been woven through this text. Indeed, the argument for this practical correlation suggests the paradigm shift of liberation theology as a transformation of modern theology. Modern theology has long been concerned about the freedom of the human subject as fulfillment of the human and the location of relation to God; liberation theology creates a new paradigm by forcing this freedom to be fully political—the quest of freedom and justice meets the religious quest of liberation and redemption.

This model of Christ liberating culture depends on two specific theological arguments that are increasingly important for liberation theologians. The reason Christians relate to culture in the liberating praxis of solidarity with those who suffer, the first argument goes, is because of God's option for the oppressed. Gutiérrez, as we have already seen, formulates this as a hermeneutical privilege wherein the Bible reveals God's option for the poor.

The love of God is a gratuitous gift. It was the intuition of Luther when he translated and understood the famous text in the Epistle to the Romans, 3:28, as justification by *sola fide*. *Sola* is not in the text, but it is in the meaning of this text because it is the affirmation of the gratuity of the action of God. Loving by preference the poor, doing that, God reveals this gratuity. And by consequence as followers of Jesus Christ, we must also do this preferential option for the poor. That is the main reason—the God of our faith, the God of Jesus Christ.[37]

Christ liberating culture as the model of the relationship of Christianity to the world depends on this understanding of God; the relationship of liberating praxis is a theological interpretation of the meaning and truth of the Christian tradition.

The second argument for the model of Christ liberating culture identifies justice as a primary analogue for faith.[38] Faith, for liberation theology, sets us free—from sin and for God and world. Freedom has been interpreted, across the Christian tradition, as the love of God and neighbor, the two commandments given by Jesus. If faith itself is now constituted and mediated through history, love of God and neighbor must include responsibility for the whole of God's creation. As Schubert Ogden has observed:

Because nothing of ourselves is to be withheld from our love for God, all of our powers and all of the uses of our powers are regulated by this single commandment. Nor is this in any way qualified by the fact that there is also the second commandment that we are to love our neighbor as ourselves. On the contrary, because God's own love boundlessly includes all our neighbors as well as ourselves, the second commandment but makes explicit what is implicitly contained in the first. As a matter of fact, it is precisely by withholding nothing of ourselves from our love for our neighbors as well as for all of our fellow creatures that we can alone obey the first commandment.[39]

Faith and love, in liberation theology, are joined with the practice of justice as the exemplification of responsibility for freedom. Justice refers to new ways of being human that are, in the discernment and judgment of the members of the polis, the best possible ways for all. Faith works through love in the bringing about of human justice through structural and personal change.

Christianity relates to the world through the liberating activity of solidarity. This includes the denunciation of oppressive structures and the conscientization of the oppressed. Christianity must criticize that which oppresses the human subject, from cultural values to global exchange, from nuclear arms to the writing of history, from language to economic systems. Christianity works for liberation by participating in new systems and structures, by suggesting alternative ways of being in the world, and by enabling persons to be and to do in history. But Christianity carries forth this praxis not as an implication of its faith, not as a time-filling device, and not as liberal charity, but as the very constitution of faith, the mysterious experiencing of God, and the following of Jesus Christ.

From the vantage point of Christ liberating culture, we can conclude that liberation theology offers a new understanding of human existence and a new interpretation of Christianity. Within this paradigm of Christ liberating culture comes a new way of conceiving and constructing theology. Theology comes second, the liberation theologians remind us, reflecting upon faith and human experience. To this second act, which has been making its presence felt throughout the text, we now turn in the following chapter.

8

Toward Praxis: A Method for Liberation Theology

The method of modern theology, judges liberation theology, was part and parcel of modernity's fault: method was reduced to a technical operation and an oppressive procedure within the theological enterprise. Consequently, the liberation theologians demand, theology must find a new way of doing theology. The logically odd language of "doing theology" suggests a paradigm shift in the nature and process of theological method. In this paradigm shift, the rupturing claim of theological method is twofold: liberation theology must find a way to uncover the distortions within modern theology and a way to transform theology in light of its new understanding of human existence and its new interpretation of Christianity. Theological method in liberation theology is, then, nothing else than the double demand to think in new ways on a new subject.

This stress on a "new way" can also alert us to the fact not only that this is a different kind of theological method, but also that it has a preliminary status, for this method is in the first stages of formulation. Reflection on method comes last in the theological enterprise, and the preliminary nature of this method demonstrates the developing character of liberation theology. With this assessment of the preliminary nature of theological method in liberation theology, this writer reveals her disagreement with a variety of interpreters and critics of liberation theology who argue either for the hopeful prospects or for the essential inadequacy of liberation theology's method. Indeed the intent of this book is to demonstrate that liberation theology is much more than some new variation of methodological finesse; rather, it is a paradigm shift in the context, the content, the experience, and the interpretation of Christianity. Those interpreters who rush in to bare methodological techniques either for literal imitation or for quick dismissal fail, in this writer's judgment, to understand the nature of liberation theology as a paradigm shift. Indeed, rather than reading theological method in liberation theology as either a well-established, easily imitated operation or a nonsubstantive, popular-activist fad, it seems preferable to locate the initial steps of liberation theology's method within the broader attempts among a variety of disciplines for practical reflection. The status of "newness" in liberation theology's method shares much in common with the status of current trends in a variety of disciplines seeking to understand their own foundations in praxis and concentrating attention on practical reason, reason as itself shaped by social practices.

The turn to praxis in liberation theology can be examined through six theses in order to distinguish and relate the various aspects of theological method. The first through the third theses discuss the sources of theology, in particular the ways of investigating human existence and Christian witness. The underlying turn to praxis, the use of practical reason, and the role of practical hermeneutics constitute the fourth thesis. The final two theses treat the defining nature and tasks of liberation theology: the fifth thesis considers the role of ideology critique, and the sixth thesis calls into question liberation theology's formulation of ideology critique and suggests the need for a social theory in the method of liberation theology.

THESIS 1: THE TWO SOURCES FOR LIBERATION THEOLOGY ARE HUMAN EXISTENCE AND CHRISTIAN TRADITION

The two sources of theology are human existence and Christian tradition: from these sources theology draws material, criticizes positions, and anticipates new ways of being and doing in the world.[1] Though the sources of theology remain the same, theological paradigms differ in how sources are understood, how issues are ordered, and what categories are used for interpretation. But in all theological paradigms, there is the attempt to become a faithful interpretation of Christian tradition as well as a credible representation of human existence. Theology must be, at least in principle, accessible to human understanding and appropriate to the tradition of which it seeks to be a representation.[2]

Liberation theology utilizes a variety of disciplines and theories to investigate the full political nature and intersubjective character of human experience. In light of anticipatory freedom, human existence is examined through the present reality of existence, the causal relations of past and present, and the future possibilities for change. Liberation theology interprets Christian tradition with the explicit theological intent of, as Míguez Bonino says, being obedient to God's action in history.[3] Liberation theology employs a variety of methods in its project of deideologization in the interpretation of biblical texts.

Whether explicitly recognized or not, theology always has an active relationship to what it examines, interpreting existence and tradition in its own practical activity. Theology's subject matter of human activity is extremely flexible, adopting and adapting insights from the various forms of reflection upon it. Liberation theology investigates human existence and Christian witness in light of the categories and concerns that it receives from its own participation in existence and tradition and, likewise, it contributes new terms, symbols, and perspectives to current existence and Christian praxis. Thus theology is itself a practical activity with a constant interplay between interpreting the interpretations of culture and providing new interpretations of human activity. This might be called the double hermeneutic of theology, and in liberation theology this entails the explicit purpose of seeking both to interpret the language of God by the victims of history and to be one voice of history's victims.[4]

THESIS 2: LIBERATION THEOLOGY INTERPRETS THE SOURCE OF HUMAN EXISTENCE POLITICALLY, USING, AMONG OTHER DISCIPLINES, THE SOCIAL SCIENCES TO REFLECT ON THE FULL CONCRETENESS OF HISTORICAL EXISTENCE

Liberation theology interprets human existence politically through the categories of its anthropology of praxis. The demand that the source of human existence be investigated politically, that is, in its historical concreteness, has two specific implications for liberation theology: (1) there must be a real dialogue with other methods of interpretation and transformation, and (2) theologians must be constantly self-critical, aware of their own particular location and involvement with the material being interpreted.

As we have already seen in the previous chapter, to investigate human existence in its full political character, theology must engage in dialogue with other models of interpretation and transformation as Míguez Bonino has remarked, "incorporating socio-political instruments and categories in our theological reflection, realizing that the political sphere is the realm of structures, ideologies, and power."[5] The argument for dialogue with other disciplines can be summarily stated: if theology is going to attend to concrete situations, then it must use theories that can analyze the various factors involved in the situation.[6] Due to anticipatory freedom of human existence and the future-oriented temporality of Christianity, any and all theological interpretation must include an analysis of present reality and the projection of future possibilities through models of transformation and concrete theories of change. Liberation theology, in its attempt to avoid both abstractness and reductionism, must also use political ethics to formulate moral and social norms in conjunction with theological interpretations. As James Gustafson has persuasively argued, political-ethical concepts offer the precision and clarification for the relation between social reality and theological symbols—a precision and clarification that liberation theology demands, both through its own reading of the tradition and through its turn to praxis.[7] Thus if theology wishes to be a critical reflection within a community wanting to lobby for the release of political prisoners, it will have to analyze the political systems, the prison systems, and the use of public pressure in that society. It may have to use educational methods to train people in their rights and organizational methods to mobilize persons for action. Specific ethical arguments will have to be advanced for the rights of dissent, free speech, and so forth. Whether they are utilizing socio-scientific explanations, ethical reflections on moral positions, or models of transformation and strategies for change, liberation theologians must always be able to give arguments as to the relative adequacy of the particular model, strategy, or interpretation.

As theologians dialogue with various theories of interpretation and models of transformation, the political source of human existence requires a reflective awareness and critique of the theologian's own values and commitments. Indeed, the double hermeneutic of theology implies that there is no value-free interpretation and, therefore, that the line between the categories used in interpretation and the subject matter of interpretation is always situated and flexible. Liberation theologians are called to be suspicious of motives for interpretation; in the preference for one theory over another there is always the danger of simply inserting one's own values and commitments into theology. Yet theologians are not reduced to merely reflecting any particular interests and values operative in a particular situation; rather, constant awareness, dialogue within the community, and the ongoing analysis of arguments used within theological interpretation all contribute to the ability of theologians to position themselves.[8] To be able to interpret *at all* is the possibility that one is not enslaved or reduced to literal reproduction, that the theologian can see alternatives, perspectives, and possibilities for change. Liberation theology emphasizes participation and involvement in human existence, but only through a constant mode of self-critical awareness.

THESIS 3: THEOLOGY EMPLOYS A HERMENEUTICS OF LIBERATION, INCLUDING A PROJECT OF DEIDEOLOGIZATION IN RELATION TO THE SOURCE OF CHRISTIAN TRADITION

The second major source for liberation theology is the Christian tradition, including the Bible, ecclesiological statements, and former theological interpretations. As the founding document of the living tradition, the Bible has a privileged place as the originary witness of Christian faith. Many liberation theologians intentionally give a prominent place to the Bible in their theologies, encouraging a freedom of understanding and interpreting that makes this theology a new "biblical" theology. Liberation theologians call for a hermeneutical circulation among the text, former interpretations, and the interpreter—a circulation within which the Bible is both disclosive and transformative of Christian praxis. As part of the hermeneutical circulation, theology studies the text as a document arising out of a particular time and place. But arguments about the historical facts or situation do not suffice for a theological interpretation; indeed historical-critical arguments and other theoretical arguments about the nature of the text only aid in formulating a theological understanding of the text. With these arguments in hand, the theologian must make an interpretation of the text for this time and place.

Within its hermeneutical circulation, liberation theology engages in a project of deideologization in a twofold sense: positively, by letting the text speak through the particularity of the time and, critically, through specific attention to false ideologies within text and tradition. As a reformulation of Rudolf Bultmann's project of demythologization, the first act of deideologization interprets the text in and through its concrete sociopolitical context.[9] Bultmann demanded that the historical particularities of the text be interpreted so that the universal event could be revealed; the myth, in other words, demands its own interpretation. In liberation theology, deideologization takes a sociological turn, requiring that the sociopolitical particularities of the text be examined. Míguez Bonino provides one example of deideologization, arguing that only by analyzing the particular historical context of a biblical account can the interpreter appropriately discern God's action in history.[10]

In the interpretation of Scripture, the theologian must pay special attention to the sociopolitical contexts and the history of effects of the text. Liberation theology continues to use historical methods of research to locate and explain the text in its historical context. Increasingly popular are sociohistorical methods to analyze the broader context of Scripture and its effects, with special attention to patterns of human relations. Norman Gottwald explains the use of both historical and sociological criticism in relation to the study of ancient Israel:

Historical method embraces all the methods of inquiry drawn from the humanities (e.g., literary criticism, form criticism, tradition criticism, rhetorical criticism, redaction criticism, history, history of religion, biblical theology). Sociological method includes all the methods of inquiry proper to the social sciences (e.g., anthropology, sociology, political science, economics). Sociological method in data collection and theory building enables us to analyze, synthesize, abstract, and interpret Israelite life and thought along different axes and with different tools and constructs from those familiar to us from historical method. Sociological inquiry recognizes people as social actors and symbolizers who "perform" according to interconnecting regularities and within boundaries of limits (social systems).[11]

Deideologization requires an explanation of the sociohistorical context of the text so that the theologian may attempt to understand the possible relevance of the text for the present day and age.

Thus far, literary modes of interpretation have not been used frequently by liberation theologians. But the role of the Bible in liberation theology as neither rule book nor literal guide demands attention to the use and reception of the Bible as a literary text. The Bible is the religious text of Christians who may have little or no idea of its original historical context—it speaks to persons as a text through its narratives, its poetry, its accounts, and its letters. Given the importance of narrative in liberation theology, literary theories can join historical and sociological methods in helping the theologian to offer an interpretation of the text.[12] Literary theories, historical methods, and sociohistorical approaches are methods to explain the text; the theologian must use these aids to render an appropriate interpretation for today. The theologian cannot confuse the explanation of the historical situation of a text or the examination of the structure of a text with theological interpretation; the project of deideologization uses explanations of the text to contribute to a new theological interpretation of the text in the current context of Christian praxis.

Deideologization also includes specific attention to the ideological distortions within the text and the ideological use of the text throughout the tradition. Given the fact that the Bible is a historical document, providing the vision of Christian praxis through narratives, letters, and historical accounts of particular persons in particular situations, distortions can appear within the text. The truth of the Bible exists in the ways of being portrayed and provoked by the text, not in the literal facts or activities reported in the text. The project of deideologization forces the recognition of distortions within the classical Christian text and through the history of interpretation of the text.[13] Indeed, some of the dangerous memories of suffering in liberation theology may well be those of the victims of the distortions in the Scriptures. For example, some New Testament texts picture the Jew as the other, the enemy, and the killer of Christ. Such texts may not have the possibility of retrieval; such instances of deideologization may force theology into a position of confession as well as conversion within its own tradition. Deideologization in this sense, is the critical demand that the classical texts, while privileged, are not secured or finalized in their systemic distortions.

THESIS 4: THE METHOD OF LIBERATION THEOLOGY CAN BE CHARACTERIZED AS A CRITICAL PRAXIS CORRELATION, WHEREIN PRAXIS IS BOTH THE FOUNDATION AND THE AIM OF THEOLOGICAL HERMENEUTICS[14]

Insisting that all life, and life as a whole, is grounded in praxis, liberation theologians seek a critical relationship between praxis and theory in theology.[15] This relationship of theory and praxis is oriented not to the mere understanding of the present, but to the active transformation of past and present into the future. Langdon Gilkey's definition of praxis indicates the orientation of this theological method:

(1) the polarity of theory with action (the purpose of thinking is to change reality not merely to comprehend it) and of action with theory (no responsible and reflective action is possible without social understanding of the structure, trends, and possibilities in social actuality), (2) the polarity of actuality and possibility: present actualities are not to be negated by future-oriented theory and practice, a negation by unified theory and practice of the negativities of actual theory and practice so that new possibilities may appear.[16]

Praxis, as the ground and aim of theology, calls for an epistemological shift within theological reflection. This epistemological shift, denying the primacy

of universal or abstract theory, assumes that the practical conditions of life—
the historical nature of existence—are the conditions for all theory and reflection. Richard Bernstein's description of Marx's epistemological insight
captures this turn to praxis: "one that shows us that man's practical relation to
the objects and the world he confronts is the basis for understanding man's
cognitive relationship to the world."[17]

This epistemological shift to recognize praxis as the foundation and aim of
theory is occurring not only in liberation theology but also within a variety of
other fields. Most startling among the various instances of "the turn to praxis"
has been the discussion of the hermeneutical dimension of scientific praxis, but
such conversations occur across the fields of science, sociology, history, political science, literary criticism, and psychology. The various discussions share in
common the realization of the practical foundation of human knowledge, and
the recognition that theories and paradigms change and develop historically.
The turn to praxis necessitates, among other things, a quest for a new form of
practical reason.

Practical reason, having to do with concrete decisions of life, suggests the
mediation of theory and praxis in sociopolitical life. It appeals not only to
theoretical knowledge and unconscious knowledge, but also to practical
knowledge—the knowledge of daily activity. Fred Dallmayr defines practical
knowledge as "insights grounded through life experience and through public
conduct, preferably in public affairs."[18] Practical knowledge must use theoretical arguments and technical applications, but both are moments within the
broader activity of understanding the full range of life in the polis and of
producing and reproducing human activity. In liberation theology practical
reason includes the knowledge of daily activity, the analysis and interpretation
of praxis, the reflexive relation of criticism to theory, and the projection of
possibilities for concrete change. Practical reason is embodied, involved, and
participative; it is reason within the polis that is oriented to the making and
changing of history.

Within the turn to praxis as the foundation and aim of theology, liberation
theology is marked by at least three new characteristics. First, theology is
known as a practical activity, characterized by its concreteness in dealing with
particular events, stories, and witnesses rather than limiting its role to the
analysis of general concepts of existence and tradition. Theology is "practical," as it is a critical and transformative reflection on the actual activity of a
Christian community and on the particular situation of its own cultural and
social context. The practical nature of theology depends upon the use of
practical reason and the nature of Christian faith as a particular praxis: thus,
reflection on the need for a new educational system or the looming apocalypse
of nuclear war is not the application of theology but part of the constitutive
activity of theology. Matthew Lamb, first to identify the method of critical
praxis correlation, summarizes the practical nature of this method:

> Common to theologians of this type is a realization that the practical and
> theoretical issues facing academics, churches, and societies can only be

met in an ongoing critical collaboration mediating the cries of the victims to those interested in transforming the structures of world and church. Both the reflex character of the relationship between theory and praxis and its question of norms involve a concomitant change (conversion) of social structures and consciousness. Such conversions—as ongoing withdrawals from bias and sin—are intrinsic to both genuine religious traditions of faith and to the realization of reason in human histories and societies.[19]

The practical nature of this method includes the three particular tasks of liberation theology as identified by Gutiérrez: the theory of a definite situation; the critique of church and society in light of the Word of God; and the projection of future possibilities in the church and in the polis. Theology is itself now a practical political activity.

Second, theology uses narrative as a basic form or structure of theology to retrieve the Christian tradition, to narrate the dangerous memories of suffering, and to effect conversion and transformation. In liberation theology the centrality of narrative is the attention to the radically historical and hermeneutical character of life and to the narrative structure of Christianity. Narrative speaks of suffering in a way that theory cannot; it matches the structure of human experience and the nature of Christian tradition. In the very telling and retelling of the stories and memories of the tradition, narrative performs; that is, it converts, informs, and changes us. Narrative demonstrates not only the new form of theology, but also the new practical activity of theology that speaks to both human existence and Christian praxis.[20]

Third, theology has a communal form as a part of Christianity's continual activity in the world. Liberation theologians insist on the importance of the theologian's own participation within a Christian community.[21] As it guides, interprets, and criticizes Christian praxis, theology is in a relationship of solidarity with those who suffer. It is a form of solidarity with the Christian tradition as it seeks to understand and interpret the Christian message in the present day. Theology has a communal form not only in its locus, tasks, and intents, but also in its content and interpretations. The communal character requires the contextualization of theology—putting theology in the language, symbols, and rituals of Christian experience in the pluralism of concrete communities that comprise contemporary Christianity.

Within the community, with the narratives and the concrete tasks of interpretation, liberation theology's method of praxis correlation consists of a practical hermeneutics. The ongoing interpretation of the tradition and the situation is, in liberation theology, itself an act of faith. Theological interpretation is not something we do and then apply but, rather, something that we are and by which we are continually transformed. The assumptions of liberation theology's practical hermeneutics are similar to those underlying the work of philosopher Hans-Georg Gadamer; for both, hermeneutics names the very nature of our being—interpreting texts and context is the activity of being human in the world.[22] In liberation theology, as with Gadamer, we are constantly in conversation: continually deciding, choosing, judging, and determining who we are and who we shall be—not as a private or an individual act, but as a public and communal activity. The paradigm shift of liberation theology is toward a method of critical praxis correlation that depends on the ongoing activity of understanding and transformation, of interpretation and appropriation, only and always in terms of historical events and situations.

THESIS 5: LIBERATION THEOLOGY'S METHOD OF CRITICAL PRAXIS CORRELATION IS, BY ITS NATURE, A FORM OF IDEOLOGY CRITIQUE

As a paradigm *shift*, liberation theology stands as a radical critique of the systematic distortions in modernity. Political theology criticizes modernity for its insidious destruction of human subjectivity by evolutionary logic. Latin American liberation theology began as a critique of the economic policies of development in third-world countries, and broadened to become a critique of the center and the margins, the rich and the poor, within the making and interpreting of history. Ideology critique marks the origins, the tasks, and the nature of liberation theology.

A curious stepchild of modernity, ideology critique considers various relations of interest, power, and belief through systematic distortions or false ideologies within the normative and legitimizing sanctions or beliefs of society. Ideology critique appeals in particular to situations of oppression, such as the poor in Latin America, or, within the first world, to distortions of historical consciousness. Theoretically formulated through various critical theories, ideology critique performs its social therapy by uncovering or revealing the distortions and moving the agent to a new future. Praxis, for ideology critique, is defined by the pursuit of freedom through the concerns of interest, knowledge, and power.

The grounds and telos of a critical theology are the solidarity of human praxis expressed either through a *transcendental argument* appealing to some universal norm or through a *contextual argument* appealing to particular social practices.[23] Liberation theology generally uses contextual arguments, appealing to properties within particular situations, such as the promise of freedom in the Enlightenment or the theme of humanization in Catholic social teaching. In its contextual appeal, liberation theology offers theological justification both for its specific ideology critiques and for its own nature as a critical theory. The relationship of ideology critique and liberation theology can be distinguished by the use of three levels: (1) ideology critique and Christian symbols, (2) Christian praxis as a critical activity, and (3) liberation theology as a critical theory.

1. *Ideology critique and Christian symbols:* Within liberation theology, theological symbols are used to break through the distortions of the present

and to anticipate a new future. The cross as a symbol of suffering is interpreted by way of the resurrection as the representation of hope and righteousness; in this symbolic identification, hope and righteousness belong to those who suffer. To take another example, redemption is a symbol that functions as the ideology critique of all ideology critique, for redemption reveals that there can be no complete realization of human freedom in history and that theories promising freedom are forever tempted to become one more form of enslavement. In liberation theology, a variety of religious symbols, narratives, and dogmas perform the function of ideology critique, ranging from the rituals and saints of popular religion to the retrieval of classical theological interpretations.

2. *Christian praxis as a critical activity:* On the second level, liberation theologians claim that Christianity is itself a critical activity, an activity forming and transforming human freedom. Míguez Bonino, for instance, in his dialogue with Marxism retrieves the radically monotheistic God and the injunction against idolatry to demonstrate the iconoclastic nature of faith. Christianity is far more critical than Marxism, Míguez Bonino argues, for the nature of Christian activity is the opposition of any and all idolatry; the proclamation of Christianity is inherently against oppression and injustice: "the Bible does not merely support the contention that religion becomes an excuse for injustice. It announces God's active purpose to overturn and destroy such idolatrous manipulation of his gifts. As a matter of fact, one of the permanent motifs in the biblical story is God's judgment against the perverse and inhuman distortions of the signs of God's humanizing mercy and righteousness."[24] Christian praxis is, for liberation theology, an activity of human freedom representing the identity of the subject in history. Religious experience is located in anticipatory freedom as the making, the doing, and the reproducing of history. As theology employs specific symbols for ideology critique, so theology reflects on Christian praxis that is engaged in the struggle for freedom, that is both enlightenment and emancipation, mediated in relation to redemption.

3. *Liberation theology as a critical theory:* On the third and final level, theology is itself a form of critical theory; on this level the paradigm shift of liberation theology includes the nature as well as the purpose of its method. Theology does not just incidentally bring about freedom because it reflects on certain symbols or doctrines in certain ways; theology does not necessarily *result* in freedom because it offers theoretical arguments as to the nature of freedom. As a form of social and religious therapy, theology anticipates freedom, calling into question the way things are, seeking out distortions, provoking a new way of being and doing in history. As part of its practical nature, theology is inherently involved with emancipation and enlightenment, and its form must be critical: uncovering, revealing, healing, and enlightening.

Consequently, ideology critique is not just a function of liberation theology, but is also part of the nature of liberation theology; somewhat rephrased, liberation theology does not just use some critical theory—it becomes a critical theory.[25] Liberation theology *claims to be a theory of freedom*, to uncover distortions of consciousnesss and systems of oppression and to anticipate new ways of being human. Raymond Geuss's definition of a critical theory could be descriptive of liberation theology: "a critical theory, then, is a reflective theory which gives agents a kind of knowledge inherently productive of enlightenment and emancipation."[26] Liberation theology attempts to correct or to clarify the knowledge of persons about their own interests and needs. As a critical theory, liberation theology also attempts to bring about emancipation, criticizing oppressive and destructive systems and freeing persons from coercive situations.[27]

As a critical theory, liberation theology is a persuasive demonstration of freedom through the critical interpretation of past, present, and future. Liberation theology's critical theory has, thus far, been a rhetoric of oppositions and contradictions—the poor vs. the rich; the nonperson vs. the person; messianic Christianity vs. bourgeois religion. Using aphorisms, stories, and examples, it interrupts, converts, and anticipates within the very act of "doing" theology, as seen in Gutiérrez's rhetoric: "wanted: a therapy for historical amnesia," or in Metz's: "the shortest definition of religion: interruption."[28] Both notions criticize the form and content of previous interpretations and anticipate new ways of interpreting and new interpretations. Liberation theology as a critical theory arises out of Christian praxis, its contents determined by the relations of context and text, and its future open to the possibilities of history.

THESIS 6: LIBERATION THEOLOGY MUST DEVELOP AN ADEQUATE SOCIAL THEORY TO ATTEND TO THE FULL MEANING OF PRAXIS

Thus far we have interpreted the method of liberation theology through its turn to praxis as including both a practical hermeneutics and a critical theory. With this final thesis we shall argue that liberation theology must now develop a social theory, that is, a new way of conceiving human praxis that considers an anthropology of human agency and social structures. In this social theory, neither the subject nor the society can be privileged, but must be brought together in order to understand the production and reproduction of social practices. The problem can be stated in the following question: Is ideology critique and practical hermeneutics, as developed, adequate to the full demands of the turn to praxis? Conversely, does praxis not demand an adequate social theory internal to the nature of theology? We can explore the problem by looking at the function of the term "praxis" in two theologians, Gustavo Gutiérrez and Johann Baptist Metz.[29]

For Gutiérrez, praxis is first used as a reading of modern history to distinguish between historical praxis and liberating praxis. Historical praxis, for Gutiérrez, is characterized by humanity's manipulation of historical and natural forces. The success of modernity has depended upon the massive contradictions between the poor nonperson and the rich person. Liberating praxis is that activity in recent Latin American history that struggles against the distortions of oppression and repression that characterize historical praxis.

Gutiérrez believes that a new stage of history is appearing, a stage due to the inevitable reality of class conflict.[30] The difference between historical praxis and liberating praxis is twofold: (1) the agent of liberating praxis is the poor nonperson who is in conflict with the rich person, and (2) the new stage of history comes about through the realization of the consciousness of the oppressed and through the movement of liberating praxis. Both characteristics place Gutiérrez's use of the term "praxis" within the broad tradition of humanism, and, more particularly, within Marxist appeals to the primacy of class conflict. Gutiérrez does not claim, in his interpretation of liberating praxis, that social structures are changing or that they have the potential for change but, rather, that the poor are breaking into history—the poor are freeing themselves from oppressive ideologies and are anticipating new ways of being human. But it is difficult to determine precisely what (rather than who) is meant by class conflict. Though Gutiérrez is influenced by dependency theory, his notion of class conflict is far more than a sociological or economic analysis. Rather, the notion of class conflict appears as a total division—economic, political, cultural, even historical. Class conflict becomes a key to the philosophy of history or, in Gutiérrez's language, a rereading and remaking of history. As it becomes a philosophy of history, it ceases to be connected, in Gutiérrez's works, with structural analysis. As a call for conscientization, class conflict demands that the poor educate themselves to change the present situation. As the symbol of the old stage of history giving rise to the new, the new is inevitable whether or not the poor realize a higher level of consciousness. But, whichever meaning may be preferred, neither suggests an analysis of the relation of human agency and social structures nor indicates a model of transformation for the new stage of liberating praxis. As an ideology critique, class conflict functions as a call for conscientization and as a description of history; it does not entail the investigation or transformation of the polis.

Parallel to the problem of analyzing class conflict runs the connection of class conflict and the state in Gutiérrez's work. For Gutiérrez, class conflict is never tied to a particular analysis of the role and the nature of the state.[31] While there is a powerful argument as to the universality of the poor, it seems impossible to offer a real critique and strategy without the analysis of major institutional structures, especially those of the state. In contemporary history *see Comblin* the state has taken on powers of nationalism and militarism that may not be connected directly to particular class divisions. Both of these problems can be located between Gutiérrez's use of ideology critique and the demands of praxis in his theology. Take, for instance, Gutiérrez's identification of the tasks of theology: theology is to criticize the church and society in light of the Word of God, to be a theory of a definite praxis, and to project future possibilities within the present situation. Though theology can certainly do the first task, given Gutiérrez's actual use of liberating praxis vs. historical praxis, theology cannot be a theory of praxis or anticipate new possibilities without an adequate social theory to relate anthropology (the conscientization of the poor) and history (the new stage of liberating praxis) to social structures. Gutiérrez has, as yet, failed to make the essential link between human consciousness and institutional structures within his own philosophy of history.

Metz's use of praxis is located within a rather searing critique of modern, rationalized society characterized by an evolutionary logic that privatizes tradition, cultural values, and religion. If Gutiérrez's critique follows a Marxist interpretation of class conflict, Metz's critique follows a Weberian-Frankfurt School interpretation of means-end rationality and the inevitablility of an iron-cage society. Though Gutiérrez may readily appeal to the obvious suffering of the poor, Metz must, in the steps of the Frankfurt School, first reveal that subjects are suffering in modernity. To counter the evolutionary logic that he believes creates the systematic forgetfulness of human subjectivity, Metz turns to what the logic suppresses, the activity of suffering.

For Metz, praxis functions in reference to the distortion of historical consciousness through evolutionary logic. Metz's critical concern is the epistemic distortion of human subjectivity in modernity. As in any good critical theory, once the distortion is uncovered, emancipation must be anticipated, and thus Metz calls for an anthropological revolution. The problems of Metz's critique are located in the adequacy of his interpretation of modernity and the possibilities for transformation of historical consciousness and society. Against Metz's portrayal of the iron cage of modernity one must balance the process of individual rights in modernity. Metz can discount these as bourgeois, but to do that he must depend on a very selective reading of the history of political, institutional, and civil freedoms of modern Western societies. Likewise, the separation between the private and the public is not as complete as Metz judges: even in nations such as the United States, with the formal separation of church and state, the public influence of religion has not been destroyed. Both the developing process of rights and the pervasive role of religion have, at least sometimes, functioned as an antidote to the evolutionary logic that Metz identifies.[32]

Metz's critical interpretation not only denies the complexity of modern society, but also makes the projection of new possibilities highly problematic in theological method. Iron-cage theories tend, as did Weber's, to deny any resources or foundation for change, for once the subject and the social system reach the more advanced stages of rationalization, it is extremely difficult to press claims for enlightenment or emancipation. This problem can be illustrated by Metz's demand for a new form of politics, which Metz hopes can be a new form of imagination. Metz argues that this imaginative vision must be kept separate from the planning of the state so that the concrete situation of life will not be dissolved into technical planning and production; thus Metz refuses to connect his transformative vision with any social conditions for the possibility of change. Working from an ideology critique that forgets the struggle of human rights, that ignores the reproductive character of social systems, and that never considers a structural analysis of institutions, Metz has no place to go but to seek some radically alternative vision. While the impulse of religious traditions may be to provide alternative vision, to dissociate these from the structural conditions of life is both naïve and inadequate to the demands of praxis, especially social praxis, as the foundation and aim of theology.

If theology is to be grounded in praxis, and praxis is distorted in the manner so powerfully shown by Metz, theology must develop a social theory that allows politics to be more than an alternative vision for the few. Though historical consciousness may be distorted and in danger of extinction, given the social anthropology of Metz's practical, fundamental theology, human consciousness is always constitutive of and constituted by social structures. If Metz remains true to his *social* anthropology, his practical, fundamental theology must reformulate its ideology critique and its hermeneutics through a theory of social praxis—an understanding of the interrelatedness of human agency and social structures. Though narrative and dangerous memories may adequately constitute hermeneutics and ideology critique as correlated to human existence and Christianity, both human subjects and Christianity also exist through and contribute to social systems. Human existence, for example, may well have a narrative structure—recalling the past in anticipation of the future as the grounds of freedom. But human existence, given Metz's own social anthropology, also has a social structure—gaining its freedom and identity through its participation in social systems. Praxis for Metz, as for Gutiérrez, promises more than it delivers, demands more than it offers.

The diagnosis is simple: praxis, in liberation theology, has been formulated through ideology critiques that displace the interrelations between human agency and social structures. In its use of ideology critique, liberation theology attends to the consciousness of the "social" subject within a philosophy of history that ignores the related structures of situated societies. To ignore these interrelations dictates that the critique will be inadequate and impotent, and that models of transformation will have to be content to envision new forms of consciousness and not new forms of sociopolitical existence. This is not to deny the importance and the necessity of Gutiérrez's and Metz's critiques, but simply to suggest that given their own demands of praxis, a social theory must be developed *within* the theological method of liberation theology. Having located both anthropology and Christianity in the praxis of the polis, liberation theology must now include a social theory adequate to the demands of sociopolitical existence. There are three equally valid arguments for this claim: first, if existence is political, intersubjective, and future-oriented, we must interpret human existence in terms of the interrelations of human agency and social structure. Second, if Christian theology mediates liberation and salvation, it must work with the theories and activities of human agents *and* social structures. Third, ideology critique demands its own transformation, for its therapeutic nature requires actual change as well as new understanding, and only an adequate social theory can allow the projection of possibilities for change in both human agency and social structures.

An adequate social theory for liberation theology might well follow Marx's dictum that "man" makes history, but not in circumstances of his own choosing, for any critical interpretation of praxis must today bring together human action and structural explanation. Praxis means that human action is always a situated practice, both temporal and social, characterized not only by knowledge—discursive, practical, and unconscious—but also by capability, the ability to determine that which could be otherwise.[33] Anthony Giddens's model of structuration provides one possibility of such a social theory.[34] For Giddens, agents exist through practices, structures exist through rules and principles, but rules and practices always exist in conjunction with each other through systems. Any reflection on praxis, in this social theory, must take account of the interdependence of human agency and social systems through what Giddens calls the duality of structure, the social nature of praxis as always both medium and outcome of the practices that constitute the system: "the structural properties of social systems do not exist outside of action but are chronically implicated in its production and reproduction."[35] Stressing the recursive nature of any theory of praxis, Giddens's social theory emphasizes both change and duration in praxis and considers the time-space relation inherent in all social interactions. Such a theory may well offer the possibility of analyzing praxis more adequately, of formulating possibilities of change within the duration of social systems, and thus in turn the "doing of theology" in a new way. Whether or not liberation theology utilizes Giddens's model of structuration or some other model of social theory, the necessity remains: the turn to praxis demands a reformulation of practical hermeneutics and ideology critique through an adequate social theory within the nature and method of theological reflection.

9

Conclusion

In conclusion, we might question the central thesis of this book—that liberation theology is a new paradigm—by asking if liberation theology is really so different from modern theology. Certainly, liberation theology is, in part, constituted as a radical critique of modern theology; it accuses modern theology of privileging the bourgeois subject, of utilizing reifying methods of reflection, of misinterpreting Christian tradition, and of legitimizing modernity's barbarism. As a counter to these systematic distortions, liberation theology claims to be a new way of understanding human existence, of interpreting Christian witness, and of formulating theological reflection. But the point of our question is neither simply to repeat the critiques nor merely to underline the claims of liberation theology, but to ask if between those critiques and claims, there lies a substantial departure from modern theology.

One answer has to be no, for liberation theology continues—albeit in a radically reformulated manner—the fundamental nature of modern theology. We can defend this answer by identifying the basic assumptions of modern theology and by demonstrating liberation theology's continuity with these assumptions. For this purpose we have to limit ourselves to six assumptions, the first three of which govern modern theology's assent to modernity, the last three of which dictate the understanding of modern religious experience: (1) the human subject is a meaning-seeker; (2) the human subject must be brought to higher consciousness; (3) history and nature are both characterized by the interrelation of cause and effect; (4) faith is located in personal experience and neither contradicts nor is reducible to scientific or historical knowledge; (5) tradition itself demands continual reinterpretation and change; (6) theology has an interpretive role, mediating the relationship of human existence and Christian tradition. Within modern theology, liberal and neo-orthodox theology gave rise to quite different expressions of these common assumptions. For instance, in liberalism the human subject found meaning in the progress of history; in neo-orthodoxy the human subject sought meaning outside of history. To take another example, liberal theology anticipated higher

149

consciousness through intellectual and moral knowledge; neo-orthodoxy explored higher consciousness in personal, existential reflection.

It certainly can be argued that these assumptions continue in liberation theology. Liberation theology believes as fervently as liberal theology that humanity must find meaning in history, but, like neo-orthodoxy, liberation theology also finds history deeply troubled. Liberation theology continues modern anthropology's project of higher consciousness, but intends this "new" consciousness to uncover coercion and distortion, to be aimed at political freedom and historical self-determination, and to be arrived at through conscientization in basic Christian communities, by the participation in some form of social therapy, or through the use of some form of critical theory. In this way, the human subject can affect the causal relations of history and nature understood now in a radically social sense as rational, historically determined, and open to change.

Within the assumptions governing the understanding of modern religious experience, the continuity through reformulation of liberation theology with modern theology also continues. Liberation theology locates faith in "personal" experience, but the personal is now properly within the community and experience is reinterpreted as activity. Theology relies upon "modern" knowledge, especially the social sciences, to aid in guidance of praxis, although theological reflection cannot be reduced to systemic analysis. As much as either liberalism or neo-orthodoxy, liberation theology realizes that tradition demands its own continual reinterpretation and, hence, argues that it is the most appropriate representation of Christianity. Indeed, liberation theology continues the interpretive role of modern theology: theology mediates the relation of tradition and existence, interpreting the meaning of existence in light of tradition and vice versa.

In sum, we might say that liberation theology is as anthropocentric as most of the rest of modern theology: Christianity is interpreted and lived in relation to the human subject. Obviously liberation theology is also related to modern theology by its sources; the philosophical, historical, and socioscientific resources that are used by liberation theology are modern and Western resources. Even the liberation theologians claim that Marxism—the source for which they offer an apologetic defense—is a form of modern humanism. Indeed, some liberation theologians forthrightly claim that they are a response to the second challenge of the Enlightenment, the challenge to change history. This claim leads one to wonder if liberation theology is not really the *true* inheritor of the Enlightenment tradition of modern theology.

But these arguments and this answer are not fully convincing. One must also answer the question "is liberation theology really different from modern theology?" with a resounding yes. With this answer, we must argue that liberation theology is a new paradigm shift—a new locus for theology, a new set of questions, a new way of ordering issues, and the inclusion of new categories and new metaphors for interpretation. We can begin the defense for this answer with the most obvious and perhaps strongest reason for liberation theology's uniqueness: liberation theology asks a quite different question from that of modern theology, the question of massive public suffering. For this logos of the Theos, suffering—*historical, human suffering*—is the focus of attention. As we have tried to portray repeatedly in this text, suffering—in liberation theology—confronts and disrupts human existence with the hunger of innocent children, the hopelessness of the poor, the marginalization of the oppressed, the extermination of the "other," and the agony of the dispossessed and despised of the earth. Suffering, according to liberation theology, is the representative experience of being human for the masses of nonpersons on the fringes or outside of modern history. Such suffering ruptures our ideologies and illusions about progress and security, revealing to us that for the majority of our fellow human beings "progress" and "history" consist of a long, dark night of tragic terror. Liberation theology stands within this rupture of suffering and does the traditional work of theology—it speaks of God. And in this question of suffering and this speaking of God, a new paradigm of theology is formed. For liberation theology risks a wager that only by standing with those who suffer—the poor and the oppressed, the living and the dead—shall we see the reality of human existence through their eyes and experience in their suffering a God of grace, of hope, of love. With this wager, liberation theology is radically different from modern theology. Liberal theologians experienced God in the progress of history; neo-orthodox theologians experienced God in the existential event of encounter; liberation theologians experience God in solidarity with those who suffer. Suffering, in sum, relocates theology—faith seeks understanding in the midst of the anguish of history.

The second reason liberation theology is a new paradigm of theology is its orientation toward transformation rather than understanding as the reconciliation of human existence and reality. Indeed, the work of Metz demonstrates that he entered a new theological paradigm as he recognized the necessity of transformation. Transformation depends on two essential points: (1) suffering demands transformation, and (2) human existence is oriented toward transformation. The first demand maintains that transformation of the causes of suffering is the urgent necessity of the moment, and the second demand discloses that transformation is central to the ontological structure of human existence. Though liberation theology has, thus far, given most of its attention to the first demand, it nevertheless assumes the second. Indeed, the second demand demonstrates one essential agreement between liberation theology and the philosophy of Marx, namely, that life implies anticipation, newness, transformation, change, reproduction. Human subjects are not simply meaning-seekers, hoping to reconcile themselves to the universe by understanding, but meaning-makers, determining and deciding their activities within the historical situatedness of the polis.[1]

Together the question of suffering and the reality of transformation lead to the third reason whereby liberation theology differs from modern theology: the emphasis on praxis. We have explored this emphasis through liberation theology's anthropology of praxis—a new understanding of human existence through the categories of the political nature, the intersubjective character, and the anticipatory freedom of human existence. With this third reason, liberation theology is very much a situated theology. As we have observed at numerous points—without being able to go into a thorough discussion—much contemporary reflection is also concerned with the centrality of praxis. Within liberation theology and other forms of contemporary reflection there are different approaches to praxis: for some it necessitates the turn to narrative, for others it forces the turn to specific ideology critique, while for still others it entails the pragmatics of conversation. The claim in contemporary reflection and in liberation theology is twofold: life is fundamentally practical, and the practical needs of the day call for discernment, judgment, and decision within the polis. Theory, even practical theory, must now take its role in the polis. The writing of books—even the study of history of science—is a political activity, and those whose vocation it is to study must now be responsible to the polis in which they participate as scholars and as human beings.[2]

Liberation theology thus shares much in common with "practical reason"; but it is also a new expression of Christian experience and a new interpretation of Christian tradition. In liberation theology, Christianity is located within the practical activity of human existence and as a specific form of praxis. Christians, as Gutiérrez repeatedly emphasizes, experience God in a praxis of solidarity with the poor that anticipates new ways of becoming human. Christianity is expressed as a praxis of solidarity, a way of following Christ by the representation of the freedom and the preciousness of created existence. The nature of Christianity as an activity is not, as is sometimes claimed, the reduction of Christian faith to social action, for in the relocation of liberation theology the activity of Christianity is both mystical and political, a way of imitating Christ in the identification of suffering and hope.

Within this enactment of Christ in the world, liberation theologians offer a quite new interpretation of Christian tradition—an interpretation demanded, of course, by the present engagement of tradition and existence. Central to this interpretation is the metaphor of liberation: God is liberator in the mediation of liberation and salvation, history is oriented toward the future in liberating praxis, grace is liberation into ways of living differently. Like any theology, liberation theology favors certain Scriptures—Matthew 25, Luke 4, 1 John, the exodus accounts, and the prophets. Central to its retrieval and reinterpretation is the belief that Christianity represents human freedom and the sanctity of created existence in history, or, as Míguez Bonino might say, Christians obey God in liberating solidarity with the poor. Christian tradition represents, as it follows Christ, the gift and the task of freedom.

The final reason is a properly theological reason: liberation theology is a different understanding of theological reflection. Its reliance on practical reason, its intent to *guide* Christian praxis, its emphasis on narrative, memories, and the social sciences—all make this theology look different from its modern predecessors. We have suggested that one way to approach this new way of doing theology is to consider its combination—somewhat and some-

times uneven—of three methodological approaches. First, theology is a practical hermeneutics—the ongoing appropriation of Christian tradition and human existence. Theology is the conversation that we are in, in the constant play
of the narrative structure of human existence and the narratives of tradition
from which we receive our freedom and project our future possibilities.
Second, theology is a critical theory—a theory of emancipation and enlightenment concerned with the ideological distortions and systematic oppressions of
all human beings. Theology helps to uncover distortions, to reveal illusions, to
form new consciousness, and to anticipate new ways of being human. Third,
theology claims to be a social theory—a theory of a definite praxis. Liberation
theology has, at least in this writer's judgment, emphasized an ideology critique
of historical consciousness and of a philosophy of history that often displaces
the structural realities of human existence. Though it is clear in the ideology
critiques of liberation theologians that social systems *oppress* the human
subject, it is not equally obvious how systems can or will *enable* or structure
human freedom. In this claim, theology must study the interrelation of human
activity and social structure; it must, in other words, carry through on its own
social anthropology.

Liberation theology, in sum, both continues and radically departs from
modern theology. As a continuation, liberation theology represents a radical
engagement of Christianity with the world, with the intent to represent human
freedom and God's gratuitous activity in the questions and issues of the day. As
a radically new paradigm and departure from modern theology, liberation
theology reflects and guides a Christianity that is identified with those who
suffer, that represents a freedom of transformation, and that proclaims a God
whose love frees us for justice and faith. Modern theology is the heritage of
liberation theology, and from it liberation theologians must both distance
themselves and return to draw the resources and visions of a project of human
freedom. Liberation theology's journey is, however, radically its own: a journey with the despised and dispossessed of history; a journey dependent upon a
wager of faith seeking understanding in the identification of suffering and
hope with a God who creates, redeems, and liberates all creation.

Notes

INTRODUCTION

1. Matthew Lamb, *Solidarity with Victims: Toward a Theology of Social Transformation* (New York: Crossroad Publishing Co., 1982), p. 3.

2. Terrence Des Pres, *The Survivor: An Anatomy of Life in the Death Camps* (London: Oxford University Press, 1976), p. 49.

3. Like all theology, liberation theology is a situated theology, formulating its center and focus through its participation in history. As Paul Tillich observed, Christian theology finds its material norm through its own participation in a particular period, see Paul Tillich, *Systematic Theology*, 3 vols. (Chicago, Ill.: University of Chicago Press, 1951), 1:47–52. To address the issues of the day is the purpose of theology; to dialogue with current forms of reflection is the nature of theology. Christologically this means that theology is an ongoing interpretation of Christianity; logically this necessitates that the criteria and norms for theology are, in part, constituted through human experience.

4. I am employing the language of "paradigm" and "paradigm shift" in its popular usage to identify a shift in basic assumptions, categories, and the ordering of issues in frameworks of interpretation. The notion of paradigm shifts became popular with the widely read work of Thomas Kuhn, *The Structure of Scientific Revolutions,* 2nd ed. enl. (Chicago, Ill.: University of Chicago Press, 1970). For a good introduction to the discussion of paradigms and paradigm shifts, see Richard J. Bernstein, *Beyond Objectivism and Relativism: Science, Hermeneutics and Praxis* (Philadelphia: University of Pennsylvania Press, 1983). For a discussion on the notion of paradigms in theology, see Sallie McFague, *Metaphorical Theology: Models of God in Religious Language* (Philadelphia, Pa.: Fortress Press, 1982).

5. For an excellent introduction to the differences between Latin American liberation theology and German political theology, see Francis Fiorenza, "Liberation Theology and Political Theology," in *Liberation, Revolution and Freedom: Theological Perspectives,* ed. Thomas F. McFadden (New York: Seabury Press, 1975), pp. 3–29.

6. Latin American liberation theologians are very critical of German political theologians for being content to reflect only theoretically on praxis. See Gustavo Gutiérrez, *A Theology of Liberation: History, Politics and Salvation,* ed. and trans. Sister Caridad Inda and John Eagleson (Maryknoll, N.Y.: Orbis Books, 1973), pp. 220–25; Hugo Assmann, *Theology for a Nomad Church,* trans. Paul Burns (Maryknoll, N.Y.: Orbis Books, 1976), p. 92; and José Comblin, *The Church and the National Security State* (Maryknoll, N.Y.: Orbis Books, 1979), p. 39.

7. For one critical review of liberation theology that emphasizes the similarities in sources and common project, see Jürgen Moltmann, "An Open Letter to José Míguez Bonino," in *Mission Trends No. 4: Liberation Theologies in North America and Europe,* ed. Gerald Anderson and Thomas R. Stransky (New York: Paulist Press;

Grand Rapids, Mich.: Eerdmans Publishing Co., 1979), pp. 59–69.
8. Alfredo Fierro, *The Militant Gospel: A Critical Introduction to Political Theologies*, trans. John Drury (Maryknoll, N.Y.: Orbis Books, 1977), p. 18.

1. LATIN AMERICAN LIBERATION THEOLOGY

1. Ignacio Castuera, "The Theology and Practice of Liberation in the Mexican American Context," *Perkins School of Theology Journal* 29 (Fall 1975):4.
2. Segundo Galilea, "Liberation Theology and New Tasks Facing Christians," in *Frontiers of Theology in Latin America*, ed. Rosino Gibellini, trans. John Drury (Maryknoll, N.Y.: Orbis Books, 1974), p. 167.
3. José Míguez Bonino, *Doing Theology in a Revolutionary Situation* (Philadelphia, Pa.: Fortress Press, 1975), pp. 22–23.
4. Arthur F. McGovern, *Marxism: An American Christian Perspective* (Maryknoll, N.Y.: Orbis Books, 1981), p. 173.
5. Portugal also settled the New World, having secured from the papacy the right to colonize and evangelize the lands it conquered. Though there are significant differences between Portugal's process of colonization and that of Spain's, the resulting colonial pact produced the same effect. Because of the lack of space, this book will trace only the history of Spanish colonization.
6. Míguez Bonino, *Doing Theology in a Revolutionary Situation*, p. 5.
7. George Pendle, *A History of Latin America* (New York: Penguin Books, 1963), p. 39.
8. Hubert Herring, *A History of Latin America from the Beginnings to the Present* (New York: Alfred A. Knopf, 1961), pp. 129–34.
9. Pendle, *A History of Latin America*, pp. 56–63; and Enrique D. Dussel, *A History of the Church in Latin America: Colonialism to Liberation (1492–1979)*, trans. Alan Neely (Grand Rapids, Mich.: Eerdmans Publishing Co., 1981), pp. 64–68.
10. Gustavo Gutiérrez and Richard Shaull, *Liberation and Change*, ed. Ronald H. Stone (Atlanta, Ga.: John Knox Press, 1977), p. 61.
11. Ibid., p. 62. See also Dussel, *A History of the Church in Latin America*, pp. 47–48.
12. Pendle, *A History of Latin America*, p. 93. Portugal's ruling house fled to Brazil in 1807 to escape Napoleon. In 1816 Don João became the king of two countries, Brazil and Portugal, leaving Brazil in 1821. In 1822 his son Pedro led the move to independence.
13. Suzanne C. Toton, *World Hunger: The Responsibility of Christian Education* (Maryknoll, N.Y.: Orbis Books, 1982), pp. 21–22.
14. Frederick B. Pike, *The Conflict between Church and State in Latin America* (New York: Alfred A. Knopf, 1964), pp. 101–8.
15. J. Andrew Kirk, *Liberation Theology: An Evangelical View from the Third World* (Atlanta, Ga.: John Knox Press, 1979), p. 6.
16. Herbert L. Matthews, "Diplomatic Relations," in *The United States and Latin America*, The American Assembly, Columbia University, 1959, ed. Herbert L. Matthews (New York: Columbia University Press, 1959), pp. 144–47.
17. Gustavo Gutiérrez, *A Theology of Liberation*, trans. and ed. Sister Caridad Inda and John Eagleson (Maryknoll, N.Y.: Orbis Books, 1973), pp. 56–58.
18. Alfredo Fierro, *The Militant Gospel*, trans. John Drury (Maryknoll, N.Y.: Orbis Books, 1977), p. 55.
19. Dussel, *A History of the Church in Latin America*, pp. 106–16.
20. Walt W. Rostow, *The Stages of Economic Growth: A Non-Communist Manifesto* (Cambridge, England: Cambridge University Press, 1960).
21. For a powerful illustration of this critique, see Penny Lernoux, *The Cry of the*

People: The Struggle for Human Rights in Latin America—The Catholic Church in Conflict with U.S. Policy (New York: Penguin Books, 1980).

22. See Gary MacEoin, *Revolution Next Door: Latin America in the 1970's* (New York: Holt, Rinehart & Winston, 1971).

23. José Comblin, *The Church and the National Security State* (Maryknoll, N.Y.: Orbis Books, 1979), p. 54.

24. Robert Calvo, "The Church and the Doctrine of National Security," in *Churches and Politics in Latin America,* ed. Daniel H. Levine (Beverly Hills, Calif.: Sage Publications, 1979), pp. 134-54.

25. Cited in McGovern, *Marxism: An American Christian Perspective,* p. 92.

26. Joseph Gremillion, ed., *The Gospel of Peace and Justice: Catholic Social Teaching since Pope John* (Maryknoll, N.Y.: Orbis Books, 1976), p. 1.

27. Ibid., pp. 143-200.

28. Renato Poblete, "From Medellín to Puebla," in *Churches and Politics in Latin America,* ed. Daniel H. Levine, p. 41.

29. Cited in Gremillion, *The Gospel of Peace and Justice,* p. 452.

30. Phillip Berryman, "What Happened at Puebla," in *Churches and Politics in Latin America,* ed. Daniel H. Levine, p. 78.

31. T. S. Montgomery, "Latin American Evangelicals," in *Churches and Politics in Latin America,* ed. Daniel H. Levine, p. 93. See also Orlando E. Costas, *Theology of the Crossroads in Contemporary Latin America: Missiology in Mainline Protestantism: 1969-1974* (Amsterdam: Rodopoi, 1976).

32. For a good introduction to Marxism, see Louis K. Dupre, *The Philosophical Foundations of Marxism* (New York: Harcourt, Brace & World, 1966); Sidney Hook, *From Hegel to Marx* (New York: Humanities Press, 1950); George Lichtheim, *From Marx to Hegel* (New York: Herder & Herder, 1971); and Nicholas Lobkowicz, ed., *Marx and the Western World* (South Bend, Ind.: University of Notre Dame Press, 1967).

33. Arthur McGovern warns against the facile assumption that positions critical of development are necessarily Marxist *(Marxism: An American Christian Perspective,* pp. 183-84).

34. Among liberation theologians there are some substantial changes in the use of Marxist theory in theology. To take a specific example, in Gutiérrez's *A Theology of Liberation,* the privileged option for the poor was formulated first through a Marxist theory of class conflict and then expressed in a spirituality of poverty. In his recent collection of essays, *The Power of the Poor in History: Selected Writings,* trans. Robert R. Barr (Maryknoll, N.Y.: Orbis Books, 1983), the option for the poor is a theological argument—God chooses to be on the side of the poor—that is then mediated through sociopolitical categories, including the Marxist category of class conflict.

35. *Underdevelopment and Development: The Third World Today,* ed. Henry Bernstein (Middlesex, England: Penguin Books, 1973).

36. See Gutiérrez's criticism of developmentalism in *Theology of Liberation,* pp. 84-92; and Míguez Bonino's criticism of development in *Doing Theology in a Revolutionary Situation,* pp. 24-36.

37. Fernando Henrique Cardoso and Enzo Falleto, *Dependencia y desarrollo en América Latina: ensayo de interpretación sociológica* (Mexico City: Siglo Veintiuno, 1969), p. 24.

38. Míguez Bonino summarizes the "history" of dependence: "This dependence is not a new fact; the Latin American countries came into 'universal' history (the history of the West) as dependent entities under the Spanish colonization, and were assigned a place in that world: that of providing resources for Spain (mainly gold and silver, then some agricultural products) in the trade-capitalism which then predominated. When capitalism developed in the Northern nations into other states: industrial and then consumer capitalism, the role of the dependent nations also changed: they were destined to provide raw materials and agricultural products first and cheap

labor and markets later" (*Doing Theology in a Revolutionary Situation,* p. 27).

39. For a criticism of Latin American liberation theology's failure to justify its use of Marxist social sciences, see John Coleman, "A Political Theology for America," in his *An American Strategic Theology* (New York: Paulist Press, 1982), pp. 280–81.

40. Karl Marx, "The German Ideology," *The Marx-Engels Reader,* ed. Robert C. Tucker (New York: W. W. Norton, 1972), p. 157.

41. Ibid., p. 157. See also Richard J. Bernstein, *Praxis and Action: Contemporary Philosophies of Human Activity* (Philadelphia: University of Pennsylvania Press, 1971), pp. 11–83.

42. Gutiérrez, *Theology of Liberation,* p. 9.

43. Míguez Bonino is especially interested in Marx's notion of the human subject as "worker"; see *Doing Theology in a Revolutionary Situation,* pp. 108–9.

44. For one critical discussion between Marxist theory and Christian theology, see José Míguez Bonino, *Christians and Marxists: The Mutual Challenge to Revolution* (Grand Rapids, Mich.: Eerdmans Publishing Co., 1976); see also Juan Luis Segundo, *Faith and Ideologies,* trans. John Drury (Maryknoll, N.Y.: Orbis Books; Melbourne: Dove Communications; London: Sheed & Ward, 1984), pp. 177–247.

45. Juan Luis Segundo, "Capitalism versus Socialism: Crux Theologica," in *Frontiers of Theology in Latin America,* ed. Rosino Gibellini, trans. John Drury (Maryknoll, N.Y.: Orbis Books, 1979), p. 249.

46. Gutiérrez, *Theology of Liberation,* p. 33.

47. Míguez Bonino summarizes the criticism of political theology by liberation theologians in his discussion of Jürgen Moltmann's work: "but is it possible to claim a solidarity with the poor and to hover about right and left as if that choice did not have anything to do with the matter?" (*Doing Theology in a Revolutionary Situation,* p. 148).

48. Gutiérrez, *Theology of Liberation,* p. 261.

49. See Thomas C. Bruneau, *The Church in Brazil: The Politics of Religion* (Austin: University of Texas Press, 1982); see also *The Challenge of Basic Christian Communities: Papers from the International Ecumenical Congress of Theology,* ed. Sergio Torres and John Eagleson, trans. John Drury (Maryknoll, N.Y.: Orbis Books, 1981).

50. Paulo Freire, *Pedagogy of the Oppressed,* trans. Myra Bergman Ramos (New York: Herder & Herder, 1970).

51. Gustavo Gutiérrez, "The Irruption of the Poor in Latin America and the Christian Communities," in *The Challenge of Basic Christian Communities: Papers from the International Ecumenical Congress of Theology,* ed. Sergio Torres and John Eagleson, p. 118.

52. English citations of the Puebla text come from *Puebla and Beyond,* ed. John Eagleson and Philip Scharper (Maryknoll, N.Y.: Orbis Books, 1979), par. 1134.

53. Ibid., par. 31.

54. Gutiérrez, "Irruption of the Poor in Latin America and the Christian Communities," pp. 108–12.

55. Gutiérrez, *Power of the Poor in History,* p. 129.

56. Galilea, "Liberation Theology and New Tasks Facing Christians," p. 179.

57. Kirk, *Liberation Theology,* p. 111.

58. For Latin American christologies of liberation, see Leonardo Boff, *Jesus Christ Liberator* (Maryknoll, N.Y.: Orbis Books, 1978); Jon Sobrino, *Christology at the Crossroads: A Latin American Approach,* trans. John Drury (Maryknoll, N.Y.: Orbis Books, 1978); and José Míguez Bonino, ed., *Faces of Jesus: Latin American Christologies,* trans. Robert R. Barr (Maryknoll, N.Y.: Orbis Books, 1984).

59. Comblin, *Church and National Security,* pp. 214–24.

60. Ronaldo Muñoz, "Ecclesiology in Latin America," in *The Challenge of Basic Christian Communities: Papers from the International Ecumenical Congress of Theology,* ed. Sergio Torres and John Eagleson, p. 157.

61. Míguez Bonino, *Doing Theology in a Revolutionary Situation,* p. 81.
62. Jon Sobrino, "Theological Understanding in European and Latin American Theology," in his *The True Church and the Poor,* trans. Matthew J. O'Connell (Maryknoll, N.Y.: Orbis Books, 1984), p. 12.
63. Ibid.
64. Ibid., p. 20.

2. POLITICAL THEOLOGY

1. Alfredo Fierro, *The Militant Gospel,* trans. John Drury (Maryknoll, N.Y.: Orbis Books, 1977), pp. 3-47.
2. For a good introduction to the broad and diverse historical period called "modernity," see Franklin L. Baumer, *Modern European Thought: Continuity and Change in Ideas, 1600-1950* (New York: Macmillan, 1977).
3. Johann Baptist Metz, *Theology of the World,* trans. William Glen-Doepel (New York: Seabury Press, 1969), p. 57.
4. Ernst Troeltsch *Gesammelte Schriften,* 2 vols. (Tübingen: J. C. Mohr, 1913), 2:729-53; see also Van. A. Harvey, *The Historian and the Believer: The Morality of Historical Knowledge and Christian Belief* (Philadelphia, Pa.: Westminster Press, 1966), pp. 14-15.
5. Harvey, *The Historian and the Believer,* pp. 102-25.
6. For a good introduction to liberal Protestantism, see Claude Welch, *Protestant Thought in the Nineteenth Century,* Vol. 1, 1799-1870 (New Haven, Conn.: Yale University Press, 1972).
7. See the major work of the "father of modern theology," Friedrich Schleiermacher, *The Christian Faith,* translation of 2nd German ed. (Edinburgh: T. & T. Clark, 1948).
8. For a good illustration of a liberal interpretation of the religion of Jesus, see Adolph Harnack, *What Is Christianity?,* trans. Thomas Bailey Saunders, 5th ed. (London: Ernest Benn, 1958).
9. Langdon Gilkey, *Naming the Whirlwind: The Renewal of God-Language* (Indianapolis, Ind.: Bobbs-Merrill, 1969), p. 76.
10. Baumer, *Modern European Thought,* pp. 367-515.
11. For a definition of neo-orthodox theology, see David Tracy, *Blessed Rage for Order: The New Pluralism in Theology* (New York: Seabury Press, 1979), pp. 27-31.
12. The notion of the infinite qualitative distinction between God and world was one of Barth's earliest contributions; see *The Epistle to the Romans,* translated from 6th German ed. (New York: Oxford University Press, 1972).
13. Rudolf Bultmann, "New Testament and Mythology," in *Kerygma and Myth,* ed. H. W. Bartsch, trans. R. H. Fuller (New York: Harper & Row, 1961), pp. 1-44.
14. Karl Rahner, *Foundations of Christian Faith: An Introduction to the Idea of Christianity* (New York: Seabury Press, 1978); for an excellent introduction to Rahner's thought, see Anne Carr, "Theology and Experience in the Thought of Karl Rahner," *Journal of Religion* 55 (July 1973): 359-76.
15. Hans-Georg Gadamer, *Truth and Method,* trans. G. Borden and J. Cumming (New York: Seabury Press, 1975).
16. Michel Foucault, *The Order of Things: An Archaeology of the Human Sciences* (New York: Vintage/Random House, 1973), and *Language, Counter-Memory, Practice: Selected Essays and Interviews,* ed. D. F. Bouchard (Ithaca, N.Y.: Cornell University Press, 1977).
17. Alasdair MacIntyre, *After Virtue: A Study in Moral Theology* (Notre Dame, Ind.: University of Notre Dame Press, 1981).
18. Jacques Derrida, *Of Grammatology,* trans. Gayatri Chakravorty Spivak (Balti-

more, Md.: Johns Hopkins University Press, 1977), and *Writing and Difference,* trans. Alan Bass (London: Routledge & Kegan Paul, 1978).

19. One display of modernity's inner contradictions is portrayed in Max Horkheimer and Theodor W. Adorno, *Dialectic of Enlightenment* (New York: Seabury Press, 1972).

20. David Tracy, *Blessed Rage for Order,* and *The Analogical Imagination: Christian Theology and the Culture of Pluralism* (New York: Crossroad Publishing Co., 1981).

21. Steven Lukes, "Relativism: Cognitive and Moral," in his *Essays in Social Theory* (New York: Columbia University Press, 1977).

22. Richard J. Bernstein, *Beyond Objectivism and Relativism*; (Philadelphia: University of Pennsylvania Press, 1983); Fred Dallmayr, *Polis and Praxis: Exercises in Contemporary Political Theory* (Cambridge, Mass.: MIT Press, 1984).

23. Jürgen Habermas, *Knowledge and Human Interests,* trans. Jeremy J. Shapiro (Boston, Mass.: Beacon Press, 1971).

24. Stanley Hauerwas, *The Peaceable Kingdom: A Primer in Christian Ethics* (Notre Dame, Ind.: University of Notre Dame Press, 1983).

25. Tracy, *Analogical Imagination.*

26. Harvey Cox, *Religion in the Secular City: Toward a Postmodern Theology* (New York: Simon & Schuster, 1984).

27. Siegfried Widenhofer, *Politische Theologie* (Stuttgart: Verlag W. Kohlhammer, 1976), p. 21.

28. Metz, *Theology of the World,* p. 109.

29. Jürgen Moltmann, *Theology of Hope: On the Ground and the Implications of a Christian Eschatology,* trans. James W. Leitch (New York: Harper & Row, 1967); and Johann Baptist Metz, "The Church and the World," in *The Word in History,* ed. T. Patrick Burke (New York: Sheed & Ward, 1966), pp. 69–85.

30. See Gerhard Bauer, *Christliche Hoffnung und Menschlicher Fortschritt: die politische Theologies von J. B. Metz als theologische Begunglung gesellschaftlicher Verantwortung des Christen* (Mainz: Matthias-Grünewald Verlag, 1976), p. 114. For a good reading of Bloch in light of political theology, see Francis Fiorenza, "Dialectical Theology and Hope," *Heythrop Journal of Theology* 9 (1968): 142–63, 384–99; 10 (1969): 26–42.

31. Adolf Lowe, "S it noch nicht P: Eine Frage an Ernst Bloch," in *Ernst Bloch zu Ehren,* ed. Siegfried Unseld (Frankfurt a. M.: Suhrkamp Verlag, 1965), pp. 135–43.

32. Ernst Bloch, *Das Prinzip Hoffnung,* 2 vols. (Frankfurt a. M.: Suhrkamp Verlag, 1959).

33. Moltmann, *Theology of Hope,* pp. 102–12.

34. Metz, *Theology of the World,* p. 114.

35. Johann Baptist Metz, "Prophetic Authority," in *Religion and Political Society,* ed. and trans. Institute of Christian Thought (New York: Harper & Row, 1974), pp. 177–209.

36. Moltmann, *Theology of Hope,* p. 388.

37. Claude Geffré, *A New Age in Theology,* trans. Robert Shillen (New York: Paulist Press, 1974), p. 84.

38. See Francis Fiorenza, "Political Theology as Foundational Theology," in *Catholic Theological Society of America Proceedings* 32 (1977): 142–77.

39. One expression of civil religion is found in Jean-Jacques Rousseau, *The Social Contract,* trans. M. Cranston (New York: Penguin Books, 1968).

40. Klaus-Michel Kodalle, *Politik als Macht und Mythos: Carl Schmitts "Politische Theologies"* (Stuttgart: Verlag W. Kohlhammer, 1973).

41. Jürgen Moltmann, "Political Theology," *Theology Today* 28 (April 1971):7.

42. See Helmut Peukert, ed. *Diskussion zur "Politischen Theologies"* (Mainz: Matthias Grünewald Verlag; Munich: Kaiser Verlag, 1969).

43. Jürgen Moltmann, *The Crucified God: The Cross of Christ as the Foundation and Criticism of Christian Theology,* trans. R. A. Wilson and John Bowden (New York: Harper & Row, 1973), pp. 329–38.

44. By the notions of the interruption of the subject and the history of freedom, Metz wants to argue the importance of the human subject (against a thinker like Foucault); to formulate a new theological anthropology (in light of Karl Rahner's works), to criticize theories of emancipation (as in the work of Jürgen Habermas), and to avoid the occlusion of suffering in a theoretical reconceptualization of God (as in Jürgen Molt- mann's theology); see Johann Baptist Metz, *Faith in History and Society: Toward a Practical Fundamental Theology,* trans. David Smith (New York: Seabury Press, 1980), pp. 123-33.

45. Walter Benjamin, *Illuminations,* ed. Hannah Arendt, trans. Harry Zohn (New York: Schocken Books, 1969), p. 257.

46. The distinctions between functional, genetic, and epistemic ideologies are ex- plained in Raymond Geuss, *The Idea of a Critical Theory: Habermas and the Frankfurt School* (Cambridge, England: Cambridge University Press, 1981), pp. 12-22.

47. Metz, *Faith in History,* p. 152.

48. For a good introduction to the Frankfurt School, see David Held, *Introduction to Critical Theory: Horkheimer to Habermas* (Berkeley and Los Angeles: University of California Press, 1980).

49. Theodor W. Adorno, *Negative Dialectics,* trans. E. B. Ashton (New York: Seabury Press, 1979). For a good introduction to Adorno, see Susan Buck-Morss, *The Origin of Negative Dialectics: Theodor W. Adorno, Walter Benjamin, and the Frank- furt Institute* (New York: Free Press, 1977).

50. Moltmann, *Crucified God,* p. 226.

51. Johann Baptist Metz, *The Emergent Church: The Future of Christianity in a Postbourgeois World,* trans. Peter Mann (New York: Crossroad Publishing Co., 1981), pp. 1-16, 48-66.

52. Johann Baptist Metz, *Followers of Christ: The Religious Life and the Church,* trans. Thomas Lintier (New York: Paulist Press, 1978), pp. 39-44.

3. GUSTAVO GUTIÉRREZ:
A THEOLOGY FOR HISTORICAL AMNESIA

1. Gustavo Gutiérrez, "Liberating Praxis and Christian Faith," in *Frontiers of Theology in Latin America,* ed. Rosino Gibellini, trans. John Drury (Maryknoll, N.Y.: Orbis Books, 1974), p. 1.

2. Gustavo Gutiérrez, "The Irruption of the Poor in Latin America and the Christian Communities," in *The Challenge of Basic Christian Communities,* ed. Sergio Torres and John Eagleson, trans. John Drury (Maryknoll, N.Y.: Orbis Books, 1981), p. 108.

3. Ibid., p. 111.

4. Gustavo Gutiérrez and Richard Shaull, *Liberation and Change,* ed. Ronald H. Stone (Atlanta, Ga.: John Knox Press, 1977), p. 92. Gutiérrez's claim is that the historical event of the poor forces us to interpret history differently and to change history. Broadly speaking, then, the claim is that events change history, that is how we understand and reproduce history. A similar claim is made by Arthur Cohen in relation to the Holocaust; see *The Tremendum: A Theological Interpretation of the Holocaust* (New York: Crossroad Publishing Co., 1981).

5. Gustavo Gutiérrez, "Liberation, Theology, and Proclamation," *Concilium* 96 (1974): 60.

6. Gustavo Gutiérrez, *A Theology of Liberation,* ed. and trans. Sister Caridad Inda and John Eagleson (Maryknoll, N.Y.: Orbis Books, 1973), p. 29.

7. Gustavo Gutiérrez, *The Power of the Poor in History,* trans. Robert R. Barr (Maryknoll, N.Y.: Orbis Books, 1983), pp. 90-94, 171-85. Gutiérrez's critical interpre- tation of modern religion and progressivist theology is formulated after the general interpretation of modernity's industrial and cultural revolutions that appear in *Theol- ogy of Liberation.*

8. Gustavo Gutiérrez, "Faith as Freedom: Solidarity with the Alienated and Confidence in the Future," *Horizons* 2 (Spring 1975): 36.

9. Ibid., p. 37.

10. Gutiérrez, "Liberating Praxis and Christian Faith," p. 8.

11. Gutiérrez, "Faith as Freedom," p. 34. Gutiérrez is using the term "politics" in a fashion similar to the Aristotelian sense of the "polis"—the public space of human decision making. Politics is not here confined to the operational management of the state. Gutiérrez's notion of politics is similar to Hannah Arendt's use of "political action" or "praxis" (see Hannah Arendt, *The Human Condition: A Study of the Central Dilemmas Facing Modern Man* [Garden City, N.Y.: Doubleday Anchor Books, 1959]).

12. Gutiérrez, *Theology of Liberation*, pp. 32-33.

13. Ibid., p. 108.

14. Gustavo Gutiérrez, *We Drink from Our Own Wells: The Spiritual Journey of a People*, trans. Matthew J. O'Connell (Maryknoll, N.Y.: Orbis Books; Melbourne: Dove Communications, 1984), p. 136.

15. Gutiérrez, *Theology of Liberation*, pp. 63-66.

16. Gutiérrez, "Liberation, Theology, and Proclamation," p. 60.

17. Gutiérrez, *We Drink from Our Own Wells*, p. 112.

18. Gutiérrez, *Theology of Liberation*, pp. 190-94.

19. Ibid., p. 152.

20. Ibid., p. 176.

21. Ibid., pp. 158-59.

22. Ibid., p. 161.

23. Ibid., p. 168.

24. Ibid., p. 255.

25. Ibid., pp. 36-37. By distinguishing the levels of liberation, Gutiérrez can avoid the reduction of redemption to any one historical event, thus ensuring the Christian claim of ultimate fulfillment from God and providing a locus for a critique of any and all historical projects of emancipation. By introducing the second level, the utopian aspirations of history, Gutiérrez secures his theology in a philosophy of history but also provides a place for a religious experience: hope in the future and participation in the project of history are, in Gutiérrez's theology, experiences of God. The question remains if the third level, the level of ultimate fulfillment, functions in any way but as a negative limit to human aspirations and revolutions.

26. Ibid., p. 177.

27. Ibid., p. 231.

28. Ibid., p. 234.

29. Ibid., p. 237. Again, the claim is quite explicit: participation in the planning of history is a religious act—a participation in or communion with God. This is not to suggest that Gutiérrez intends a new form of anonymous Christianity but, rather, to indicate that Gutiérrez does hold to the nature of human, religious experience—though his own concern is the explication of Christian faith in the new paradigm of liberation theology.

30. Ibid., p. 260.

31. Gutiérrez, "The Irruption of the Poor," pp. 116-18.

32. Gutiérrez, *Theology of Liberation*, p. 300.

33. Gustavo Gutiérrez. *Lineas pastorales de la Iglesia en América Latina* (Lima: Centro de Estudios y Publicaciones, 1976), p. 1. A paradigm shift in theology must include this very important third claim—that there is a new way of reflection, a new procedure of interpretation, a new orientation of knowledge, otherwise the new theology might just be a different interpretation within an older paradigm. Method is a way of asking questions and making interpretations. Liberation theology claims that other forms of theological method cannot ask the questions of massive public events of

human suffering. In this text Moltmann will demonstrate the problem of a theologian who addresses questions of suffering but within the paradigm of a neo-orthodox theological method.

34. Ibid., p. 1. In a presentation at the Academy of Religion, December 1984, in Chicago, Illinois, Gutiérrez described liberation theology as a new language for something very old—talking about God. Though Gutiérrez may now shy away from claims of liberation theology as a Copernican revolution (itself a quite "progressivist" claim), Gutiérrez insists that liberation theology is a new way of theological reflection.

35. Gutiérrez, *Power of the Poor in History,* p. 93.

36. Ibid., p. 179. It must be noted that Gutiérrez reads the liberal theologians—and especially Schleiermacher—in a general manner, attempting to discern the questions asked by liberal theology.

37. Ibid., p. 213.

38. For an interesting interpretation of this point by a North American theologian, see Schubert M. Ogden, *The Point of Christology* (New York: Harper & Row, 1982), pp. 91–92.

39. Gutiérrez and Shaull, *Liberation and Change,* p. 82.

40. Gutiérrez, *Power of the Poor in History,* p. 200. The first insight, theology as a critical reflection, deals with the formal nature of theology, including issues of epistemology, criteria of truth and meaning, use of other disciplines, tasks, and purposes; the second insight covers the substantial nature of theological reflection, that is, its relation to Christian tradition and hence its uniqueness as *theological* reflection.

41. See Schubert M. Ogden, "The Concept of a Theology of Liberation: Must a Christian Theology Today Be So Conceived?" in *The Challenge of Liberation Theology: A First World Response,* ed. Brian Mahan and L. Dale Richesin (Maryknoll, N.Y.: Orbis Books, 1981), pp. 127-40. As Ogden argues, the difference between Gutiérrez and himself is how theology should be conceived; the differences between Ogden and Gutiérrez involve both the given tasks of theology and the nature of what counts as "critical" reflection. Gutiérrez's theology is a practical hermeneutics using arguments in the context of interpretations; Ogden's theology is a philosophical theology, defining and arguing the truth status of Christian claims.

42. Gustavo Gutiérrez, "Liberation Movements and Theology," *Concilium* 93 (1974):143.

43. Gutiérrez, "Liberation, Theology, and Proclamation," p. 68. Gutiérrez, at least in the judgment of this author, is more interested in a radical reorientation of theological reflection and less interested in arguing particular points of theological method within liberation theology.

44. Gutiérrez considers the relationship of Christianity and Marxism in a "Marxismo-Christianismo" (Mexico City: Centro Crítico Universitario, 1971). Mimeographed.

45. Gutiérrez, *Power of the Poor in History,* p. 36.

46. Especially in his early work, Gutiérrez sometimes indicated that "truth" could be identified with historical success. Such claims are at odds with Gutiérrez's theological warrants of the three levels of liberation and the three distinct tasks of theology. Certainly the truth of history is not identifiable with any one particular event; likewise the truth of theology as a guide to Christian praxis is not verified through the success or failure of any one particular activity.

47. Gutiérrez, *Power of the Poor in History,* p. 101.

4. JOHANN BAPTIST METZ: THE SUBJECT OF SUFFERING

1. Johann Baptist Metz, *The Emergent Church,* trans. Peter Mann (New York: Crossroad Publishing Co., 1981), p. 12.

2. Johann Baptist Metz, *Faith in History and Society,* trans. David Smith (New York: Seabury Press, 1980), p. 111.

3. Even before his constructive work on secularization, Metz was attempting to formulate a social anthropology. See, Roger Dick Johns, *Man in the World: The Theology of Johannes Baptist Metz* (Missoula, Mont.: Scholars Press, 1976); see also Metz, "Heidegger und das Problem der Metaphysik," *Scholastik* 28 (1953):1-22; Metz, *Christliche Anthropozentrik* (Munich: Kosel Verlag, 1962); Karl Rahner, *Geist in Welt,* ed. Johann Baptist Metz, 2nd ed. (Munich: Kosel Verlag, 1957); and Rahner, *Horer des Wortes,* ed. Johann Baptist Metz, 2nd ed. (Munich: Kosel Verlag, 1963).

4. Johann Baptist Metz, *Theology of the World,* trans. William Glen-Doepel (New York: Seabury Press, 1969), p. 13.

5. Ibid., p. 54.

6. Ibid., p. 23. For a discussion of Metz's secularization thesis in relation to that of Friedrich Gogarten, see Charles Davis, *Theology and Political Society* (Cambridge, England: Cambridge University Press, 1980), pp. 36-50.

7. Metz, *Theology of the World,* p. 47.

8. Johann Baptist Metz, "Freedom as a Threshold Problem between Philosophy and Theology," *Philosophy Today* 10 (Winter 1966):276.

9. Metz, *Theology of the World,* p. 42.

10. Ibid., p. 124.

11. Ibid., p. 87.

12. Metz, in "Ernst Bloch und Georg Lukacs im Gesprach mit Irving Fetscher, Johannes B. Metz, und Jürgen Moltmann," *Neues Forum* 14 (1967):841, cited in Johns, *Man in the World,* p. 107.

13. Metz, *Theology of the World,* p. 114.

14. Ibid., pp. 117-18.

15. Ibid., p. 111.

16. Later Metz recognizes that he did not, at this stage, clearly define the term "praxis" (see *Faith in History and Society,* pp. 52-53).

17. Jon Sobrino, *The True Church and the Poor,* trans. Matthew J. O'Connell (Maryknoll, N.Y.: Orbis Books, 1984), p. 11.

18. Similar criticisms of Metz's position were brought out in Helmut Peukert, ed., *Diskussion zur "politischen Theologie"* (Mainz: Matthias-Grünewald Verlag; Munich: Kaiser Verlag, 1969); see also, Willi Oelmüller, "Zur philosophischen Begrundung des Sittlichen und Politischen. Ein Beitrag zur 'politischen theologies,' " pp. 38-71.

19. It is only after this second stage that Metz moves to a new paradigm of theology. Metz's work illustrates that new paradigms can be arrived at through the intensification to the point of rupture of an old paradigm. From his early work as a student of Rahner, Metz worked on formulating an anthropology through the social categories of intersubjectivity, corporeality, and freedom, until the questions of the historical subject could no longer be asked within a transcendental theology such as Rahner's.

20. Some critics have questioned the adequacy of Metz's definition of the Enlightenment. As we shall see, Metz changes his definition and evaluation of the Enlightenment greatly in this third stage. See Henri de Lovalette, "La théologie politique de Jean Baptiste Metz," *Recherches de Sciences Religieuses* 58 (1970): 321-50.

21. Metz, *Faith in History and Society,* p. 37.

22. Metz, *The Emergent Church,* p. 35.

23. Ibid.

24. Metz, *Faith in History and Society,* p. 101.

25. Ibid., p. 5. In other words, the "structures of consciousness" in East and West are essentially the same, deriving from their common source in the Enlightenment. Metz is not criticizing the distortions of social structures but the more subtle, and for Metz, more basic distortions in how we experience and understand the world. Metz's analysis of modernity's fault is close to the Weberian emphasis within the Frankfurt School—the

emphasis on the problem of rationalization; see Paul Connerton, *The Tragedy of Enlightenment: An Essay on the Frankfurt School* (Cambridge, England: Cambridge University Press, 1980).

26. Ibid., pp. 169–70.

27. Ibid., p. 172.

28. Metz, *The Emergent Church*, p. 36.

29. Ibid., p. 29.

30. See Walter Benjamin, "Theses on the Philosophy of History," in *Illuminations*, ed. Hannah Arendt, trans. Harry Zohn (New York: Schocken Books, 1969), pp. 253–64.

31. Metz, *Faith in History and Society*, p. 108.

32. The image of the iron cage of modernity is taken from Max Weber's description of the bureaucratization of Western society. See Max Weber, *The Protestant Ethic and the Spirit of Capitalism* (New York: Scribner, 1930).

33. Metz, *Faith in History and Society*, pp. 91–92.

34. Ibid., pp. 66.

35. Metz's use of memory, narrative, and solidarity as constitutive of praxis has parallels to the emphasis on freedom and solidarity in the work of Hans-Georg Gadamer. For Gadamer, the play of understanding is both the expression and the constitution of human freedom and solidarity; see "What Is Practice? The Conditions of Social Reason," in his *Reason in the Age of Science,* trans. Frederick G. Lawrence (Cambridge, Mass.: MIT Press, 1981), pp. 69–87.

36. See Joe Colombo, "Towards a Theology of History: An Essay on the Critical Theory of the So-called Frankfurt School and the Theologies of Wolfhart Pannenberg and Johann Baptist Metz" (Ph.D. dissertation, University of Chicago, in progress).

37. Metz, *Faith in History and Society,* pp. 159–62. In this third stage Metz now recognizes that a major change in theological systems is called for; see ibid., p. 13.

38. Ibid., pp. 60–61.

39. In this stage, as in the first two, Christianity parallels the constitution of the human subject. In the first stage, freedom was located in secularity and grounded in Christianity; in the second stage, freedom was related to the new and grounded in eschatology; now, in the third stage, freedom exists in suffering and the dangerous memories of Christian tradition.

40. Metz, "Prophetic Authority," in *Religion and Political Society,* ed. and trans. Institute of Political Thought (New York: Harper & Row, 1974), pp. 188–89.

41. Metz, *Faith in History and Society,* p. 111.

42. Ibid., p. 113.

43. Ibid., p. 112.

44. Johann Baptist Metz, "Redemption and Emancipation," trans. Matthew Lamb and Jeanette Martin, *Cross Currents* 27 (Fall 1977): 327.

45. Metz, *Followers of Christ,* trans. Thomas Lintier (New York: Paulist Press, 1978), p. 39.

46. Metz, *The Emergent Church,* p. 42.

47. For an important argument for the essential linkage between time and narrative, see Paul Ricoeur, *Time and Narrative,* vol. 1, trans. Kathleen McLaughlin and David Pellauer (Chicago, Ill.: University of Chicago Press, 1984).

48. Metz, *Faith in History and Society,* p. 63.

49. Ibid., p. 73.

50. Metz recognizes the radical shift in his own theology; see *Faith in History and Society,* p. 79, note 3: "shortly after the first phase in the development of a political theology, I became aware, through the work of some of my pupils, of the practical limitations of a purely theoretical and critical theology."

51. Theology is narrative due to its convergence with the structure of human experience through memories and narratives and due to the nature of Christian tradition

as itself essentially narrative. For a similar but far more developed argument, see David Tracy, *The Analogical Imagination* (New York: Crossroad Publishing Co., 1981).

52. Metz, *Faith in History and Society,* p. 57.

53. John B. Cobb, Jr., *Process Theology as Political Theology* (Philadelphia, Pa.: Westminster Press, 1982), pp. 13–14.

54. Metz uses the German fairytale of the hedgehogs and the hare to argue that Christianity must enter the race of history (*Faith in History and Society,* pp. 163–66). My reference to running the course of history has to do with the nature of human existence as not only narrative but structural; humans exist not only through narratives but also through systems.

5. JOSÉ MÍGUEZ BONINO: THE CONVERSION TO THE WORLD

1. José Míguez Bonino, "The Historical Spectrum of Protestantism in Latin America: Historical Expressions," CICOP Working Paper (Davenport, Iowa: Latin America Bureau, 1967), p. 13 (mimeographed).

2. José Míguez Bonino, "Five Theses toward an Understanding of the Theology of Liberation," *Expository Times* 37 (April 1976):197–98.

3. José Míguez Bonino, *Doing Theology in a Revolutionary Situation* (Philadelphia, Pa.: Fortress Press, 1975), p. 103.

4. Ibid.

5. José Míguez Bonino, "Historical Praxis and Christian Identity," in *Frontiers of Theology in Latin America,* ed. Rosino Gibellini, trans. John Drury (Maryknoll, N.Y.: Orbis Books, 1974), p. 262.

6. Míguez Bonino, *Doing Theology in a Revolutionary Situation,* pp. 90–91.

7. See Karl-Otto Apel, "Types of Social Sciences in the Light of Human Interests of Knowledge," *Social Research* 44 (1977):425–70.

8. Míguez Bonino, *Doing Theology in a Revolutionary Situation,* p. 93.

9. For another liberation theologian who uses ideology in a positive sense, see Juan Luis Segundo, *The Liberation of Theology,* trans. John Drury (Maryknoll, N.Y.: Orbis Books, 1976), as well as his *Faith and Ideologies,* trans. John Drury (Maryknoll, N.Y.: Orbis Books; Melbourne: Dove Communications; London: Sheed & Ward, 1984).

10. Míguez Bonino, *Doing Theology in a Revolutionary Situation,* p. 95.

11. Liberation theologians differ as to whether ideology critique is a moment within hermeneutics—part of the act of interpretation—or a related but distinct theory of human freedom. For a nontheological version of this debate between Hans-Georg Gadamer and Jürgen Habermas, see *Continuum* 8 (1970):77–96 and 123–28.

12. José Míguez Bonino, *Toward a Christian Political Ethics* (Philadelphia, Pa.: Fortress Press, 1983), p. 44.

13. Míguez Bonino, *Doing Theology in a Revolutionary Situation,* p. 93.

14. Míguez Bonino argues for a theory of context as well as a theory of the text in theological hermeneutics. For one exploration of "contextualization," see Robert J. Schreiter, *Constructing Local Theologies* (Maryknoll, N.Y.: Orbis Books, 1985).

15. Míguez Bonino demands that theology remain, albeit in a transformed manner, theology—that it speak of God, and God acting in history through the events of the present; see *Doing Theology in a Revolutionary Situation,* p. 98, and "For Life and Against Death: A Theology That Takes Sides," *Christian Century* 97 (November 1980):1156.

16. Míguez Bonino, *Doing Theology in a Revolutionary Situation,* p. 103.

17. José Míguez Bonino, "How Does God Act in History?" in *Christ and the Younger Churches: Theological Contributions from Asia, Africa and Latin America,* ed. Georg Vicedom (London: SPCK, 1972), p. 23.

18. Ibid., pp. 24–25.

19. Ibid., p. 25.

20. This is a good illustration of the fact that even within the paradigm of liberation theology there are major theological differences between theologians. Míguez Bonino, like some of liberation theology's critics, warns against any reduction of redemption to particular acts of liberation.

21. Míguez Bonino, "Historical Praxis and Christian Identity," p. 272.

22. Ibid., p. 273.

23. Ibid., p. 276.

24. For a more detailed argument on the use of theory and "explanation" to arrive at an understanding of the text, see Paul Ricoeur, *Interpretation Theory: Discourse and the Surplus of Meaning* (Fort Worth, Tex.: Texas Christian University Press, 1976).

25. Míguez Bonino, *Doing Theology in a Revolutionary Situation,* p. 94.

26. Ibid., p. 102; see also José Míguez Bonino, "Doing Theology in the Context of the Struggles of the Poor," *Mid-Stream* 20 (October 1981):370.

27. Míguez Bonino, "How Does God Act in History?" p. 29.

28. José Míguez Bonino, *Ama y haz lo que quieras: Hacia una ética del hombre neuvo* (Buenos Aires: Editorial Escatón, 1972).

29. Míguez Bonino, *Doing Theology in a Revolutionary Situation,* p. 88.

30. Míguez Bonino, "For Life and Against Death," p. 1154.

31. José Míguez Bonino, "Violence and Liberation," *Christianity and Crisis* 32 (June 1972):169.

32. Míguez Bonino, *Doing Theology in a Revolutionary Situation,* p. 126.

33. Míguez Bonino, "Violence and Liberation," pp. 169–70.

34. Ibid., p. 170.

35. José Míguez Bonino, *Christians and Marxists* (Grand Rapids, Mich.: Eerdmans Publishing Co., 1976), p. 16.

36. Ibid., p. 49.

37. Ibid., p. 50.

38. Ibid., p. 65.

39. Ibid., p. 73.

40. For an excellent interpretation of the "two schools" of Marxism, see Alvin Gouldner, *The Two Marxisms: Contradictions and Anomalies in the Development of Theory* (New York: Oxford University Press, 1980).

41. Míguez Bonino, *Christians and Marxists,* p. 84. Note that Míguez Bonino is in essential agreement with Metz that Marxism, as a theory of interpretation, is basically an expression of modern humanism.

42. Míguez Bonino, *Doing Theology in a Revolutionary Situation,* p. 108.

43. Ibid., p. 113. Note that Míguez Bonino offers a somewhat different theological interpretation of the option for the poor from Gutiérrez's. For Gutiérrez, the option for the poor is based first upon God's own choosing to be with the poor; solidarity with the poor is itself a religious experience. Míguez Bonino bases the option for the poor on the obedience of faith to a God of love, which necessarily implies justice. Said differently: for Gutiérrez, the poor manifest God's presence; for Míguez Bonino, Christians are in solidarity with the poor out of obedience to the proclamation of God's Word. With these two theologians we see a "manifestation model" and a "proclamation model" of Christian theology.

44. Míguez Bonino, *Doing Theology in a Revolutionary Situation,* p. 123.

45. Ibid., p. 127.

46. Ibid., p. 128.

47. Míguez Bonino calls for the necessary inclusion of theoretical arguments within theology to aid understanding and transformation; see "From Praxis to Theory and Back," in *Toward a Christian Political Ethics,* pp. 37–53.

48. Míguez Bonino does argue for the use of dialectical sociology instead of functional sociology, based on the philosophy of history of conflict. While I agree with his

criticism of functionalist sociologies, his preference for dialectical sociology is still not enough to provide adequate criteria for the use of empirical analysis or specific strategies for change. See Míguez Bonino, *Toward a Christian Political Ethics,* pp. 46–47.

49. Míguez Bonino, "Doing Theology in the Context of the Struggles of the Poor," p. 367.

6. JÜRGEN MOLTMANN: THE LANGUAGE OF GOD AS THE LANGUAGE OF SUFFERING

1. Jürgen Moltmann, "Political Theology," *Theology Today* 28 (April 1971):7.
2. Ibid.
3. Jürgen Moltmann, *Theology of Hope,* trans. James W. Leitch (New York: Harper & Row, 1967), pp. 44–45.
4. Ibid., pp. 50–58. For an excellent discussion of Barth's influence on Moltmann, as well as a general introduction to Moltmann's theology, see M. Douglas Meeks, *Origins of the Theology of Hope* (Philadelphia, Pa.: Fortress Press, 1974).
5. Moltmann, *Theology of Hope,* pp. 42–69.
6. Ibid., p. 30.
7. Jürgen Moltmann, *The Crucified God: The Cross of Christ as the Foundation and Criticism of Christian Theology,* trans. R. A. Wilson and John Bowden (New York: Harper & Row, 1973), pp. 332–35.
8. Jürgen Moltmann, *The Future of Creation: Collected Essays,* trans. Margaret Kohl (Philadelphia, Pa.: Fortress Press, 1979), pp. 97–98.
9. Moltmann, *Theology of Hope,* p. 16.
10. Ibid., p. 84.
11. Ibid., p. 85.
12. Ibid. Here the influence of Ernst Bloch is brought into relationship with the influence of Karl Barth in Moltmann's theology. Although Moltmann wants to make the resurrection a historical event and a history-creating event, he wants it to transcend historical verification; see A. D. Galloway, "The New Hegelians," *Religious Studies* 8 (1972):367–71.
13. Moltmann, *Theology of Hope,* p. 16.
14. Ibid., p. 86.
15. Ibid., pp. 124–33.
16. Ibid., pp. 133–38.
17. Christopher Morse, *The Logic of Promise in Moltmann's Theology* (Philadelphia, Pa.: Fortress Press, 1975), pp. 49–81.
18. Moltmann, *Theology of Hope,* p. 108.
19. Moltmann, *Future of Creation,* p. 29.
20. Morse, *Logic of Promise,* pp. 65–67.
21. Moltmann, "The Future as a New Paradigm of Transcendence," in *Future of Creation,* pp. 1–17.
22. Jürgen Moltmann, *Religion, Revolution and the Future,* trans. R. A. Wilson and John Bowden (New York: Harper & Row, 1973), p. 195.
23. For criticisms of Moltmann's inability to affirm present religious experience, see Langdon Gilkey, *Reaping the Whirlwind: A Christian Interpretation of History* (New York: Seabury, 1976), pp. 233–36. For Moltmann's inability to give norms and criteria for ethics, see James Gustafson, *Ethics from a Theocentric Perspective,* Vol. I (Chicago, Ill.: University of Chicago Press, 1981), pp. 43–48.
24. Moltmann, *Theology of Hope,* pp. 199–200.
25. Ibid., p. 198.
26. Moltmann, *Crucified God,* pp. 112–14.

27. Ibid., p. 123.
28. Ibid., p. 126.
29. Ibid., p. 128.
30. Ibid.
31. Ibid., p. 136.
32. Ibid., p. 114.
33. Ibid., p. 147. Moltmann executes some very poor biblical scholarship when he makes statements such as "the flight of the disciples can be regarded as historical, because it conflicts with any kind of veneration for a hero and forebear," (p. 132).
34. Ibid., p. 148.
35. Ibid., p. 151.
36. Ibid., pp. 151–52.
37. Ibid., p. 171.
38. Ibid., p. 174.
39. Ibid., p. 185.
40. Ibid., pp. 217–27.
41. Ibid., p. 249. For Moltmann's distinctions on the forms of the Trinity, see his *The Trinity and the Kingdom: The Doctrine of God,* trans. Margaret Kohl (New York: Harper & Row, 1981).
42. Moltmann, *Crucified God,* p. 246. For a critical review of Moltmann in relation to the occlusion of the Holocaust and Jewish suffering into a preconceived idea of Christianity, see A. Roy Eckardt "Jürgen Moltmann, the Jewish People and the Holocaust," *Journal of the American Academy of Religion* 44 (December 1976):693–703.
43. Jürgen Moltmann, *The Church in the Power of the Spirit: A Contribution to Messianic Ecclesiology,* trans. Margaret Kohl (New York: Harper & Row, 1977), and *The Passion for Life: A Messianic Lifestyle,* trans. M. Douglas Meeks (Philadelphia, Pa.: Fortress Press, 1978).
44. Moltmann, *Theology of Hope,* p. 224.
45. Moltmann, *Church in the Power of the Spirit,* p. 127.
46. Ibid., p. 19.
47. Moltmann, *Theology of Hope,* pp. 304–25.
48. Ibid., p. 320.
49. Moltmann's view of the church's critical relation to society is similar to Metz's interpretation, in his second stage, of the church as a critical institution.
50. Moltmann, *Passion for Life,* p. 117.
51. Ibid., pp. 37–49.
52. Ibid., p. 45.

7. CHRIST LIBERATING CULTURE

1. The model of "Christ liberating culture" is intended as a sixth model to the five models proposed by H. Richard Niebuhr in *Christ and Culture* (New York: Harper & Row, 1951). The term "culture" refers to the total constitution of the polis.
2. Walter Benjamin, *Illuminations,* ed. Hannah Arendt, trans. Harry Zohn (New York: Schocken Books, 1969), pp. 257–58.
3. For one theological interpretation of the need for anamnestic solidarity as universal solidarity, see Helmut Peukert, *Science, Action, and Fundamental Theology: Toward a Theology of Communicative Action,* trans. James Bohman (Cambridge, Mass.: MIT Press, 1984).
4. Arthur Cohen, *The Tremendum* (New York: Crossroad Publishing Co., 1981), p. 7. Cohen notes the debasement of language that occurred in the Nazi era, with the extermination of the Jews articulated in terms of "disinfecting" and "purifying," thus avoiding words such as "murdering" and "killing."

5. Contemporary works on "praxis" are numerous. To cite a few: Karl-Otto Apel, *Towards a Transformation of Philosophy,* trans. Glyn Adey and David Frisby (London: Routledge & Kegan Paul, 1980); Jürgen Habermas, *Communication and the Evolution of Society,* trans. Thomas McCarthy (Boston, Mass.: Beacon Press, 1979); Richard Rorty, *Philosophy and the Mirror of Nature* (Princeton, N.J.: Princeton University Press, 1979).

6. Both contemporary philosophical discussions and liberation theology might well agree to Marx's Second Thesis on Feuerbach: "the question whether objective truth can be attributed to human thinking is not a question of theory but is a *practical* question. Man must prove the truth, that is, the reality and power, the this-sidedness of his thinking in practice," "Theses on Feuerbach," in *The Marx-Engels Reader,* ed. Robert C. Tucker (New York: W. W. Norton, 1972), p. 144.

7. The shift from liberal to neo-orthodox theology occurred, in part, because the questions of despair and meaningfulness could not be asked as primary questions within the paradigm of liberal theology. Likewise, the question of suffering and liberation—with the attending issues of praxis, justice, and ideology critique—cannot, liberation theologians argue, be formulated adequately within modern theology.

8. Of course, liberation theologians must always introduce arguments for the adequacy of their analysis and the appropriateness of their theological interpretations; see José Míguez Bonino, *Toward a Christian Political Ethics* (Philadelphia, Pa.: Fortress Press, 1983), p. 9.

9. Johann Baptist Metz, *Faith in History and Society,* trans. David Smith (New York: Seabury Press, 1980), p. 172.

10. For contrasting interpretations of the notion of historicity in Heidegger, see Terry Eagleton, *Literary Theory: An Introduction* (Minneapolis: University of Minnesota Press, 1983), pp. 61-66, who uses the line from Lukacs; and Fred Dallmayr, "Ontology of Freedom: Heidegger and Political Philosophy," in *Polis and Praxis,* (Cambridge, Mass.: MIT Press, 1984), pp. 104-32, who argues that Heidegger formulates an ontology of freedom wherein freedom is the ground for human solidarity.

11. Gustavo Gutiérrez, *The Power of the Poor in History,* trans. Robert R. Barr (Maryknoll, N.Y.: Orbis Books, 1983), p. 175.

12. *Puebla and Beyond,* ed. John Eagleson and Philip Scharper (Maryknoll, N.Y.: Orbis Books, 1979), pars. 32-39.

13. Terrence Des Pres, *The Survivor* (London: Oxford University Press, 1976), p. 37.

14. Richard J. Bernstein, *Praxis and Action: Contemporary Philosophies of Human Activity* (Philadelphia: University of Pennsylvania Press, 1971), p. 306.

15. David Tracy, "The Foundations of Practical Theology," in *Practical Theology: The Emerging Field in Theology, Church, and World,* ed. Don Browning (New York: Harper & Row, 1983), pp. 76-77.

16. For an interpretation of the importance of this theme in Marx and Benjamin, see Christopher Lenhardt, "Anamnestic Solidarity: Proletariat and Its Manes," *Telos* 25 (Fall 1975):133-54.

17. Hannah Arendt, *Between Past and Future: Eight Exercises in Political Thought* (New York: Meridian Books, 1963), p. 148.

18. Metz strongly emphasizes the need for a new understanding of time, which should include both a new understanding of the nature and purpose of history and a new understanding of human freedom and solidarity; see Metz, *Faith in History and Society,* pp. 175-76.

19. Tracy, "Foundations of Practical Theology," pp. 76-77.

20. Jürgen Moltmann, "The Future as a New Paradigm of Transcendence," in *The Future of Creation,* trans. Margaret Kohl (Philadelphia, Pa.: Fortress Press, 1979), pp. 1-17.

21. Gustavo Gutiérrez, *A Theology of Liberation,* trans. and ed. Sister Caridad Inda and John Eagleson (Maryknoll, N.Y.: Orbis Books, 1973), pp. 232-39.

22. In other words, most liberation theologians argue for some type of "religious experience" in the anticipation of the future through solidarity with others.

23. Richard J. Bernstein, *Beyond Objectivism and Relativism* (Philadelphia: University of Pennsylvania Press, 1983), especially pp. 109-231.

24. Dallmayr, *Polis and Praxis*, p. 1.

25. Gutiérrez, *Theology of Liberation*, p. 108; Johann Baptist Metz, *The Emergent Church*, trans. Peter Mann (New York: Crossroad Publishing Co., 1981), pp. 1-16.

26. Johann Baptist Metz, *Unterbrechungen* (Gütersloh: Mohn, 1981).

27. See Gutiérrez, *Theology of Liberation*, pp. 287-302; Jürgen Moltmann, *Theology of Hope*, trans. James W. Leitch (New York: Harper & Row, 1967), pp. 50-76.

28. Biblical symbols, in the words of Langdon Gilkey, "challenge the way we concretely are, they call for a new way of being, a new attitude to ourselves and to others, new forms of our actual relations in community and a new kind of action in the world" *Reaping the Whirlwind: A Christian Interpretation of History* (New York: Seabury, 1976), p. 138.

29. Gutiérrez, *Theology of Liberation*, pp. 175-76.

30. J. Andrew Kirk, *Liberation Theology* (Atlanta, Ga.: John Knox Press, 1979), p. 111.

31. Gustavo Gutiérrez, "Theology and Spirituality in a Latin American Context," *Harvard Divinity Bulletin* 14 (June-August 1984):4.

32. For one expression of the many christological images in liberation theology, see José Míguez Bonino, ed., *Faces of Jesus: Latin American Christologies*, trans. Robert R. Barr (Maryknoll, N.Y.: Orbis Books, 1984).

33. The point is not so much that Jesus consciously intended a particular revolution or realized any one particular way of life but, rather, that Jesus is the revelation of God. Said differently: the historical reconstruction of Jesus is not equal to the christological representation of Jesus. In the words of Schubert Ogden, the point is that "the meaning of Jesus for us is precisely the possibility of the existence of freedom," *The Point of Christology* (New York: Harper & Row, 1982), p. 122.

34. Moltmann, *Theology of Hope*, pp. 304-38; Metz, *The Emergent Church*, pp. 1-17.

35. Gustavo Gutiérrez, "The Irruption of the Poor," in *The Challenge of Basic Christian Communities*, ed. Sergio Torres and John Eagleson, trans. John Drury (Maryknoll, N.Y.: Orbis Books, 1981), pp. 119-20.

36. The church and sect typology is another major contribution to theology by Ernst Troeltsch; see *The Social Teaching of the Christian Churches*, 2 vols., trans. Olive Wyon (New York: Macmillan, 1931), vol. 2.

37. Gutiérrez, "Theology and Spirituality in a Latin American Context," p. 4.

38. The first theological base for the model of Christ liberating culture is an argument about God; the second and related theological base is an argument about the nature of faith.

39. Ogden, *The Point of Christology*, pp. 158-59. For another expression of faith as justice, see Jon Sobrino, *The True Church and the Poor*, trans. Matthew J. O'Connell (Maryknoll, N.Y.: Orbis Books, 1984), pp. 69-79.

8. TOWARD PRAXIS: A METHOD FOR LIBERATION THEOLOGY

1. For the explication of the two sources for theology, see Schubert Ogden, "What Is Theology," *Journal of Religion* 52 (1972):22-40; and David Tracy, "A Revisionist Model for Contemporary Theology," in his *Blessed Rage for Order* (New York: Seabury Press, 1979), pp. 43-63.

2. Tracy, *Blessed Rage for Order*, pp. 64-78; and Ogden, "What Is Theology," pp. 25-27.

3. José Míguez Bonino, *Doing Theology in a Revolutionary Situation* (Philadelphia, Pa.: Fortress Press, 1975), p. 81.

4. Anthony Giddens, *The Constitution of Society: Outline of the Theory of Structuration* (Berkeley and Los Angeles: University of California Press, 1984), p. xxxv. Though Giddens is concerned with the double hermeneutic of the social sciences, given the nature of theology to reflect on human experience, the same must be said of theology. Theology and the social sciences both reflect on frames of reference, and their findings are, or at least can potentially be, incorporated back into the frame of reference.

5. José Míguez Bonino, "Historical Praxis and Christian Identity," in *Frontiers of Theology in Latin America,* ed. Rosino Gibellini, trans. John Drury (Maryknoll, N.Y.: Orbis Books, 1974), p. 262.

6. See Johann Baptist Metz and Trutz Rendtorff, eds., *Die Theologie in der interdisziplinaren Forschung* (Düsseldorf: Bertelsmann Universitatsverlag, 1971).

7. James Gustafson, *Ethics from a Theocentric Perspective,* Vol. I (Chigago, Ill.: University of Chicago Press, 1981), p. 73.

8. José Míguez Bonino, *Toward a Christian Political Ethics,* (Philadelphia, Pa.: Fortress Press, 1983), p. 44.

9. Schubert Ogden, *The Point of Christology* (New York: Harper & Row, 1982), pp. 94–96, 164–65; and "The Concept of a Theology of Liberation," in *The Challenge of Liberation Theology,* ed. Brian Mahan and L. Dale Richesin (Maryknoll, N.Y.: Orbis Books, 1981), pp. 130–31, 136–39. See also Alfred T. Hennelly, *Theologies in Conflict: The Challenge of Juan Luis Segundo* (Maryknoll, N.Y.: Orbis Books, 1979), pp. 177–78.

10. Míguez Bonino, *Doing Theology in a Revolutionary Situation,* p. 91.

11. Norman Gottwald, "Sociological Method in the Study of Ancient Israel," in *The Bible and Liberation: Political and Social Hermeneutics,* ed. Norman Gottwald (Maryknoll, N.Y.: Orbis Books, 1983), p. 27.

12. These various theories all aid in understanding. A historical reconstruction of Jesus or a literary construal of the sense of the text does not complete a theological interpretation of the text for the present situation.

13. An excellent feminist deideologization of Scripture is presented by Elizabeth Schüssler Fiorenza, *In Memory of Her: A Feminist Theological Reconstruction of Christian Origins* (New York: Crossroad Publishing Co., 1983), and "Towards a Feminist Biblical Hermeneutics: Biblical Interpretation and Liberation Theology," in *The Challenge of Liberation Theology,* ed. Brian Mahan and L. Dale Richesin, pp. 91–112.

14. For the notion of a "critical praxis correlation," I am indebted to Matthew Lamb, *Solidarity with Victims* (New York: Crossroad Publishing Co., 1982), pp. 82–87.

15. For a treatment of the relation between theory and praxis, see Richard J. Bernstein, *Praxis and Action: Contemporary Philosophies of Human Activity* (Philadelphia: University of Pennsylvania Press, 1971); Nicholas Lobkowicz, *Theory and Practice: History of a Concept from Aristotle to Marx* (South Bend, Ind.: University of Notre Dame Press, 1967). For a succinct statement of the terms "theoria" and "praxis" in Aristotle, see Thomas McCarthy, *The Critical Theory of Jürgen Habermas* (Cambridge, Mass.: MIT Press, 1981), pp. 1–4.

16. Langdon Gilkey, *Reaping the Whirlwind: A Christian Interpretation of History* (New York: Seabury, 1976), p. 369.

17. Bernstein, *Praxis and Action,* p. 73. See also Leszek Kolakowski, "Karl Marx and the Classical Definition of Truth," in his *Toward a Marxist Humanism,* trans. Jane Zielonko Peel (New York: Grove Press, 1968), p. 46.

18. Fred Dallmayr, *Polis and Praxis* (Cambridge, Mass.: MIT Press, 1984), p. 167.

19. Lamb, *Solidarity with Victims,* p. 87.

20. The recognition of narrative as central to the theological enterprise is not unique

among liberation theologians. It occurs in theologians as diverse as David Tracy, *The Analogical Imagination* (New York: Crossroad Publishing Co., 1981), and Stanley Hauerwas, *The Peaceable Kingdom* (Notre Dame, Ind.: University of Notre Dame Press, 1983).

21. Gustavo Gutiérrez, *The Power of the Poor in History,* trans. Robert R. Barr (Maryknoll, N.Y.: Orbis Books, 1983), p. 212.

22. Hans-Georg Gadamer, *Truth and Method,* trans. G. Borden and J. Cumming (New York: Seabury Press, 1975), pp. 235–341.

23. Raymond Geuss, *The Idea of a Critical Theory* (Cambridge, England: Cambridge University Press, 1981), pp. 63–68.

24. José Míguez Bonino, *Christians and Marxists* (Grand Rapids, Mich.: Eerdmans Publishing Co., 1976), p. 65.

25. I am proposing that critical theory and practical hermeneutics must be related but distinguished in theology. I am influenced in this judgment by Paul Ricoeur, "Hermeneutics and the Critique of Ideology," in *Hermeneutics and the Human Sciences: Essays on Language, Action, and Interpretation,* ed. and trans. John B. Thompson (New York: Cambridge University Press, 1981), pp. 63–100.

26. Raymond Geuss, *The Idea of a Critical Theory,* p. 2.

27. Ibid.

28. Gutiérrez, *Power of the Poor,* p. 77; Johann Baptist Metz, *Faith in History and Society,* trans. David Smith (New York: Seabury Press, 1980), p. 171.

29. I have chosen Gutiérrez and Metz, since they have, in this text, provided the basic arguments for the paradigm shift and the constructive interpretations of the "praxis" of Christianity. Míguez Bonino's theology includes a hermeneutics of context and should be, at least on internal grounds, agreeable to my argument for the need of a social theory. The problem with Míguez Bonino is his refusal to give equal weight to ideology critique, preferring to see it as one moment within the hermeneutics of the world. Moltmann, at least in my interpretation, methodologically denies any relevance to incorporating a social theory in theological method; the unique foundation of Moltmann's theology is to serve as its own social theory.

30. Gutiérrez thinks this new stage of history presents a *kairos,* a decisive time for the encounter of God in history (*We Drink from Our Own Wells,* trans. Matthew J. O'Connell [Maryknoll, N.Y.: Orbis Books; Melbourne: Dove Communications, 1984], p. 136).

31. There is some difference between liberation theologians who rely on the social analysis of dependency theory and those who rely on the analysis of a national security system. Gutiérrez represents the former, José Comblin the latter. See Gutiérrez, *A Theology of Liberation,* ed. and trans. Sister Caridad Inda and John Eagleson (Maryknoll, N.Y.: Orbis Books, 1973); José Comblin, *The Church and the National Security State* (Maryknoll, N.Y.: Orbis Books, 1979).

32. Ignoring events such as the civil rights movement and the current peace movement, Metz portrays the human subject as almost completely determined by the sociopolitical realm through the rationalization of consciousness. Metz succumbs to a common temptation of critical theory—the reduction of the individual. A related criticism can be directed to Metz's insistence, shared with Frankfurt School critical theorists such as Adorno, on the negativity of critical thought. What Buck-Morss said about Adorno could also be said of Metz, that by abandoning any use-value of reason (as a way of abolishing instrumental reason), Adorno abrogated any political utility for critical theory: "Hence in the name of revolution, thought could never acknowledge a revolutionary situation; in the name of utopia, it could never work for utopia's realization" (Susan Buck-Morss, *The Origin of Negative Dialectics* [New York: Free Press, 1977], p. 189).

33. Anthony Giddens, *Central Problems in Social Theory: Action, Structure and Contradiction in Social Analysis* (Berkeley and Los Angeles: University of California

Press, 1983), p. 56. As Giddens notes, this notion of "could have done otherwise" must be understood in the context of historically located modes of activity.

34. Ibid., pp. 49–95, and *The Constitution of Society: Outline of the Theory of Structuration* (Berkeley: University of California Press, 1984). Giddens attempts to combine structuralism, dialectical materialism, and philosophical hermeneutics to formulate a social theory of human praxis. In this he is critical of much of the functionalist bias of much modern social theory, the view that society has needs that it inevitably must satisfy apart from human intentionality and practical knowledge. Giddens offers one way of formulating a "social" anthropology, which, though it decenters the human subject, does not "deconstruct" the subject's participation in the reproduction of history.

35. Giddens, *The Constitution of Society*, p. 374.

9. CONCLUSION

1. Nicholas Lobkowicz, *Theory and Practice: History of a Concept from Aristotle to Marx* (South Bend, Ind.: University of Notre Dame Press, 1967), pp. 340–41.

2. See Frank Lentriccha, *Criticism and Social Change* (Chicago, Ill.: University of Chicago Press, 1983).

Index

Adorno, Theodor, 43, 72
aggiornamento, 14-15
alienation, 18, 24, 52, 56, 74
Allende, Salvador, 18
anthropology, 5, 42, 43, 64, 94, 120, 121-
126, 130, 136, 147, 150, 151, 153; see
also subject
apocalypticism, 77, 79-81, 104, 109
Arendt, Hannah, 125
Aristotle, 59, 60, 122, 123
Augustine, 59, 63, 88
Auschwitz, 28, 73, 102, 123
Banquet, parable of the, 130
Barth, Karl, 19, 32, 101
basic Christian communities, 8, 21, 22,
26, 35, 56, 123, 150
Beatitudes, 129
Benjamin, Walter, 42, 43, 74, 118
Bernstein, Richard, 123, 126, 140
Bible, 52, 67, 83, 87, 88, 90-95, 97, 99,
104-106, 129, 131, 135, 137, 138
black theology, 3
Bloch, Ernst, 39, 40
Bonino, José Míguez, see Míguez Bonino
bourgeois religion, 26, 27, 39, 72, 77,
127, 144
bourgeois theology, see modern theology;
liberal theology; neo-orthodoxy
bourgeoisie, 4, 19, 20, 26, 27, 32, 33, 34,
38, 39, 64, 65, 72, 73, 75, 77, 80, 81,
93, 114, 121, 127, 144, 149
Bultmann, Rudolf, 84, 101, 138
Calvo, Robert, 14
capitalism, 10-15, 23, 48
Cardoso, Fernando Henrique, 17
Castuera, Ignacio, 7
Catholic Action, 13
Catholic social teaching, 14-15, 142

Catholic Trade Unions, 13
Catholicism, 9-16, 48
Chile, 13
Christ, 6, 24, 25, 32, 44, 45, 52, 64-66,
75-78, 95, 96, 106-112, 118, 130-133;
dangerous memories of, 44, 45, 64,
65, 75, 76; as liberating culture, 6, 24,
118, 131-133
Christian Democracy, 13
"Christianization" of Latin America, 9,
10
Christians for Socialism, 19
Christologies, 76, 107, 109, 129
class conflict, 16, 60, 93, 94, 97, 120, 145,
146
colonialism, 3, 5, 7, 9, 12, 15
Comblin, José, 13
comunidades eclesiales de base, see basic
Christian communities
congregation, 114, 115
conquistadors, 9
conscientization, 15, 21, 125, 130, 132,
145, 146
conversion, 21, 42, 45, 46, 50, 56, 57, 59,
63, 64, 74, 77, 78, 80-82, 98, 125, 127,
141; of the bourgeoisie, 64, 77, 80, 81;
of theology, 57, 59, 64, 98
Cortez, 9
creation, 53, 66, 67, 109, 110, 128, 129,
132, 153
cross, 2, 103, 106, 107, 110-113, 127, 129
cross-resurrection, 76, 103, 106, 109-113
crucifixion, 103, 109, 110, 114
Dallmayr, Fred, 126, 140
deideologization, 137-139
demythologization, 138
Derrida, Jacques, 34
Des Pres, Terrence, 2, 122

developmentalism, 2, 3, 13, 17, 22
dialectic of contradiction, 100, 106, 110, 111, 115, 116
dialectic of identification, 100, 103, 106, 107, 111, 112, 115
Docetism, 107
"double location" of the text, 90
dualism, 88, 89
Ebionitism, 107
Encuentro Latinoamericano de Teología, 26
enlightenment, 143, 146, 153
Enlightenment, the, 10, 26, 29, 31, 34, 35, 37, 39, 57, 58, 69, 71, 72, 74, 80, 81, 127, 142, 150
epistemological shift, 140
"eschatological proviso," 68-70, 76
eschatological theology, 102-106
eschatology, 39-41, 44, 53, 55, 65, 67-71, 100, 101, 103, 107, 109, 110, 112, 113, 114
European theology, 26
evangelical poverty, 23, 56, 62
evangelization, 12, 16, 25
evolutionary logic, 72-74, 77-80, 142, 146
exchange, the principle of, 71-72
exodus, 3, 24, 53, 100, 116, 117, 129
exodus church, 112, 114
Falleto, Enzo, 17
feminism, 2
Feuerbach, Ludwig, 34
Fierro, Alfredo, 5, 7, 21
freedom, 1, 19, 21, 30, 31, 34, 45, 65-66, 67-69, 72, 74-76, 97, 115, 116, 119, 121, 125, 129, 142, 143, 145, 150, 152; anticipatory, 123, 125, 131, 135, 136
Freire, Paulo, 5, 7, 21-22
Freud, Sigmund, 34
futur, 105, 106, 107, 125
Gadamer, Hans-Georg, 34, 141
Galilea, Segundo, 7
German Idealism, 43
German political theology, 3-5, 19, 20, 28-48, 64-81, 100-117, 118, 120
Geuss, Raymond, 144
Giddens, Anthony, 148
Gilkey, Langdon, 31, 139
God as Liberator, 6, 22, 24, 25, 44, 152
gospel, 57, 61, 90, 102

Gottwald, Norman, 138
Gregory XVI, 11
Gustafson, James, 136
Gutiérrez, Gustavo, 5, 10, 18, 19, 22, 23, 82, 121, 126, 127, 129, 130, 141, 144-147, 152
Harvey, Van, 30
Hegel, G. W. F., 18, 69, 119
hermeneutics, 6, 82-84, 88, 90, 93, 94, 97, 98, 99, 130, 137, 141, 144, 148, 153; of liberation, 49, 62, 98; practical, 37, 96, 98, 141-142, 144, 148, 153; of suspicion, 127-128, 130; of violence, 83, 92-97; of the Word, 6, 83, 88, 90, 92-94, 97, 98; of the world, 83-87, 92, 97-99
history, 1-3, 8, 24, 25, 27, 30, 33, 42, 43, 48, 53, 55, 56, 59, 62, 72, 74, 91, 101, 103, 104, 113, 128, 143; church as sacrament of, 24, 25, 55, 56; underside of, 27, 48, 62; victims of, 1, 2, 33
Holocaust, 2, 34, 116, 119, 122, 123
Horkheimer, Max, 43, 72
humanism, 94, 95, 145
humanization, 142
identity-in-difference, 53, 55
ideology critique, 6, 33, 34, 39, 43, 83, 85-87, 93, 98, 142-144, 146-148, 152, 153
Ignatius of Loyola, 59
immanence, 105-107
imperialism, 10, 11, 13, 14
incarnation, 66, 67, 103, 129, 130
independence movements, 10, 11
individualism, 48, 121, 128, 130
Institute for Social Research, 43
intersubjectivity, 43, 66, 72, 73, 75, 116, 117, 123-126, 128
Irenaeus, 89
John XXIII, 14
Judgment, the parable of, 128
Kant, Immanuel, 69
kerygma, *see* gospel
Kingdom of God, 88, 89, 91, 95-98, 109, 112, 130
Kirk, Andrew, 24
Klee, Paul, 118
Lamb, Matthew, 1, 140
las Casas, Bartolomé de, 10

Latin America, 2, 5, 8-16, 51, 56, 60, 82, 83, 92, 116, 119, 145
Latin American Council of Evangelization, 16
Latin American Evangelical Conference, 16
Latin American Protestantism, 11, 12, 16
Latin American socialism, 19
liberal Protestantism, 30, 31, 48, 49
liberal theology, 31-33, 41, 78, 149, 150, 151
liberation, 10, 23, 54-58, 60-63, 77, 82, 94, 95, 125, 130, 131, 147, 152, 153; and salvation, 10, 60, 63, 128-129, 147, 152
liberation theology, 2-7, 7-27, 45-64, 80-100, 115-131, 133-144, 147, 149-153; Latin American, 4, 5, 7-27, 45-63, 82-99; as a new paradigm, 3, 22, 62, 99, 117, 120, 131, 149, 151; as a paradigm shift, 4, 5, 23, 46, 47, 64, 80, 82, 118, 127, 134, 142, 150
Lukacs, Georg, 121
MacIntyre, Alasdair, 34
Marcuse, Herbert, 43
Maritain, Jacques, 13
Marx, Karl, 16-18, 34, 59, 69, 93, 94, 95, 122, 123, 140, 151
Marxism, 5, 7, 16, 17, 18, 19, 60, 93-96, 126, 143, 145, 150
Medellín Conference, 15-16, 23
memory, 64, 74-76, 78-81
messianic Christianity, 44, 78, 114-115, 120
Metz, Johann Baptist, 5, 20, 38, 40, 43, 44, 64-81, 82, 127, 130, 146-47, 151
Míguez Bonino, José, 5, 6, 9, 19, 26, 82-99, 135, 137, 138
Modalism, 107
modern theology, 3, 5, 19, 26, 29, 31, 45, 46, 57-58, 64, 77, 81, 85, 98, 100, 101, 121, 127, 131, 134, 149, 150, 153
modernity, 29-33, 37, 38, 42, 43, 47, 48-50, 64-66, 71-74, 113, 144
Moltmann, Jürgen, 5, 6, 20, 40, 44, 82, 88, 100-117, 126, 130
monism, 89
Monroe Doctrine, 12
Moses, 108

multinational corporations, 13-14
narrative, 44, 74-76, 78-80, 88, 90, 100, 101, 104-107, 109-112, 114, 115, 138, 141, 143; of Christ, 107, 109, 110-112; of God, 104-107, 111, 114, 115; of the Spirit, 112, 114
"national security system," 13-14
Nazi Germany, 41
neocolonialism, 10-13
neo-orthodoxy, 31-33, 38, 40, 41, 78, 100, 101, 149, 151
New Christendom Movement, 12, 13, 15
new creation, 109, 110, 128
Nietzsche, Friedrich, 34
nonidentity, 48, 67, 89, 119
nonperson, 47-50, 61, 64, 144, 145
nonviolence, 96
Ogden, Schubert, 132
Origen, 89
"other," 8, 14, 21, 27, 51, 52, 122, 151
Panama Conference on Christian Work in Latin America, 12
patronage system, 9
Pendle, George, 11
Pius IX, 14
pluralism, 35-36, 39, 43
polis, 84, 119, 122, 126, 141, 147, 152
political ethics, 136
political theology, 4, 5, 20, 28, 29, 38-45, 64, 69, 70, 71, 74, 78, 81, 101, 102, 111, 146
politics, 50, 62, 79, 84, 123, 124, 146
poor, 3, 7-9, 13-14, 15, 17, 21-25, 27, 41, 46-52, 55-56, 58-64, 98, 102, 116, 119, 123, 126-128, 130-132, 142, 144-146, 151, 152; interruption of, 102, 144; irruption of, 27, 46-49, 56, 64, 127; option for, 21-24, 60-62, 116, 131-132; solidarity with, 23-25, 46, 51-52, 56-58, 61, 62, 126, 152
popular culture, 129
popular movements, 23, 35
popular religion, 10, 16, 24, 47
praxis, 3-6, 8, 26, 36-38, 40-44, 46, 47, 49, 51-54, 56-62, 64, 69, 76-79, 82, 83, 85-88, 91, 97-100, 102, 115, 116-120, 122-124, 126-129, 131, 132, 134-137, 139-148, 152, 153; Christian, 8, 44, 47, 53, 55, 58, 59-61, 78, 83, 97, 100,

114, 116, 131, 135, 137, 139, 141; historical, 49-52, 57-62, 86, 144, 145; human, 100, 116, 118, 120, 142; liberating, 46, 49-52, 56-59, 61, 62, 64, 78, 99, 117, 131, 132, 144-146, 152
progress, 2, 30-33, 118, 151
progressive theology, 3, 5, 27, 32, 33, 57-58; *see also* modern theology
proletariat, 93, 95
promise, 53, 103-106, 109, 112, 113, 115, 116
Puebla Conference, 15-16, 121-122
Rahner, Karl, 19, 32
rationalism, 48
reconciliation, 87
redemption, 77, 91, 128, 129, 131, 143; *see also* salvation
reformation, a new, 79
relativism, 36, 39, 43
resurrection, 103, 109-112, 114, 127, 129
revolution, 38, 45, 96
rhetoric, 47, 114, 118, 144
Rostow, Walt W., 13
sacrament, church as, 20, 25, 55-57, 130
salvation, 10, 52-56, 59, 60, 62, 63, 76, 77, 80, 91, 103, 128, 130, 147, 152, 153
Schleiermacher, Friedrich, 30, 58
Schmitt, Carl, 41
Scriptures, 88, 99, 106, 126, 138; *see also* Bible
secularity, 28, 65-67, 80, 127
secularization, 65-67
Segundo, Juan Luis, 19
sin, 24, 52, 128
Sobrino, Jon, 26, 70
social ethics, 3, 4
social gospel, 12, 13
social theory, 97, 98, 135, 144-148, 153
socialism, 13, 15, 19
Socrates, 108
solidarity, 24, 25, 43-46, 51, 52, 57-58, 61, 62, 74-76, 78-81, 96, 114, 118-120,

125-127, 129-132; with the dead, 76, 78, 79, 125; with the poor, 24, 25, 46, 51, 52, 56-58, 61, 62, 126, 152; with those who suffer, 43, 44, 78, 79, 114, 118, 120, 127, 129-131, 141, 151
Spirit, 100, 101, 110-112, 114, 115, 117, 127, 130
subject, 19, 28, 34, 36, 39, 41, 42, 43, 45, 46, 51, 57, 64-81, 94, 101, 116, 120-122, 124, 131, 132, 134, 142, 143, 146, 147, 149, 150, 151; bourgeois, 39, 64, 65, 71-73, 77, 80, 122, 147; new, 28, 51, 57, 64, 65, 71, 80, 121, 134; of suffering, 28, 65, 80, 101, 121, 122, 146
subjectivity, 142, 146
suffering, 2, 4, 28, 38, 64, 74, 76, 77, 79-81, 101, 102, 110-112, 115, 116, 117, 118-119, 122, 128-130, 139, 141, 146, 153
"Syllabus of Errors," 14
Teilhard de Chardin, Pierre, 19
time, 39, 40, 42, 74, 77, 80, 105, 124
Tracy, David, 36
transcendence, 105-107
Trinity, 110, 111, 116
Troeltsch, Ernst, 30
truth, 60-61
underside, 8, 27, 48, 62, 121
United Nations Decade of Development, 13
unity-in-difference, 89, 97
universal solidarity, 61
universalism, 36, 58, 61
universality and particularity, 38
utopia, 54-55, 56, 57
Vatican II, 14, 15, 28, 55
Vietnam, 28
violence, 83, 92, 94, 95, 97
Word of God, 52, 59, 83, 87, 98-99, 102, 141, 145
Zealots, 108
zukunft, 105, 106, 107, 126

Other Orbis Titles . . .

A THEOLOGY OF LIBERATION
by Gustavo Gutiérrez
One of the classics of liberation theology now in its tenth printing.
"This book must be read, not once but several times, by those who are interested in doing theology today." *Commonweal*
"This is one of the most acute and the most readable theological essays of today on the meaning and mission of the Church." *Catholic Library World*
no. 478-X   334pp. pbk. $10.95

THE POWER OF THE POOR IN HISTORY
by Gustavo Gutiérrez
Eight major essays that examine developments in liberation theology since Medellín with a focus on the option for the poor and the historical role of the poor in the liberation process.
"Gutiérrez is the first person in modern history to reactualize the great Christian themes of theology starting from a fundamental option for the poor. . ." *Edward Schillebeeckx*
no. 388-0   256pp. pbk. $10.95

WE DRINK FROM OUR OWN WELLS
by Gustavo Gutiérrez
"Gustavo Gutiérrez develops a spirituality which grows out of the lived experience of the Latin American people. Rooted in the reality of oppression and repression, this book calls forth a conversion from self-complacency and self sufficiency to that of solidarity with the poor." *Catholic New Times*
". . . it powerfully and beautifully provides a guide for 'the spiritual journey of a people,' a people of whom we too are a part." *Robert McAfee Brown*
no. 707-X   176pp. pbk. $7.95

THE LIBERATION OF THEOLOGY
by Juan Luis Segundo
Juan Luis Segundo analyzes the methodology of liberation theology, which is integrally linked to the structural realities of Latin American societies, and challenges the supposed impartiality of academic theology in Europe and North America.
"Makes for exciting reading and should not be missing from any theological library." *Library Journal*
no. 286-8   248pp. pbk. $10.95

FRONTIERS OF THEOLOGY IN LATIN AMERICA
edited by Rosino Gibellini

Rosino Gibellini invited thirteen of the most prominent Latin American theologians to contribute to this comprehensive survey of liberation theology in the Southern hemisphere. The authors represented are: Alves, Assmann, Boff, Bonino, Comblin, de Valle, Dussel, Galilea, Gutiérrez, Muñoz, Scannone, Segundo, and Vidales. Includes extensive biographical information about the contributors.

"If there is any one college textbook best suited to introduce students to Latin American liberation theology, this is it."   *Religious Studies Review*
no. 144-6   **333pp. pbk.**   **$10.95**

SALVATION AND LIBERATION
In Search of a Balance Between Faith and Politics
by Leonardo and Clodovis Boff

After an introduction to the basic propositions of liberation theology, the authors discuss their stance on the relationship between faith and politics, salvation and liberation. The expositional chapters are rounded out by a lively, imaginary "conversation" among a parish priest, a theologian, and a Christian activist confronting the challenges posed by the present social reality in Latin America.

"The book serves well to introduce the reader to the theology of liberation while at the same time being self-critical and adopting a needed historical perspective. Recommended for undergraduate and graduate libraries that desire to stay abreast of one of the century's most significant religious and theological movements."   *Choice*
no. 451-8   **128pp. pbk.**   **$6.95**

THE IDOLS OF DEATH AND THE GOD OF LIFE
A Theology
by Pablo Richard, et. al.

Ten Latin Americans look at the biblical, economic, and ideological implications of a liberating, life-giving God in contrast to "the false gods of the system," which through militarism, oppression, and economic exploitation deny life and usher in death. Richard, Croatto, Pixley, Sobrino, Araya, Casanas, Limon, Betto, Hinkelammert, and Assmann contribute to this ecumenical endeavor.

"Even where their way is not our way, we need to listen to what they have learned. These essays make an excellent listening post."   *Walter Wink,*
Auburn Theological Seminary
no. 048-2   **240pp. pbk.**   **$12.95**